LANDSCAPE TREKS

LANDSCAPE TREKS

A PHOTO LOCATION GUIDEBOOK

PAUL ALLEN

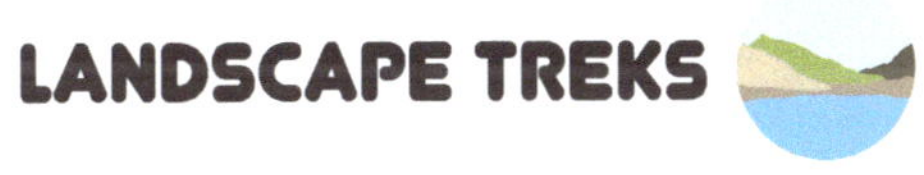

YOUCAXTON PUBLICATIONS

OXFORD & SHREWSBURY

ISBN 978-1-909644-92-2
Printed and bound in Great Britain.
Published by YouCaxton Publications

Contents

Introduction

This collection of routes is designed for photographers and hikers of all levels of experience, with options of relatively simple, flat walks, to two day expeditions into the hills. They will allow you to access some stunning locations, some of which are well known and others that are off the beaten track, offering exciting new angles on a range of landscape subjects. The routes and the images in this guide give you an idea of what to expect and help you to plan your visit. However, part of the excitement and anticipation of heading out on your own adventure is the chance to be creative in forming your own images and to capture the unique conditions that you experience. The in depth route descriptions will allow you to be flexible in the walk that you take as the weather and your goals change throughout the trip. Although they are exciting walks in their own right, focussing on the photography allows you to take time over your craft so that you can fully appreciate and enjoy your surroundings. In doing so you can really immerse yourself in what is around you and capture moments in time that not only form great images but lasting personal memories as well.

For each route there is a 'Focal Point' that forms the main subject matter for the walk. Also, several 'Photographic locations' are described to enable you to fully plan your visit and to give you a real flavour of what the area offers. A detailed map gives you plenty of options for extending or shortening your trip and suggests a number of photographic opportunities. The shorter route options are also really useful when the weather is less than perfect as they offer lower level alternatives to some photogenic locations. The map and route description also offer wild camp options if you wish to camp out in the hills and attempt to experience them during the glorious sunset and sunrise hours. By wild camping out in the mountains you get to stay out at a beautiful location and have time to capture the changing light without the time pressures of getting up or down a hill in the dark. More on wild camping can be found in the 'Wild Camping' section later.

This guide covers a number of photography walks in Snowdonia, The Brecon Beacons, The Lake District, The Peak District, The Pennines and the Scottish Borders giving you a range of areas to explore and a chance to experience some of the most dramatic landscapes in the UK.

You can't beat the joy of slinging your rucksack on your back and heading out into the hills to have an adventure. So choose your route, grab your camera gear and get out exploring.

Acknowledgements

I would like to dedicate this book to my family and friends without which it would never have happened.

To Sally and Sophie, for your love and support and for sharing many adventures, and our dogs Penny and Millie for pulling me up many a hill and for never questioning my route choices. To my Mum, Dad (and Sally again) for all the proof reading.

The AZ walking and climbing group who have shared both highs, and lows, on many wild camping trips and have helped make this project a realty:

Catherine Barber, Roger Bonnert, Moya Caffrey, Rhona Cox, Adrian Fisher, Anna Karin-Tieden, Liz Kinchin, Lee Kingston, Chris Luckhurst, Andy Mather, Andrew Morlin, Austen Pimm

A special mention must go to Larry Coe who inspired many of this group to explore and enjoy wild places. He introduced me to the joys of wild camping for which I shall be eternally grateful. He also introduced me to the joys of whiskey! You are sorely missed.

Simon Hoult for some fantastic support in getting this book off the ground and for joining me on some extreme weather trips.

To the friends of Landscape Treks who have backed this project; a big thank you especially goes to Paul Willgoss and David Albans.

To share a memorable experience in the hills with some great friends is truly one of life's most simple and enjoyable pleasures.

Snowdonia

Snowdonia in North Wales offers something rather special to the landscape photographer with its small number of compact regions delivering fantastic vantage points to some stunning peaks. Whilst mountains such as Snowdon and Tryfan have numerous enjoyable routes to their tops, to really get to know and photograph them you need to seek out the best viewpoints which are often tucked away on less visited peaks.

1.1 A Circuit of Tryfan

Focal Point – this route takes in a full circumnavigation or photo-circumnavigation around Tryfan, allowing you to capture the full character of this fantastic peak. You also get to take in the mighty Glyders and all their outstanding rock architecture.

Route Summaries

Full route – the northern shores of Llyn Ogwen then on to Llyn Idwal before an ascent of Foel Goch with an optional wild camp at the summit. The route then traverses the central Glyder range, starting with Y Garn, before climbing up onto the highest Glyders (Fawr then Fach). A descent is made via Y Foel Goch and Galt Yr Ogof.

26 km; 1650m ascent

This is quite a long route to undertake in one day so if you're not camping out you might want to split it into two. The easiest point to split the route is at the Devils Kitchen.

Shorter route – a circuit of Llyn Ogwen and Llyn Idwal

9km; 120m ascent

Why Try this Route

Tryfan is probably one of the most iconic mountains in Wales with its stunning north ridge rising like a shark fin straight up from the road as the latter winds its way through the superb Ogwen valley.

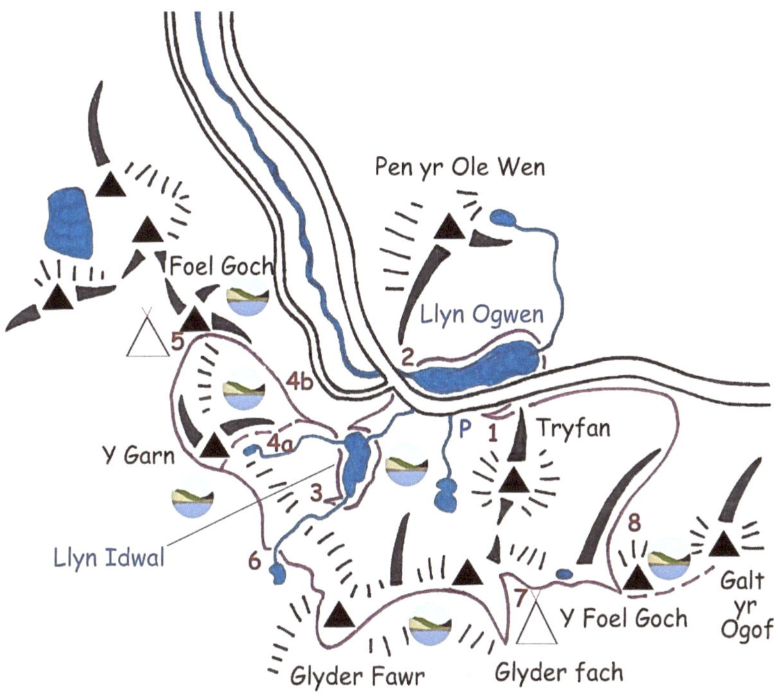

Key to Maps

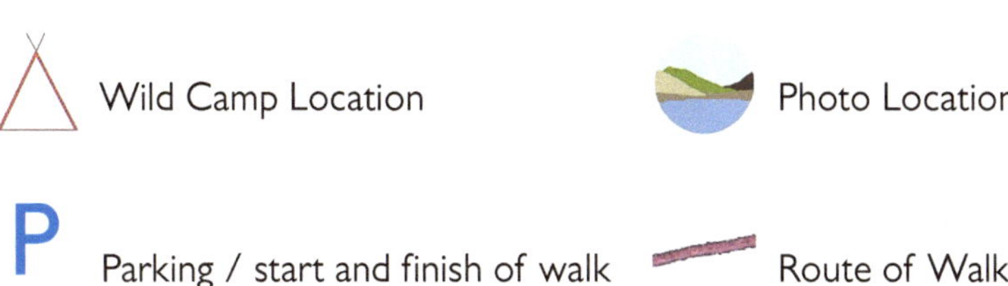

Clockwise from top left:

The wild camp view from Foel Goch over Tryfan and the main Glyders... Llyn Caseg-fraith and the east face of Tryfan... Ogwen sunrise from Foel Goch... Llyn Caseg-fraith and Bristly ridge... The Castle of the Wind... Llyn Idwal and Pen Yr Ole Wen

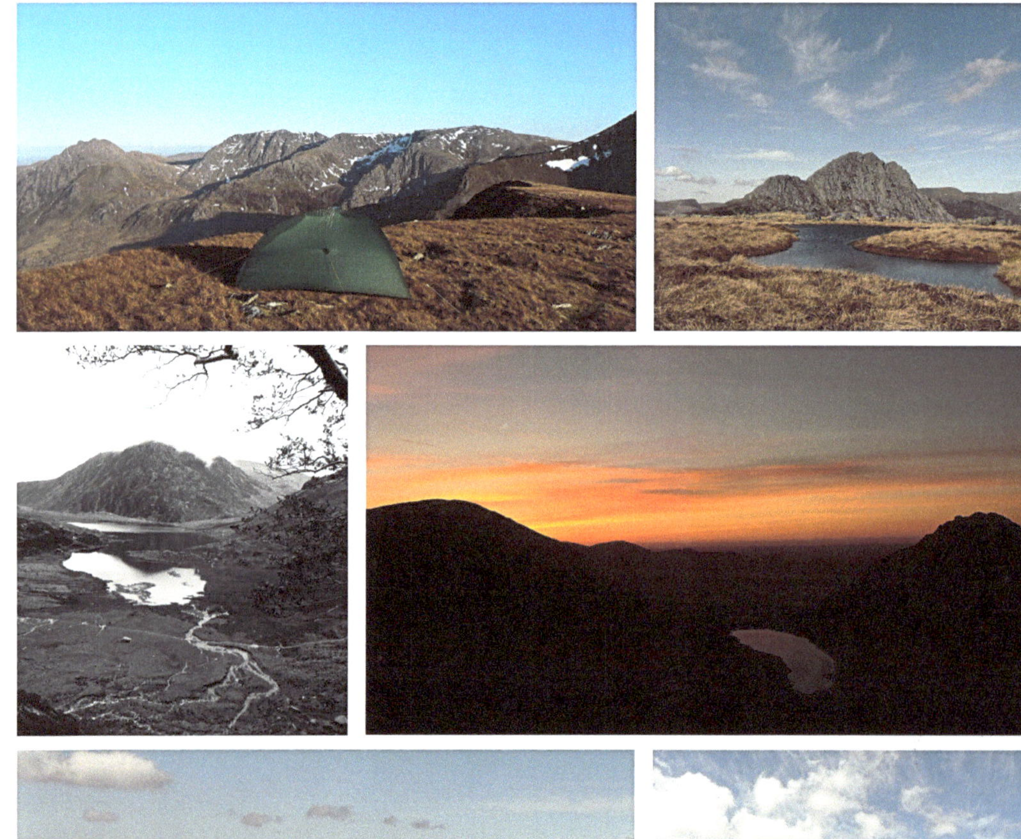

Route Description

1) The route starts at the very foot of Tryfan's north ridge Grid Ref. SH 658601 which gives you a close up of the immense boulders that make up this mountain of rock. Whilst most people will be heading directly up the scramble in front of you, our route starts with a significantly less lung busting amble round Llyn Ogwen's eastern end. Despite the busy A5 being just a stones skim across the lake you quickly feel like you are away from the crowds that can flock to this area as a faint track winds its way along the northern shoreline. As you begin to distance yourself from Tryfan the views start to open up offering numerous camera stops with interesting lake level foreground.

Cramming enough kit for a night into my 34L sack I arrived in the Ogwen valley just in time for the evening light to do its special thing and to take in my first views of the mighty Tryfan.

Heading further west towards Ogwen Cottage the steep slopes of Pen Yr Ole Wen start to encroach forcing the path to wind its way over some large boulders. Whilst not requiring too much 'hands on rock', care will need to be taken when the water levels are high and the rock is wet. Similarly there are a number of stunning waterfalls further down river but the slopes and access to these are very steep. If this all sounds too much or it's too wet underfoot this whole section can be avoided by following a path next to the A5 on the southern side of Llyn Ogwen.

2) Once across the A5, you can make good use of the visitor centre before heading back into the wilds. You only need to step a few paces along the main path heading up to Llyn Idwal before the next geological feature grabs your attention. A deep gash in the rock face to

the right of the path leads up through a dramatic fissure. On climbing out the far end of this fissure it makes an interesting foreground to the brooding steep southern ridge of Pen Yr Ole Wen.

The route follows some faint tracks over often boggy terrain towards your first view of Llyn Idwal. On your way to the lake check out the views that open up to your right down the Nant Ffrancon valley. Despite the A5 tracing its route along the side of the valley it has a glorious wild feel to it. It is well worth arriving at the northern shores of Llyn Idwal early as this is one of the easiest 'classic' viewpoints in the area, being less than 500m from the carpark at Ogwen Cottage.

Photo Location – Llyn Idwal

Seek out some low level viewpoints along the stony beach at the northern end of the lake and if still conditions prevail, the reflections of the Devil's Kitchen across the water can be sublime. Maybe more impressive and less sought out is the opposite view from the southern shore of Llyn Idwal. To reach this follow the eastern shore where there is an excellent path to guide you. However, you'll no doubt make several detours down to the waters edge to seek out some more images; the sweeping ridges of Y Garn look very impressive from here. You'll soon reach a path junction and the stunning Idwal slabs (superlative climbing, if a little popular). Perhaps my favourite viewpoint over the narrow but shapely Llyn Idwal is from a small rocky outcrop on the way up the Devils Kitchen. This can be located as the path up the cliffs crosses the stream that falls from above. To gain this spot requires a short out and back climb. If you don't fancy this take the path that drops down to the right allowing you to follow the western shore of the lake. However, if you make the short climb, the outcrop delivers a stunning vantage point.

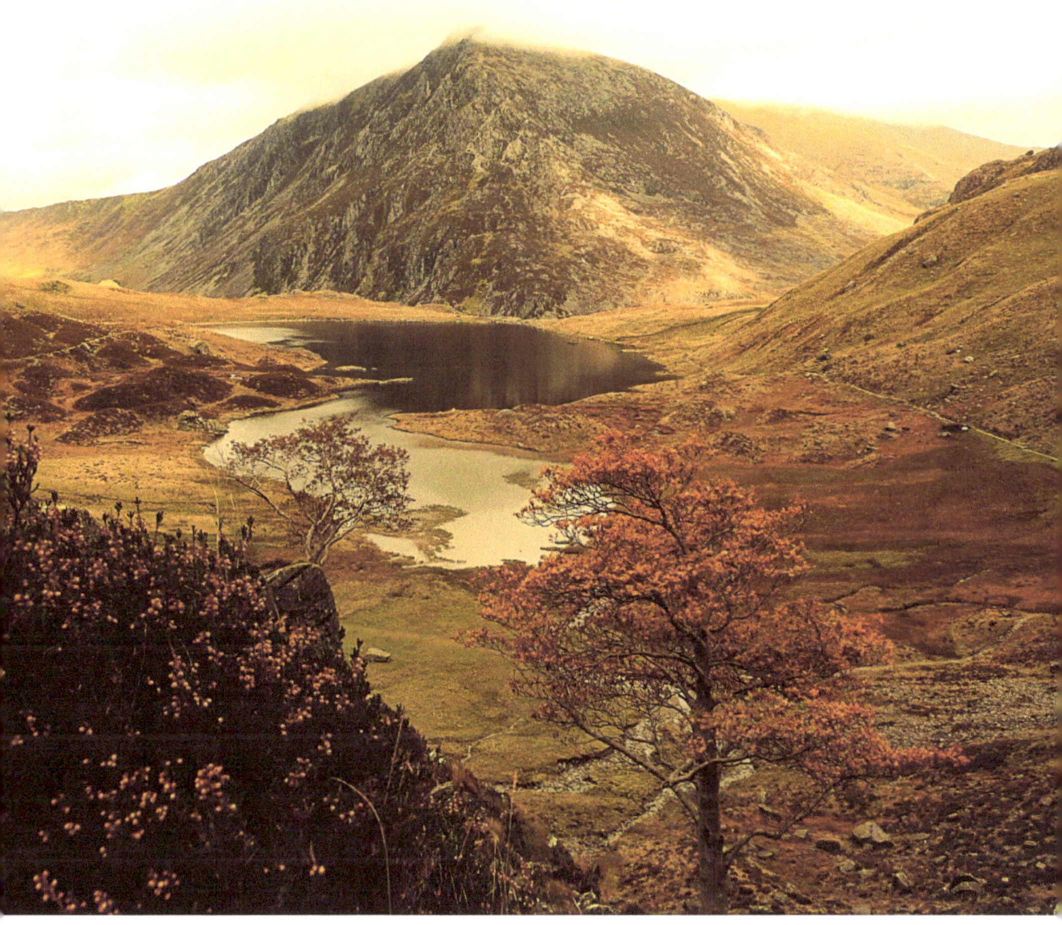

8.30am 14th October – Discovering this viewpoint was a real joy especially as I was able to later share it with Vivek and Ahmed for a fine autumn shoot.

It has a couple of small trees adding to the foreground interest, colour and framing opportunities. The outline of Llyn Idwal forms a good mid-distance focal point and the rocky bulk of Pen Yr Ole Wen forms a towering but not oppressive backdrop. The feeder stream also acts as a useful lead in line to aid the composition. This area is also a great place to see Arctic plants such as moss campion, alpine saxifrage and the rare Snowdon lily which can be found hidden amongst the crags in late Spring.

If you are short of time, an ascent of the main Glyders can be continued from here by following the good path up Devils Kitchen to the pass above. This route is quite popular as it is the most direct ascent, but there are better options, which offer better views.

3) If you are planning on making a night of it, a summit wild camp on Foel Goch is a superb option. From the viewpoint at the southern end of Llyn Idwal, head back towards the lake and pick up a path that leads round its western shoreline. There are several interesting views over the lake with the backdrop of Tryfan dominating the skyline.

4a) At the northern end of the lake, pick up a path that goes through a wall and starts to head west up Y Garn's imposing north east ridge. This ridge is a good route up and can be followed all the way to the summit of Y Garn. A good detour can be made half way up the climb by visiting the snug shores of Llyn Clyd. If you're after a sheltered spot for a wild camp there are a few dotted around this small llyn. Although the remaining ascent up to the summit is hard work, it does offer great views back over to Tryfan, necessitating many camera breaks.

4b) However, to take in the summit of Foel Goch a more devious ascent can be made up this peaks little visited eastern ridge. Just before reaching this ridge the route passes above the delightfully named Mushroom Garden. After crossing through the wall on the start of the ascent up Y Garn from Llyn Idwal the path zigs left and then zags to the right. The path then turns steeply to the left, where a faint path leads off to the right aiming for a grassy ridge. This path traverses around the ridge and then contours the hillside slightly above a stone wall.

Photo Locations
Ascents of Y Garn or Foel Goch

On either ascent the classic scrambling lines of Tryfan's north ridge and Glyder Fach's Bristly ridge dominate the skyline and are now hopefully, your almost constant companions.

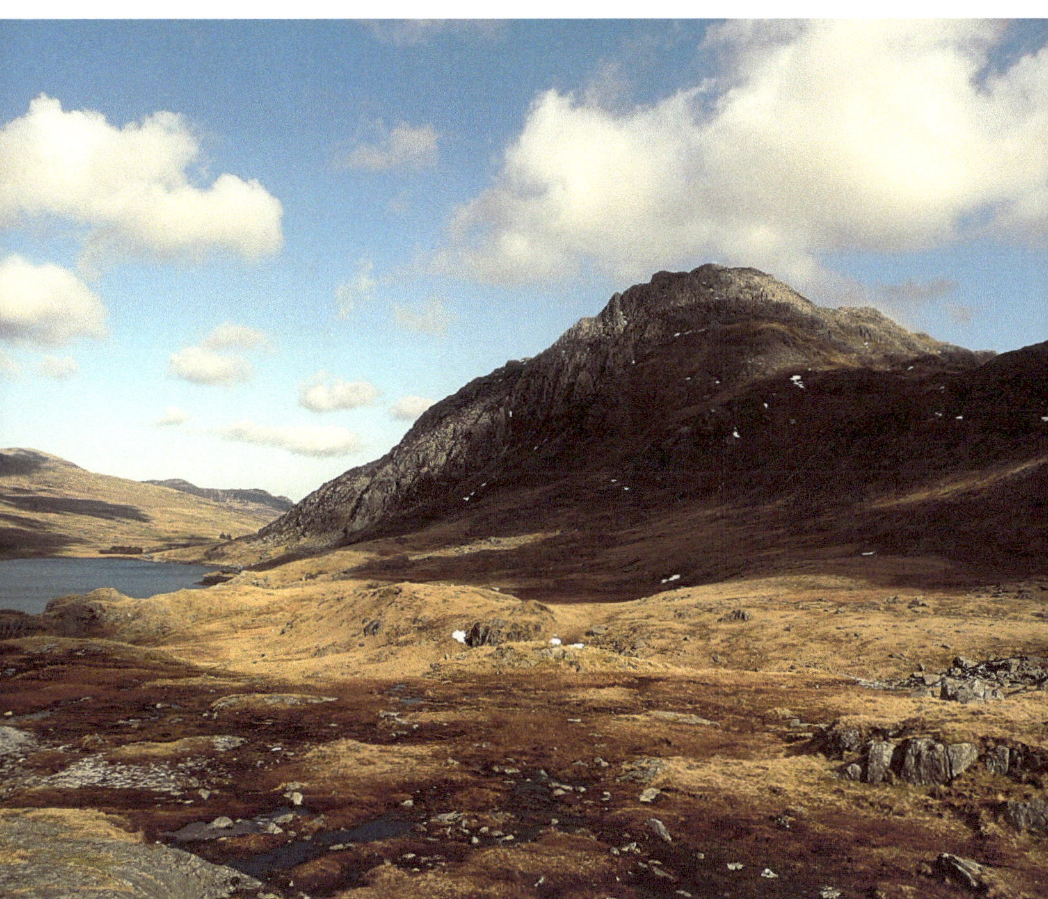

4.30pm 19th April – the ascent of Y Garn; The clouds started to dissipate and the light just got better and better. From this elevated spot, Tryfan rears up from a landscape that looks more like the far north of Scotland rather than one that is only a few hundred meters from the busy A5.

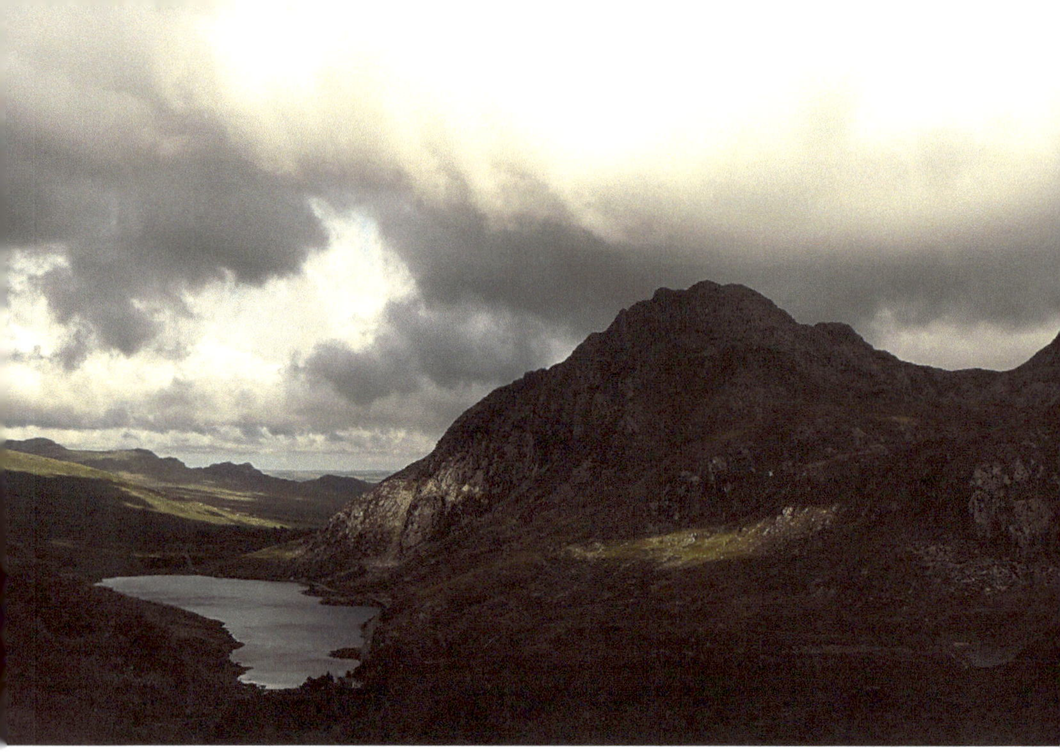

4.30pm 2nd August – the ascent of Foel Goch; My mate Simon and I had battled through heavy rain and thick cloud but we were rewarded for our efforts. The cloud level was no longer around our knees and the views opened up.

After crossing a small stream, spilling down from the diminutive Llyn Cywion, the path winds up through a patch of scree. Once on the broad grassy spur above the scree, a reasonable path climbs steadily upwards, aiming for, what looks from below to be a large flat area. It's another great place to stop and take in the ever expanding scene over your shoulder.

Once you reach this area the ground drops away precipitously in front of you. This opens up superb views down to the Nant Ffrancon valley below your feet. There are a number of precarious rocky outcrops from which you can take in this beautiful panorama. This is the start of the ridge proper and whilst it never requires any hands on action it offers excellent walking. An eroded path, although probably more eroded by weather than footfall, leads you first gently downwards before the final climb up to the summit.

You soon reach the grassy summit area of Foel Goch, the actual summit being slightly off to the right. This offers a great wild camp spot. Relatively flat but well drained grass makes for a comfortable pitch and a water supply just to the south west down towards Llyn Cywion add to its attraction.

Most folks were heading down by the time I was making the acscent and in fact on reaching the summit I met the last person I was to see until late morning the next day. I had the Glyders all to myself and it looked like the weather was going to play ball. There was plenty of light left for me to decide on a spot for a cracking wild camp.

Photo Location - Foel Goch

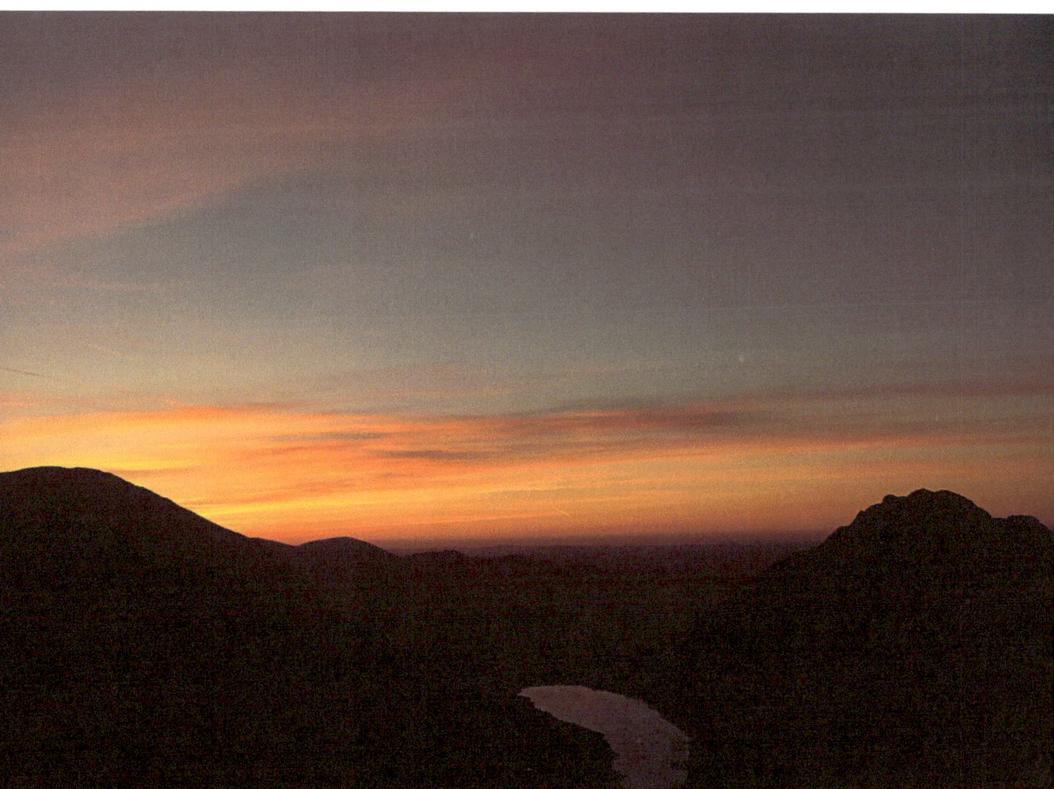

5.50 am 20th April - Sunrises are usually special experiences and this one, seen from my summit camp was truly memorable. It took a while for the sun's warmth to melt the frost that had settled in the night, although the ascent of Y Garn was enough to get me warm again. I spent the next few hours exploring some of the finest scenery in Wales, maybe the UK, taking in some of the highlights of the spectacular Glyders.

The views over to the distant Llyn peninsula offer great sunset potential (in fact these westerly outliers offer a great sunset focus from a number of locations – see Nantlle ridge walk later). The views to the east, over Llyn Ogwen and Llyn Idwal with the outline of Tryfan, make for an excellent start to the photography in the early morning light.

This wild camp is quite exposed so in high winds a couple of spots on the alternative ascent up to Y Garn can be found in the sheltered cwm around Llyn Clyd. However, this high level camp makes for an exciting and photogenic viewpoint.

5) From Foel Goch you can follow the cliff edge that heads south towards the pointy summit of Y Garn. You descend steadily down Foel Goch's grassy flanks, keeping the fence to your right, to the small pass of Bwlch y Cywion, and then make a small re-ascent over a rocky knoll. Climb over the ladder stile then pick up a good, stoney path that leads you up the climb to the summit of Y Garn. It is quite hard work; especially as you reach the scree and the gradient increases, however, with luck your efforts will be rewarded.

Photo location – Y Garn

Y Garn is a well situated peak with its pointy summit offering an amazing 360 degree panorama. The views to the north, especially from the northern end of the summit area, stretch all the way over the tail end of the Glyders to the distant Isle of Anglesey. To the east, over Y Garn's near vertical cliffs the three llyns of Clyd, Idwal and Ogwen align up with Tryfan as a shapely backdrop.

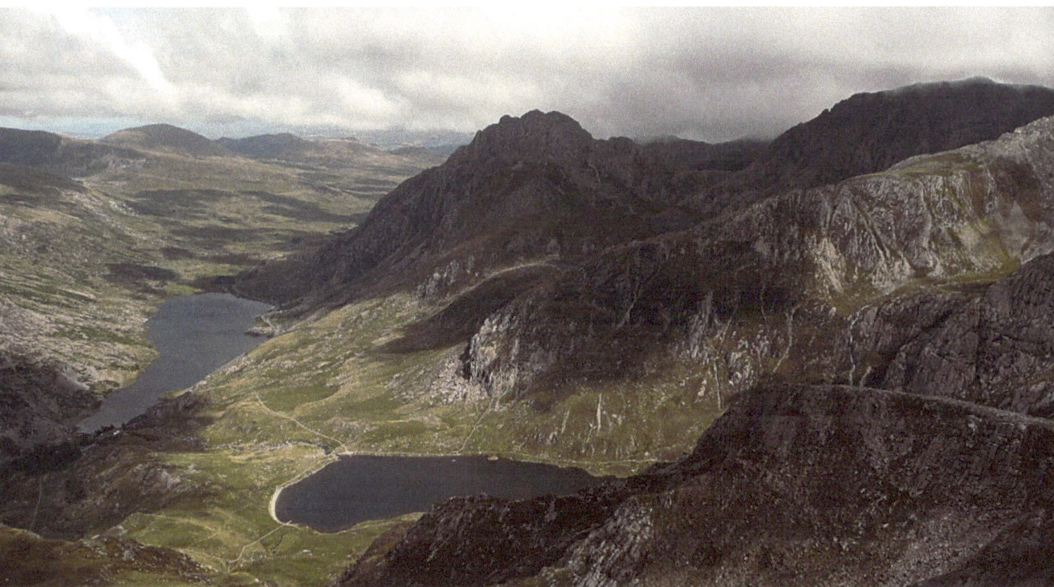

3.30pm 2nd August – Simon was keen to climb Y Garn as on his previous visit the mist had come down denying him the glorious views. Standing on this summit we traced out numerous routes we had done. Moreover, there was a lifetime of exploring to be had in this peaks hinterland.

Also to the east the enormous bulk of Pen Yr Ole Wen shows off its rocky flanks as they sweep down to the Ogwen Cottage which is just a speck at the northern end of Llyn Ogwen.

5.45pm 19th April – there are times when you toil up a hill in bad weather and wonder why you are doing it. Then, there are times like this when the ascent is enjoyable, the views are sublime and even the weather is working in your favour.

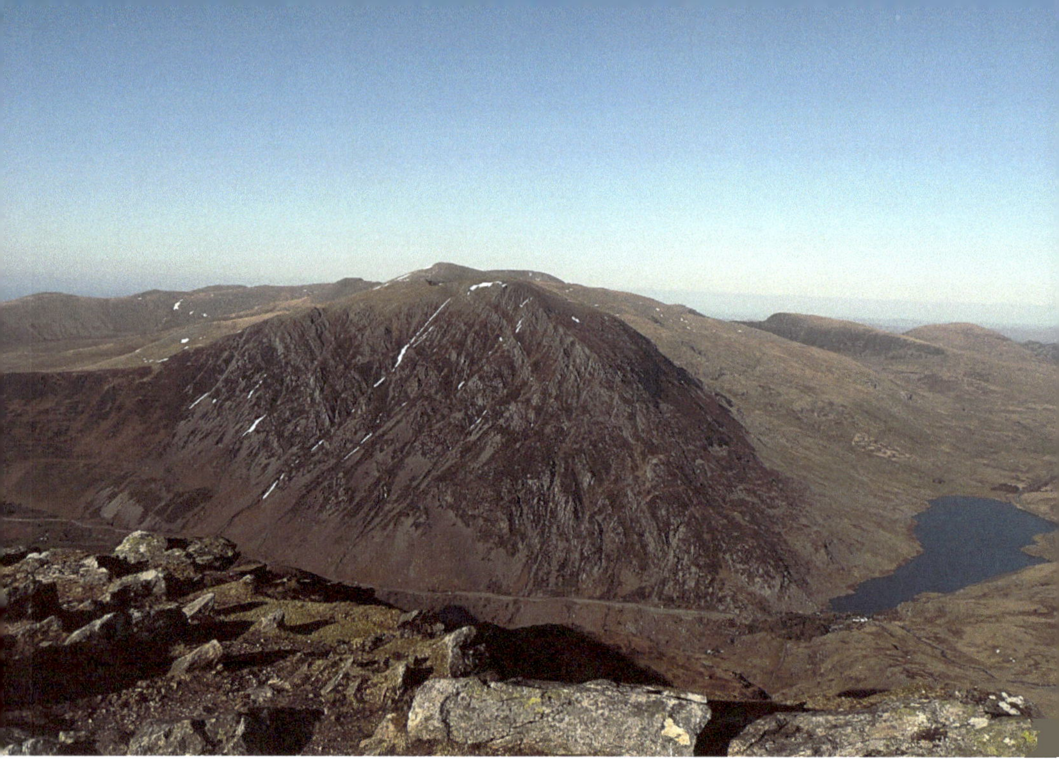

Then to the south your descent route to Llyn y Cwn is dominated by the bulk of the main Glyders and all their craggy good features. If all this wasn't enough, you look southwest where Snowdon's arcing horseshoe grabs your attention. On panning round to the west, to complete the 360 degrees, the vista stretches off over a multi ridge layered bonanza all the way to the wonderful Lleyn peninsula.

The descent from Y Garn is relatively straightforward as you drop south east, then south, on good paths. You can stick to the cliff edge to get a peek down over the Devils Kitchen, although be sure not to follow the steep south eastern ridge off Y Garn. As you trend south the ground soon levels out at the surprisingly broad pass around Llyn y Cwn. Cross a boggy section just to the left of the lake, around which there are some large rocks where you can shelter if needs be. If time and energy levels are lacking you can of course descend from here on the path down Devils Kitchen and back to the Ogwen valley. However, whilst the next section requires some girding of your loins it really is rather special.

6) On reaching the pass the climbing is far from over and in fact the next section is quite tough if thankfully relatively short. Another 280m of steep ascent up quite loose scree never sounds attractive but if good conditions prevail then the slog up on to the main Glyder summits is more than worth the effort. In fact even if the conditions are less than ideal, the stunning rock features on and around the two main Glyder summits make for some of the best photographic opportunities in the whole area. So pick your line up on one of the many paths that heads south up the steep climb in front of you.

If you fancy a really high wild camp there are a number of relatively limited spots to be found about 300m to the east and west of the summit of Glyder Fawr.

Photo Locations – Glyder Fawr and Glyder Fach

Whilst the climb might have been hard, the route between Glyder Fawr and Glyder Fach makes for a relatively flat and easy going walk with so many photography shoots that you'll soon be burning your way through your memory cards. Black and white images really come into their own up here in this monochrome but beautifully sculptured environment.

It is well worth checking out the following opportunities but it is also a great place to just spend some time exploring, especially around the plateaus edges.

As you approach the highly photogenic Castle of the Wind, the spiky rock pile that lies between the two summits, head to the north edge to take in the views down the Y Gribin ridge and the dramatic rock faces that make up the steepest side of the Glyders.

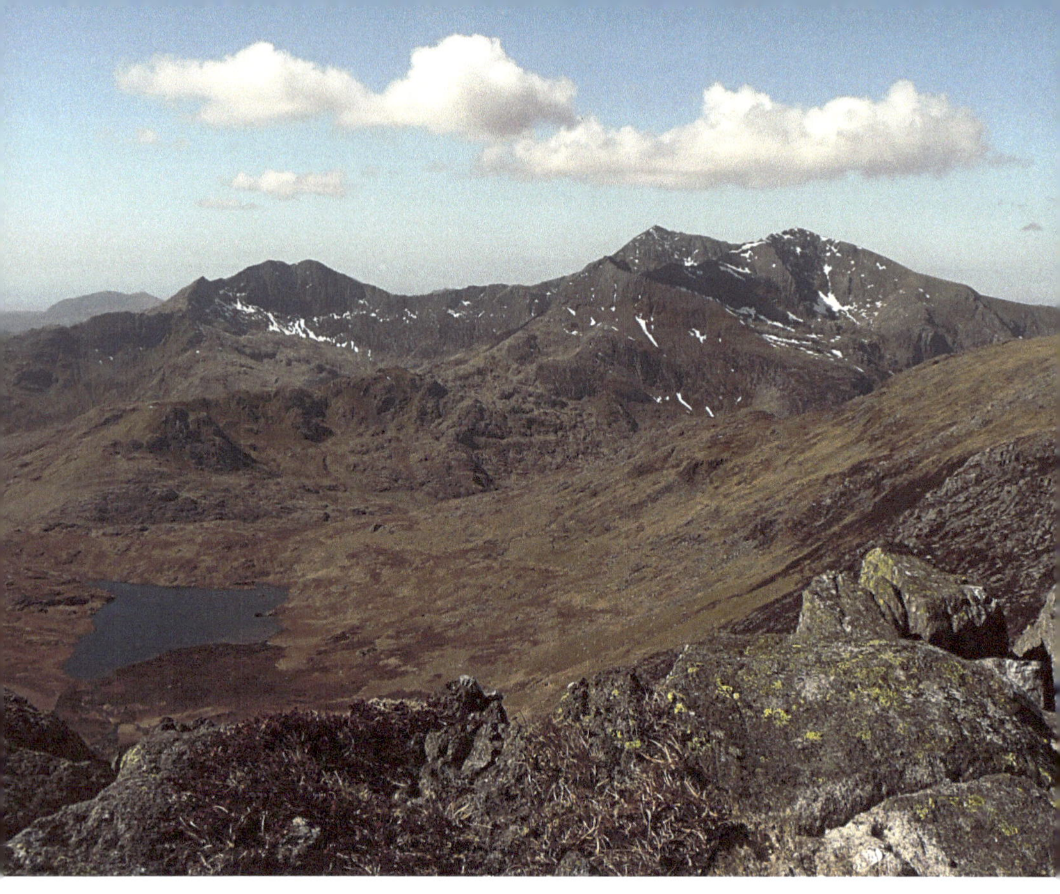

2.20pm 20th April - Despite the extra effort required to seek out this viewpoint it was more than worthwhile. Even more rewarding was the fact that I had it all to myself.

The view back over the Castle in the Wind from the summit or just before the summit of Glyder Fach is a classic but a well deserved one. As is the Cantilever stone, found just along from the summit of Glyder Fach and features in numerous shots of people trying to tip the balance of this massive see saw of a rock. If it's busy wait a while to get it for yourself so you can explore the image possibilities.

The thick cloud that we had been walking in started to dissipate and we were treated to a special hill walking reward; a beautiful panorama that started to reveal itself to our visually deprived brains.

The view over to the Snowdon horseshoe, across to the south west, is a well sought out one. Probably the best spot takes some seeking out to the south of the path as it drops down east from Glyder Fach. There's a small plateau about 500m south south east from the summit which offers great camping potential and stunning views over to the Snowdon massif. It is also suitably far from the main route giving it that extra feeling of being 'in the wild'.

7) Either way the route heads east down past the top of the aptly named Bristly ridge (whose cracking profile you get to see later) and on down to where the Miners track crosses our path. The quickest route back to your car takes you north west down the Miners track through the high pass between Bristly ridge and Tryfan. If you can't resist climbing this stunning peak then this gives you access to the easiest of its routes, the south ridge. Whilst still hands on, this route is not a graded scramble, however it does take a good while to clamber up and over the rocks to the summit and back. On heading back down the Miners track the stunning Llyn Bochlwyd makes for a fantastic spot although it is better shot from the lower edge of the Y Gribin ridge to the west which also takes in this side of Tryfan.

If you have more time then stick with the main path heading east from Glyder Fach and drop down to the rather boggy Llyn Caseg-fraith.

Photo Location - Llyn Caseg-Fraith to Gallt Y Ogof

The eastern shore of Llyn Caseg-fraith offers amazing views over to Tryfan and Bristly ridge with the unusual shape of the lake making an interesting foreground.

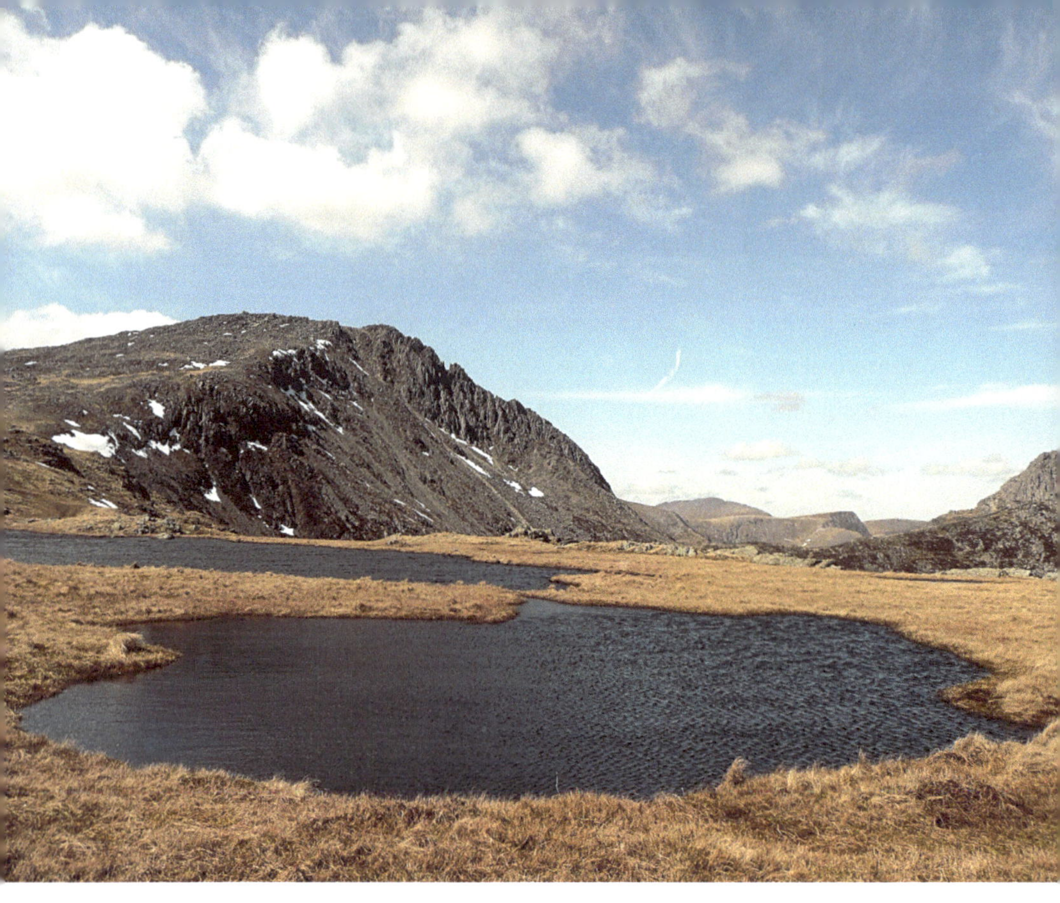

3.40pm 20th April - A few years ago I walked passed this spot in thick cloud and horizontal rain. I was on a navigation course at the time and just finding the lake was a real challenge. So coming back some years later in such fine weather felt like a special gift.

A short climb leads to the little visited summit of Y Foel Goch which offers great but somewhat distant views over to the Snowdon horseshoe. The main attraction of heading out this far east however is to carry on over to the even less visited rocky summit of Gallt Y Ogof. There are unrivalled views which take in the glorious profiles of both the Bristly ridge and what is possibly the best angle of Tryfan's north ridge.

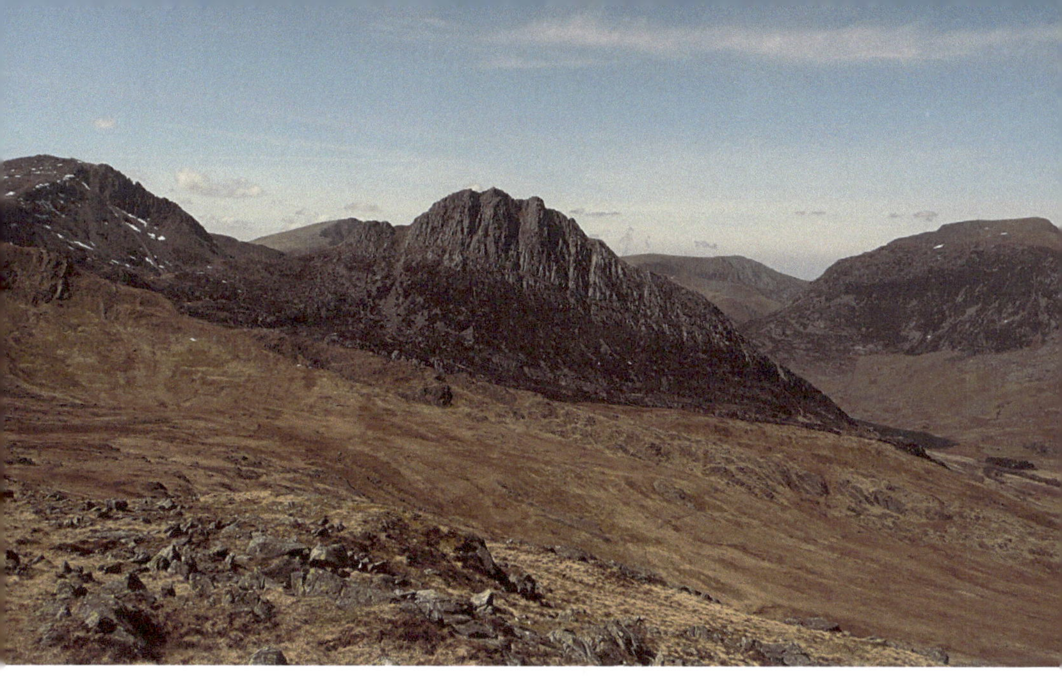

4.20pm 20th April – Scramblers paradise; whilst the gradient doesn't look too bad from here, when you are at the foot of these ridges your heart starts to beat a bit faster and your palms start to sweat.

The area also has numerous wild camp spots in amongst the last two summits.

Whilst there is a descent route off Gallt Yr Ogof the going is very rough and in fact feels almost Scottish being pathless, tough terrain. If you do fancy this route follow the ridge down a fair way but head north west to avoid the cliffs that start to appear on your right.

8) An easier option is to backtrack to Llyn Caseg-fraith and take the north east ridge that leads you down to the campsite at Gwern Gof Isaf. Either way, on reaching the campsite, there is a reasonable track that heads west, first to the Gwern Gof Uchaf campsite and then under the looming north face of Tryfan. The track then brings you out onto the A5 near the entrance you took earlier to Glen Dena. From here follow the path alongside the road back to your car.

The circuit of Tryfan is now complete, as are no doubt a number of your memory cards.

On reaching the car, after spending two days on the hill, I was tired and ready to return to civilisation. However, I was buzzing from the experience and I knew that I would not only have some special images on my camera but also some special memories stored away in my head.

1.2 Nantlle Ridge Exploration

Focal Points – the dramatic Mynydd Drws-y-coed as seen from the summit of Y Garn and the views over to the distant Lleyn peninsula from the remote summit of Moel Lefn.

Route Summaries

Full route – starting the Nantlle ridge with Y Garn then on to Mynydd Drws-y-coed and Trum y Ddysgl. Leave the main ridge to take in the Hebog range (Moel Lefn, Moel-yr-Ogof and Moel Hebog). Return to Rhyd Ddu by heading north up Cwm Pennant then through Beddgelert forest.

20 km; 1650m ascent

Route extension

Continuing on the Nantlle ridge from Trum y Ddysgl to Mynydd Tal-y-mignedd, Craig Cwm Silyn and finally Garnedd-goch. Descending south east off the ridge into Cwm Pennant then climbing to the pass, Cwm Meilionen via Cwm Llefrith. Return to Rhyd Ddu over the Hebog range.

12km; 830m ascent

Shorter route - the Nantlle ridge including Y Garn, Mynydd Drws-y-coed and Trum y Ddysol before returning via Beddgelert forest.

9 km; 690m ascent

* *Some hands on sections of low grade (around grade 1) scrambling*

Why Try this Route

An exploration of the series of peaks that make up the Nantlle ridge, with options to take in the even less visited Hebog range, is not only a sublime walk in itself but offers the photographer a wealth of opportunities. The peaks themselves are varied underfoot, give excellent views over the whole route and beyond to the coast. There are also excellent vistas over to the neighbouring Snowdon massif. The wild Pennant valley has a rich industrial past with its small, now redundant mines adding to the experience.

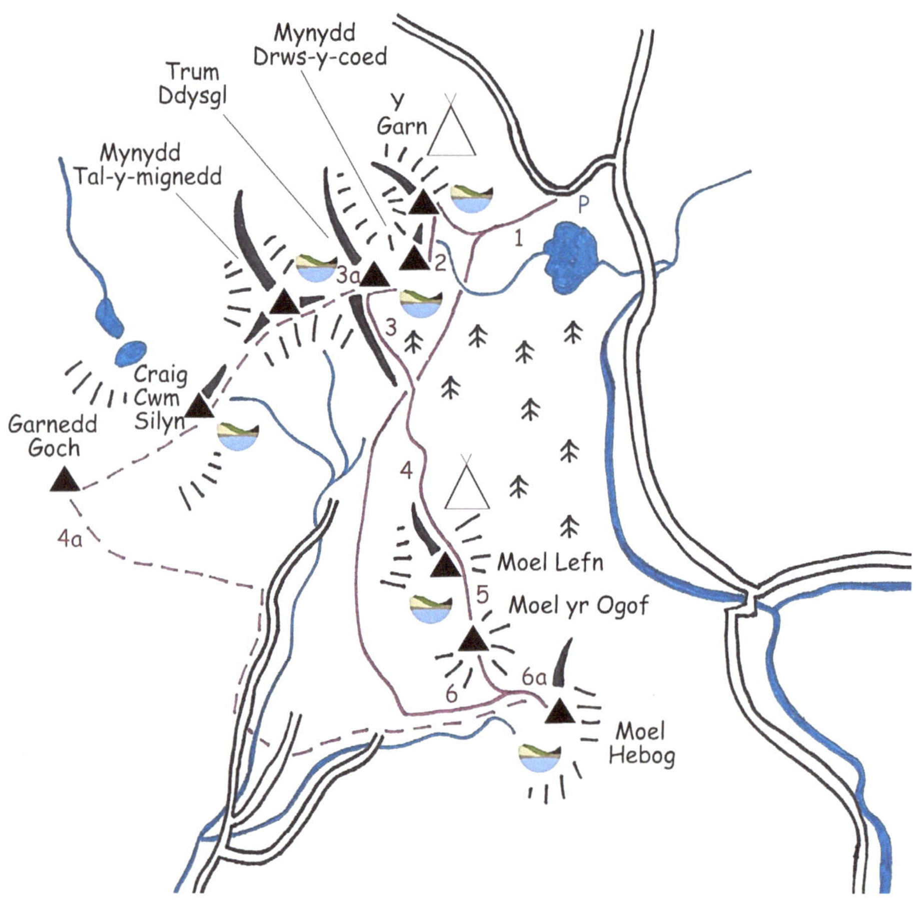

Clockwise from top left:

The Nantlle ridge from Moel Lefn... Sunrise over Y Lliwedd, Yr Aran and Moel Siabod from Moel Lefn wild camp... Mist over Trum y Ddysgl from Y Garn wild camp... The Llyen hills from Moel Lefn wild camp... View back to Trum y Ddysgl on the ascent of Mynydd Tal-y-mignedd... Shooting the sunset from Moel Lefn wild camp

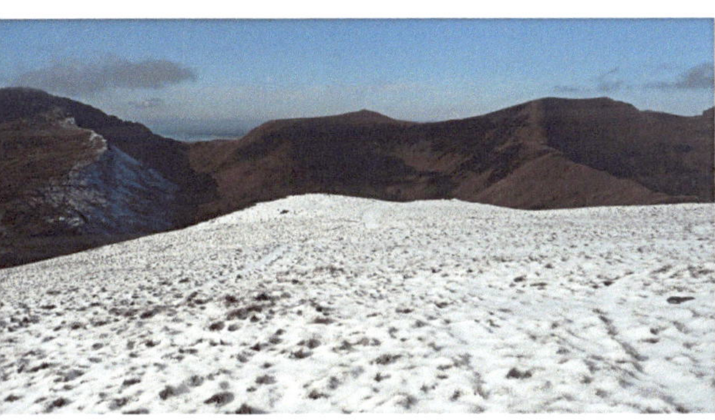

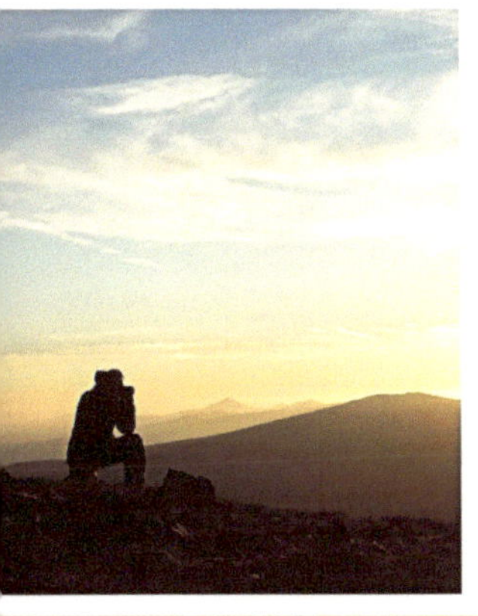

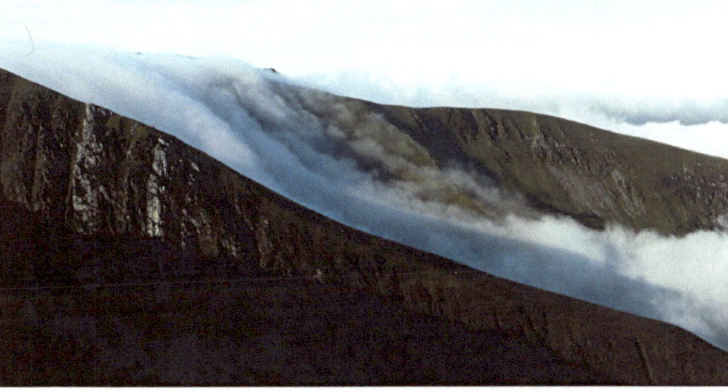

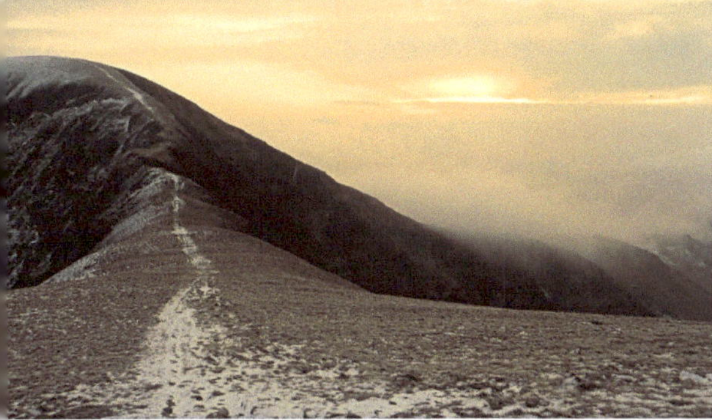

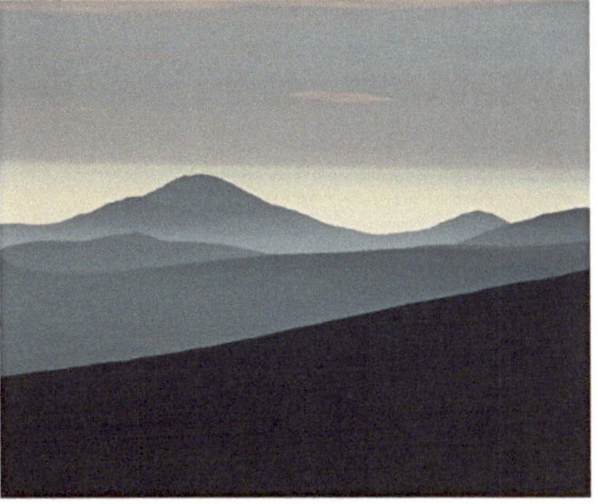

Route Description

1) Starting from Rhyd Ddu on the western side of Snowdon, the best place to park is on the small pull in (SH566526) on the B4418 as it leaves the village on its way to Nantlle. The start to the walk is quite unforgiving with the ascent of Y Garn starting only a few hundred meters from the road.

After a bit of a late start on Friday evening, well almost Saturday morning, we made a somewhat, shall I say 'interesting' climb up some rather steep pathless terrain in the dark. We topped out on a clear, windless summit of Y Garn.

There are a few paths crossing this area but keep heading upwards in a westerly direction and after a fair bit of effort you'll gain the rocky summit of Y Garn after crossing over the stone wall.

Photo Location - The Summit of Y Garn

The summit has, rather surprisingly, a flat grassy top, but with steep drops on three out of its four sides you find yourself at an amazing vantage point. In fact it also makes a great spot for a wild camp. There is a good area just beyond the summit cairn near the stone wall, before it drops precipitously down the north western ridge.

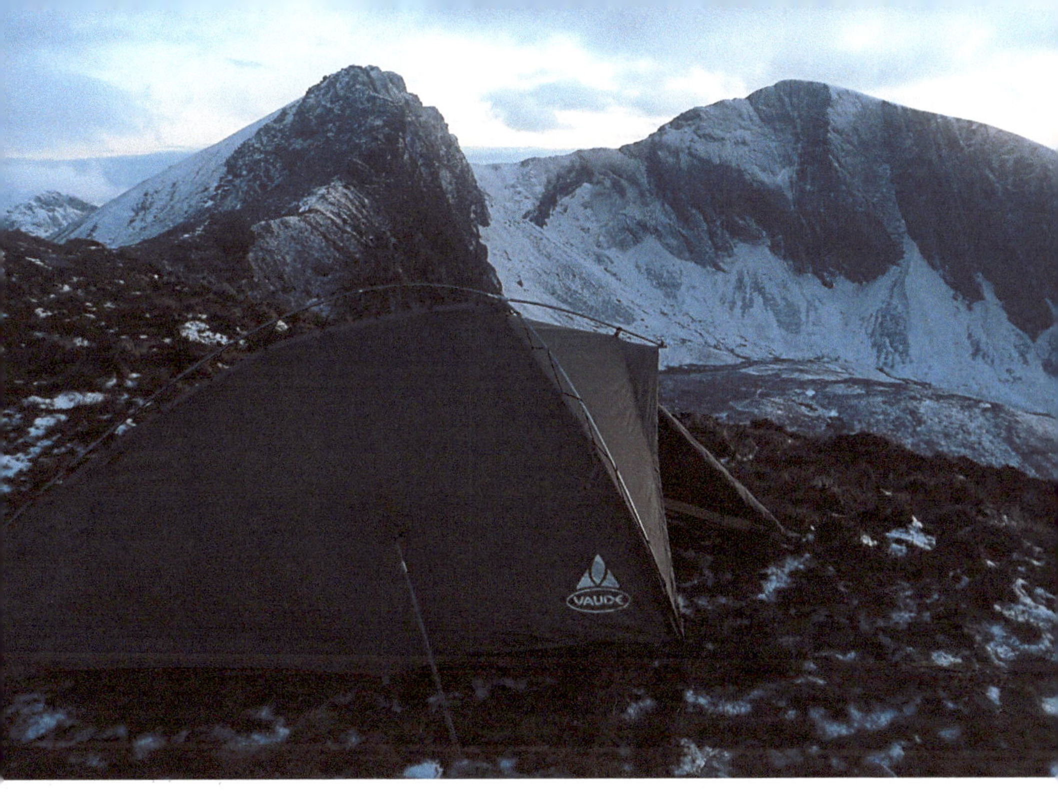

16.10am 16th February – the sun was starting to drop over the horizon and the temperature was plummeting too. Still, this was a wild camp to savour.

On another trip to this summit we made a night ascent, camping out at the top.

After quickly pitching our tents we clambered into our bags for a few hours kip. I woke with a start, some time before my alarm was due to go off and quickly extracted myself from my tent. I stumbled, bleary eyed, out onto what is possibly the most stunning morning vista I have had the privilege to experience.

This summit offers a full 360 degree view, with the most dramatic from its northern edges. These take in the rugged side of Mynydd Mawr across the valley to the north.

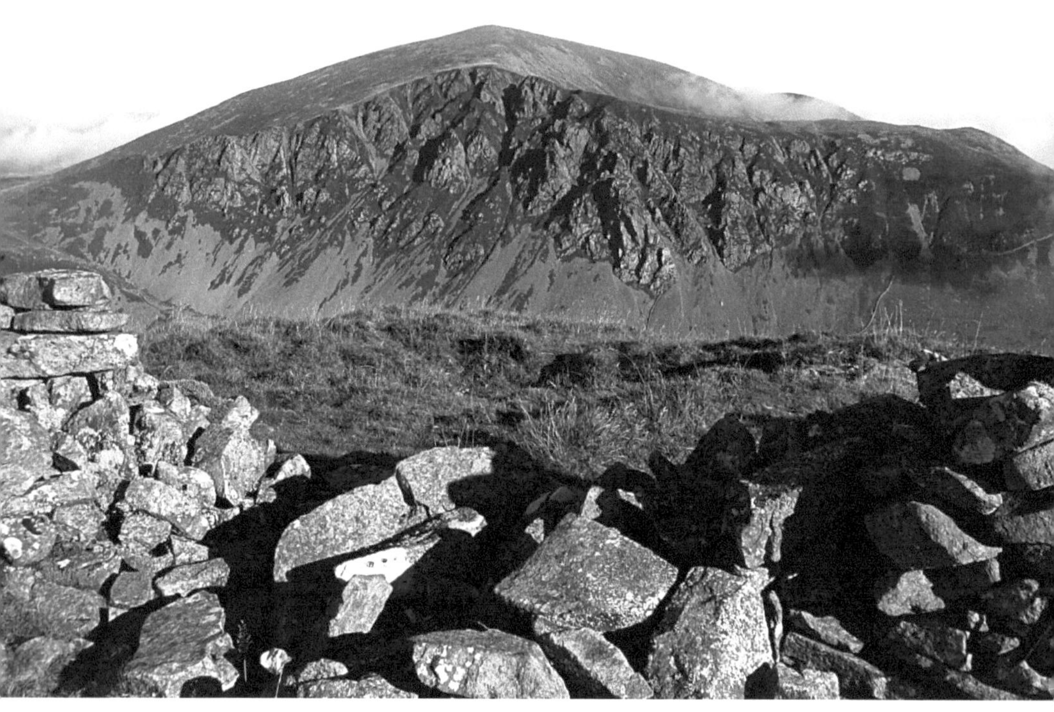

7.10am 8th September – We had chosen our summit well, just above a cloud inversion and with the top half of the Snowdon range poking through a sea of fluffy white clouds. Needless to say we spent a fair bit of time shooting the view from the many vantage points and watching the inversion slowly burning away as the sun came up. The cloud seemed to be streaming over the craggy summits and tumbling into the valley before our eyes.

This peak looks quite rounded and uninspiring from most of it's aspects but from here it looks anything but with a huge scoop taken out of the hillside to reveal some impressive cliffs. To the east you get an interesting aspect on Snowdon and the pointy satellite peak of Yr Aran. To the west the show stopping ridge of Mynydd Drws-y-coed not only looks fantastic but gets the pulse racing as this is where you're headed next.

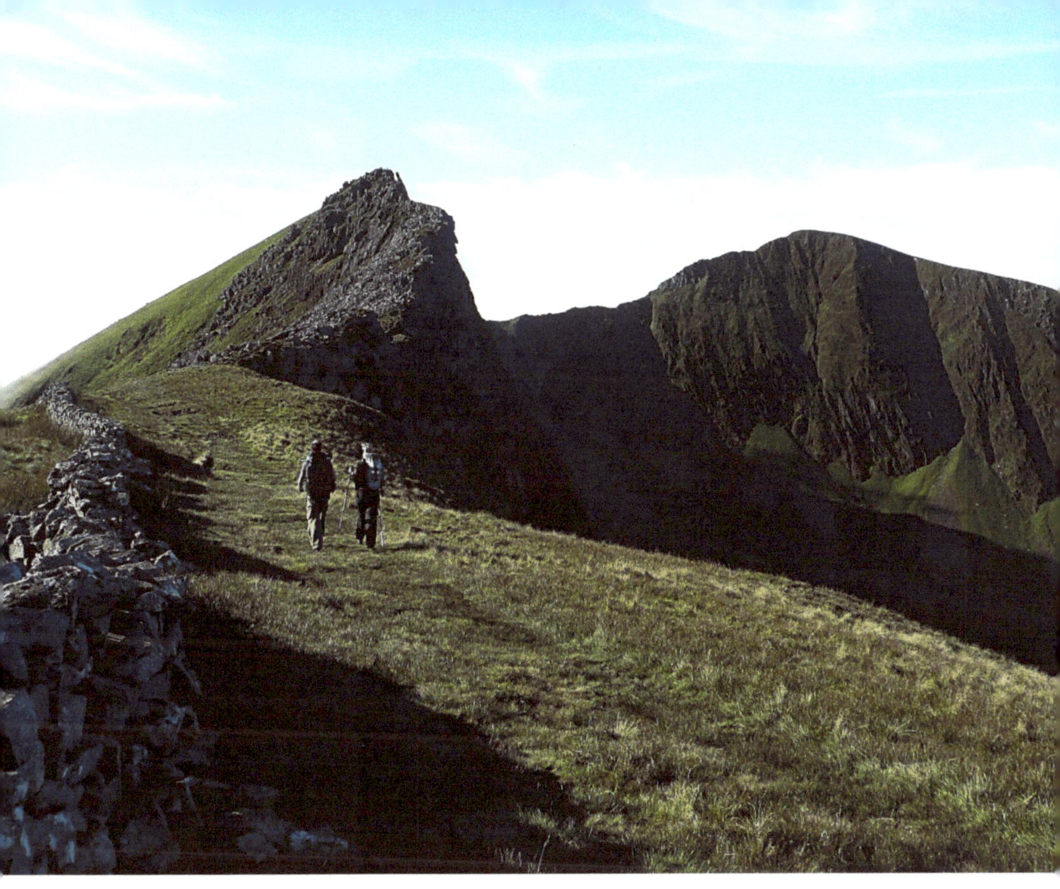

8.10am 8th September – Pete and Helen leaving camp to take on the Nantlle ridge.

Even if you are not camping here there is plenty of shelter to be had behind the stone wall offering you a good chance to spend some time making the most of your surroundings.

2) When you can finally tear yourself away, the next section of the walk tackles the north east ridge to Mynydd Drws-y-coed, which from here looks quite intimidating. The peak's name means 'the mountain at the door to the forest' which is quite appropriate as it stands proud above Beddgelert Forest. So follow a good, grassy path that runs alongside the stone wall to the ridge proper and then pick your way up the fine scramble. Whilst it does require some hands on rock, most of the steeper, exposed stuff can be avoided by taking a line to the left of the crest.

Photo Location – Mynydd Drws-Y-Coed

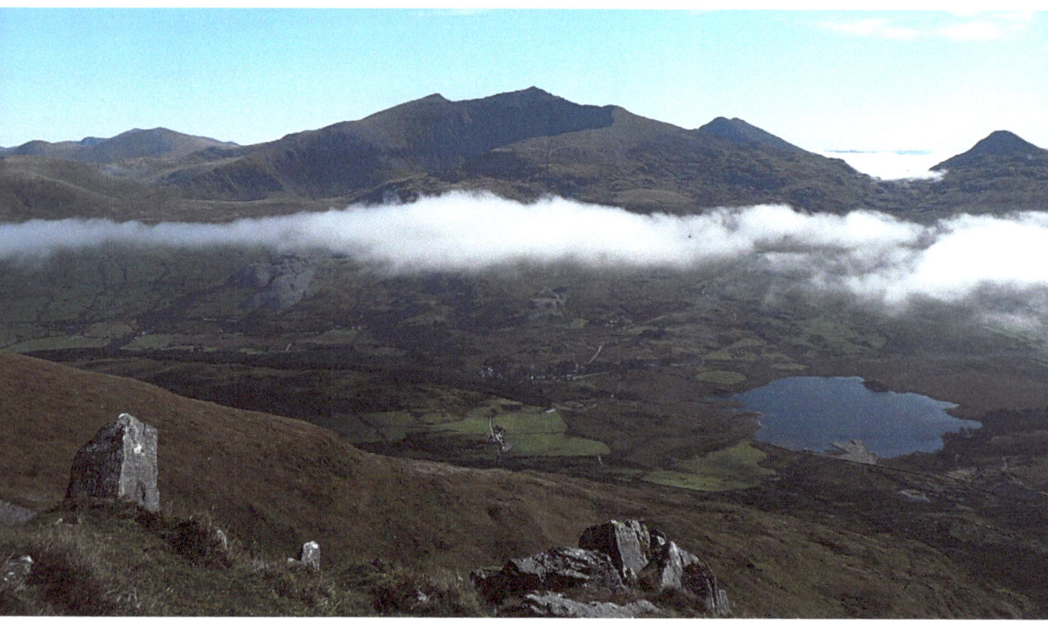

9.20am 8th September – the scramble had been good fun and pretty absorbing. So, as we topped out on the summit, it was time to take in our surroundings again. The view back over to Snowdon was clamouring for our attention, where a thin layer of mist was still hanging in the valley.

As expected, the view from the very top of the scramble gives a wonderful perspective back over to Y Garn with the stone wall snaking over the lush grass and the cliffs dropping away steeply to the left.

On reaching the summit the route is pretty obvious as it follows the ridge south west and then westwards onto the next summit, Trum y Ddysgl ('dish shaped ridge'). This summit is a bit of a surprise being quite flat and grassy again but it does offer stunning views over to the rest of the Nantlle ridge.

Photo Location – Trum Ddysgl

The view looking back over the route so far takes in the precipitous cliffs of Mynydd Drws-y-coed which, whilst in shade in the morning, add to the drama of the shot. The Snowdon range fills the skyline and you can start to appreciate there is more to this bunch of hills than just one mountain and one route up it.

Looking in the other direction, the eye is drawn to the south western end of Trum y Ddysgl's summit plateau. With luck you should be able to see the beautifully sculptured crags of Craig Cwm Silyn and the obelisk on the top of Mynydd Tal-y-mignedd.

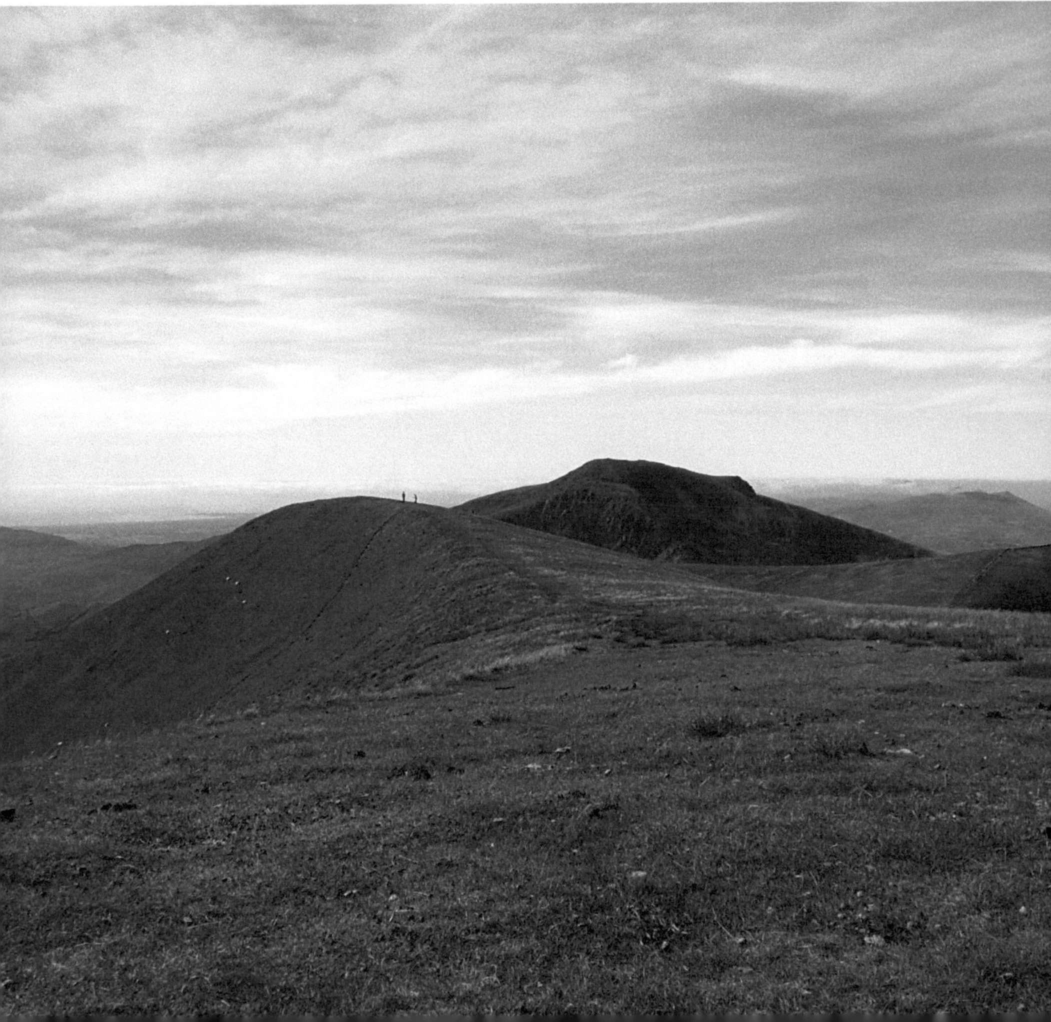

10.05am 8th September - finally after our early and high altitude start some folks had made the climb up from the valley below and broken our solitude. Whilst the conditions were still excellent we did feel rather smug (if a little tired) to have experienced the earlier cloud inversion.

Route Extension

Here you have to make a choice of where to go next. The main route heads away from the Nantlle ridge for the Moel range of hills; see point **3)**. However, with the remaining peaks of the Nantlle ridge stretching off in front of you it is hard to leave it here. So, if time and energy permits you might want to consider this route extension.

3a) To continue on the Nantlle ridge, head down the steep and ever narrowing western spur. As you drop into the col there is a superb little nick in the ridgeline that allows you to peer into the valleys below. There are also excellent views to the peaks you are about to explore. You then climb up towards the obelisk on the summit of Mynydd Tal-y-mignedd ('mountain at the end of the bog').The obelisk was built to commemorate Queen Victoria's Diamond Jubilee and was once considerably higher than it is now. On topping out, the view back over the route you have just walked, is impressive. The path over this narrow section acts as a great lead in line and accentuates this delightful part of the ridgeline.

Just before reaching the summit I looked back along the ridge and saw the rising sun break through the wintry skies. The snow had accumulated on the path picking out the route I had just taken.

To gain the next peak along the ridge, Craig Cwm Silyn, you sadly have to lose a fair bit of height, heading along the obvious path south, south westwards to the pass, Bwlch Dros-bern. The climb up from the pass is a real delight and can be made as scrambly as you like. For those wishing to avoid the rocks, trend rightwards of the wall on a meandering path. For those wanting to put hand to rock, scramble your way up the ridge in front of you, starting to the left of the wall, where you can make up your own route. Both routes reach another plateau, although this time a rocky one. From here it is a great place to take stock of your journey so far.

Photo Location – the Summit of Craig Cwm Silyn

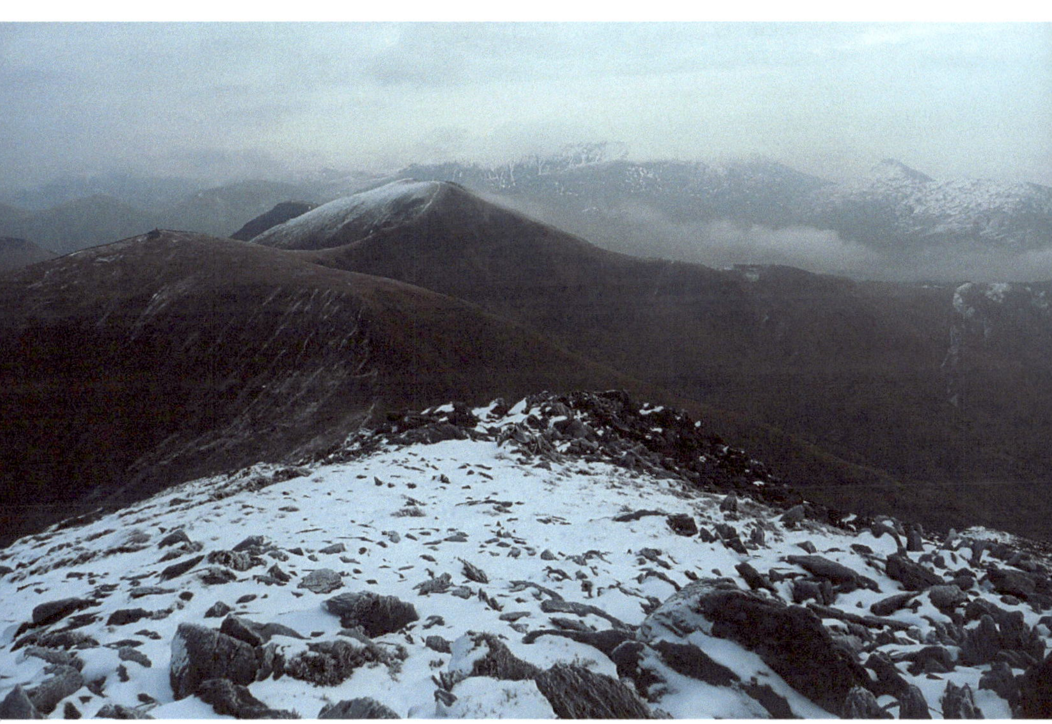

10.15am 17th February – after enjoying a slightly icy scramble I decided to stop, get a brew on and see if the low cloud

would shift. Whilst it still clung to the distant high ground around Snowdon, the rest of the Nantlle ridgeline appeared stretched out in front of me.

Craig Cwm Silyn is a truly wild summit that whilst being attached to the Nantlle ridge, it, along with its attached neighbour Garnedd-goch, is sufficiently aloof to be able to offer a unique vantage point

You face another choice here; either reverse your route along the ridge and head back to Trum y Ddysgl, where if time is short, head back to your car over Y Garn and down to Rhyd Ddu; or at Trum y Ddysgl taking the south eastern ridge as on point **3)**. This has the advantage of taking in more of the views that have been behind you and experiencing the ridge quite literally in a different light to that on your way out.

4a) However, if you are happy with taking a rougher, pathless descent, head south west across the plateau from Craig Cwm Silyn to its far end at Carnedd-goch. Here take the south eastern ridge down to the road at Braich-y-Dinas. On reaching the road turn right and follow it for 2 km or so to a footpath on the left. Cross the river on stepping stones (if the river is in spate or you don't fancy this shortcut keep heading down the road for another 500m then take a left turn up the joining road) and continue on a path that crosses the next road. Head up a green lane that brings you out at Cwrt Isaf. Note this can be used as an alternative starting point to a circuit of the hills described here. Take the path that leads you up Cwm Llefrith (fill up you water bottles along here if camping later) to reach the pass between Moel Hebog and Moel yr Ogof. From here you can reverse the route over these hills, see points **6a, 5 and 4)**.

3) If you decided not to continue along the Nantlle ridge, head down the relatively broad south eastern spur leading off Trum y Ddysgl which winds its way above the woodlands on your left. Follow the path until you come to a kink in the ridge where you trend southwards down to the disused mines littered round the head of the Pennant valley.

Again you have to make another route decision which depends on your time and energy levels. If both are fading, then the best option is to take the bridleway that heads through the woods in a north easterly direction. Leave the trees below Y Garn to rejoin the path that takes you back to the car and Rhyd Ddu.

If you do have time, or just want to spend a night out on the hills, then the climb up onto the Moel Hebog range of hills is worth the effort. Note, if you are wild camping, you'll need to make sure you have enough water for the evening and following morning, as from this point onwards there are few streams.

After carefully exploring some of the interesting mine entrances we shouldered our packs and then started the ascent of Moel Lefn. However, half way up, with the sun beating down we stepped off the path and decided to take a siesta.

4) The climb up Moel Lefn might seem like hard work at the time but the views from this relatively wild peak more than make up for the effort.

From the old mined area pick up a path that heads south east around a rocky outcrop where you reach a wall. This wall leads you around the edge of the forest, across an often boggy area. Ignore a path that crosses the wall to your left and start climbing a narrow path that leads in a southerly direction. You are soon on the northern flanks of Moel Lefn following a path that climbs around some pretty steep cliffs off to your right. As you approach the rocky outcrops that mark the summit of Moel Lefn the view of a resplendent Nantlle ridge should have you reaching for you camera.

Photo Location - Moel Lefn

This area offers spectacular views over to the Snowdon range, back over the Nantlle ridge and to the distant Lleyn hills, so it is worth spending a night out here if possible. As the peak lies on a north-south trending ridge it makes a great place to experience a sunset and following sunrise. There are numerous, flat grassy spots to pitch a tent where, with minimal effort, you'll be able to position yourself in some stunning locations. Some of the finest areas can be found just after the first rocky outcrop but before you reach the main summit.

The sunset shoot takes in the shapely tail end of the Nantlle ridge and the distant hills on the Lleyn peninsula, making for an interesting layered composition.

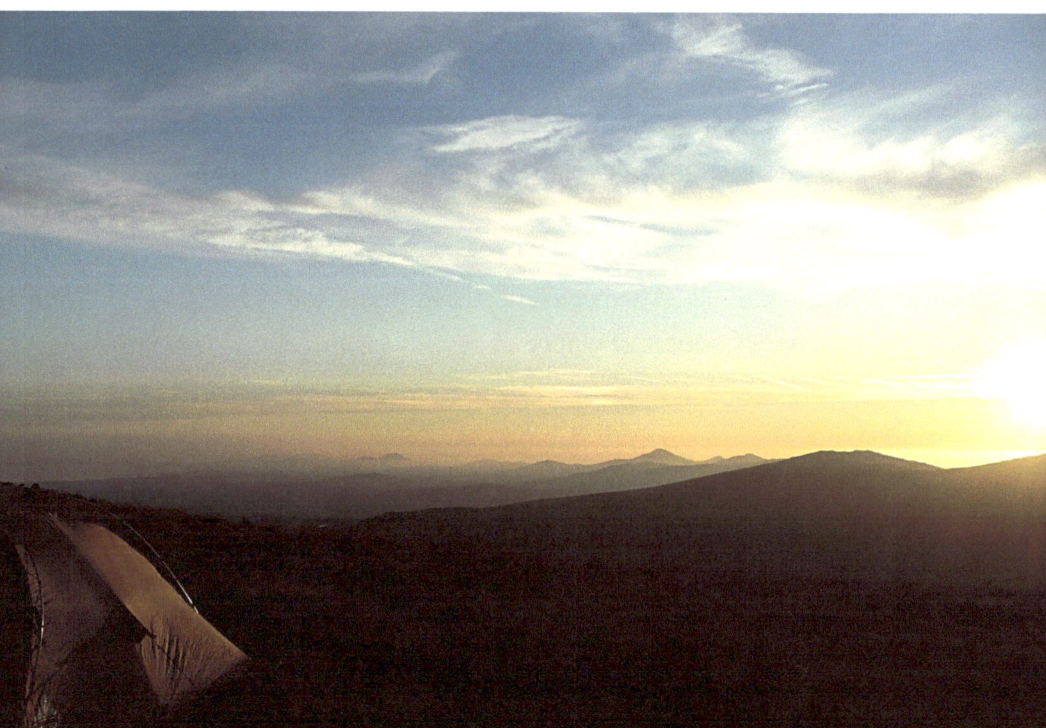

19.05 pm 8th September – Pitching up in the late afternoon allowed us to take in our surroundings in a rather leisurely way and plan our sunset shoot. More importantly it allowed us to pitch our tents with great foresight for the following morning's dawn spectacular.

Looking east the following morning, any sunrise will be over the pointy summits of Moel Siabod, Yr Aran and Y Lliwedd which lie to the south of Snowdon. Once the sun has risen, the light should start to illuminate the Nantlle ridge in the opposite direction. One area to focus on is the Craig Cwm Silyn ridgeline which is seen in profile from here and looks particularly striking as the early light picks out its fine buttresses.

5.50 am 9th September – How many times can you capture a mountain sunrise without even having to get out of bed? This sunrise shoot was a real delight as we didn't even need to climb out of our sleeping bags. It really was a sublime place to experience the golden hours.

5) From Moel Lefn continue south eastwards over the craggy summit of Moel yr Ogof. A short but steep descent over rocky ground leads you down to a stone wall and a couple of small lakes. This is an interesting area to explore with rocky outcrops and the lakes forming good foreground interest to a distant Snowdon. Follow the path down alongside the wall towards the small pass at Bwlch Meillionen. Just before you reach this col the path squeezes itself through a narrow gap between two enormous boulders. From the pass, this makes a nice image as the wall snakes its way back towards the gap.

Route Extension

6a) Gazing up at the steep, uninviting flanks of Moel Hebog it would be understandable not to want to undertake this climb. However, looking head on at a climb always makes it look far more daunting than it really is and with only 230m of ascent, how hard can it be? In truth it is not the most exciting of climbs as you plod on up next to the stone wall. Nonetheless, there are some superb views waiting for you at the summit.

Kicking steps into the snowy flanks of Moel Hebog made the climb rather enjoyable. I was also spurred on by the fact that I could see the low cloud starting to dissipate. Would I get lucky and get a weather window from this fine summit?

Photo Location – Moel Hebog

For a start you get your first real views of the rough and wild Moelwyn range of hills which from here look very exciting. Moving further round, the hills peter out towards the nearby coast. To the west, the familiar but never dull vista of the Lleyn hills can be composed with

Moel Hebog's summit as the foreground. Looking over Moel yr Ogof, the now distant Nantlle ridge can be seen in all its glorious profile.

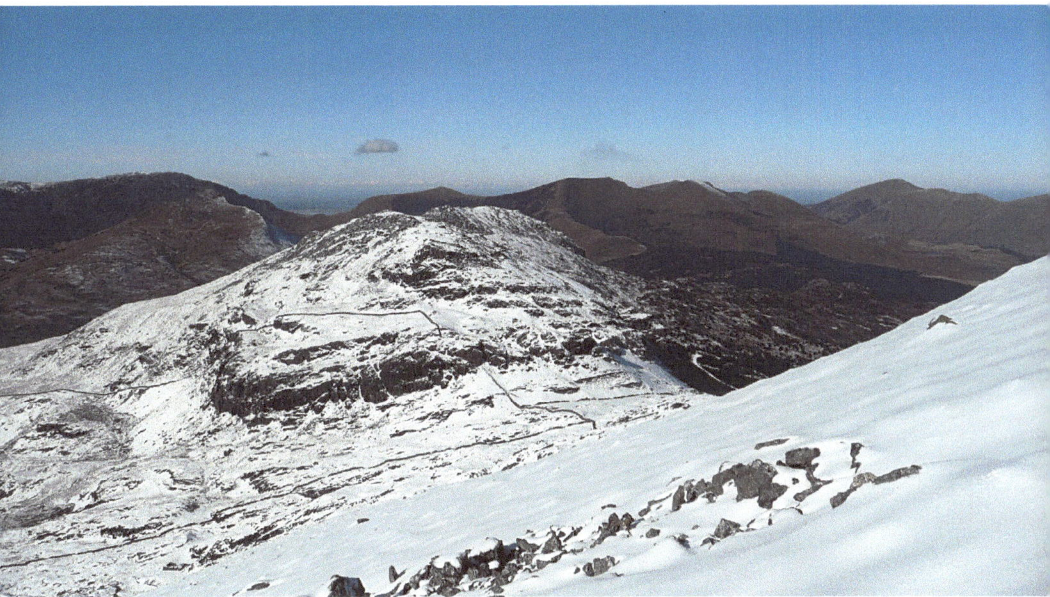

11.10 am 17th February - the snow had plastered the Moel range but left the Nantlle peaks pretty much devoid of any covering. This made a great contrast between the two ranges.

The steep cliffs on the summits eastern side offer a dramatic viewpoint down to the distant village of Beddgelert and beyond. What a fine place to sit and saviour the last elevated viewpoint on the route.

Whilst you can return via the main route off Moel Hebog down to Beddgelert, the walk through the forest is quite dull. A better option is to reverse your steps down to the pass.

6) From the pass the easiest return route is to head south west along Cwm Llefrith for 2km. Just before you reach the road at Cwrt Isaf, follow the bridleway that heads north up to the head of the valley and over the pass at Bwlch-y-ddwy-elor. You head past the old mines again before crossing the col and dropping down into the forest. As you leave the forest a reasonable, if a bit boggy at times, path winds its way along the flanks of Y Garn. After 1km you turn right on the path that leads you back to the road and Rhyd-Ddu. From here you can gaze back up to the towering summit of Y Garn where it all began.

Which ever route you take you'll experience a day or two in one of the best areas that North Wales has to offer the adventurous landscape photographer.

1.3 Y Lliwedd and Snowdon – the Alternative Snowdon Horseshoe

Focal Point – the area between Gallt y Wenallt and Y Lliwedd is little visited and offers an alternative perspective of the classic Snowdon horseshoe.

Route Summaries

Full route – starting up the Watkin Path, traverse the lower slopes of Y Lliwedd before reaching the fine vantage point of Gallt y Wenallt. Head over Y Lliwedd and on to Snowdon (Yr Wyddfa) by re-joining the upper reaches of the Watkin Path. Return via the south ridge of Snowdon, taking in the outlying peak of Yr Aran.

17 km; 1730m ascent

Shorter routes – Starting as above to Gallt y Wenallt then on over Y Lliwedd before descending the Watkin path

12.5 km; 1150m ascent

Or

The lower stretches of the Watkin Path taking in Yr Aran

* *Some hands on sections of low grade (around grade 1) scrambling*

Why Try this Route

Snowdon is a mountain with a split personality. If it's not in cloud it offers unrivalled views over the whole of Snowdonia and has a number of exciting approaches. However, being one of the 'Three Peaks' and with a mountain railway and 'tourist track' up it's northern ridge, makes it ridiculously busy at times. Therefore it could easily be discounted as not being worth exploring. If however you approach from the south and especially if you camp out at a reasonable altitude, you have a good chance to experience this mountain at its best. If you add in the glorious descent on the south ridge of Snowdon and the outlying viewpoint of Yr Aran then you are in for a view packed trip.

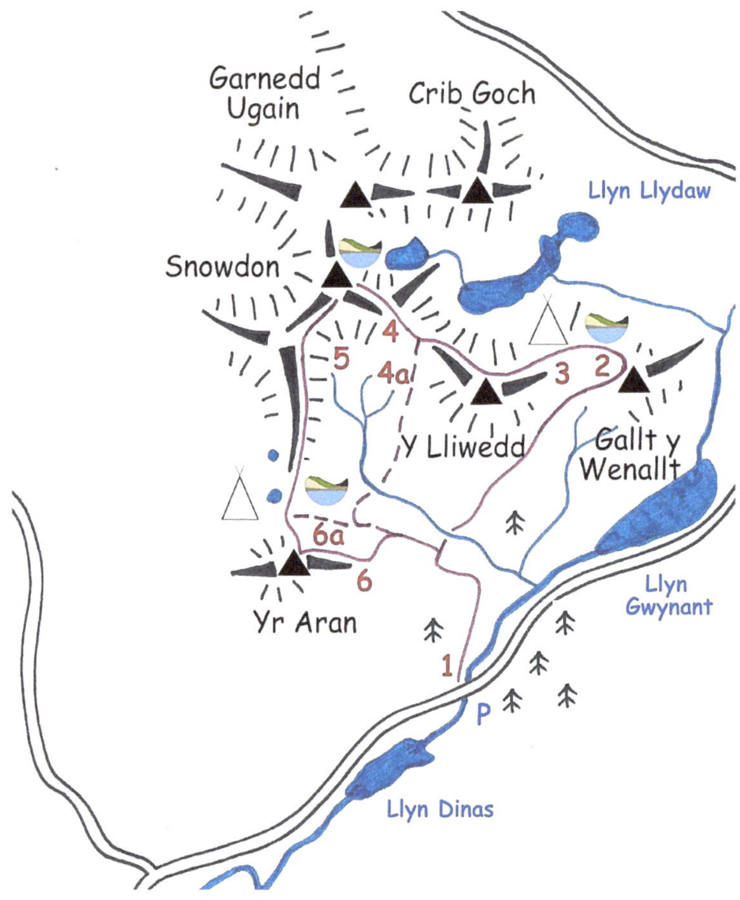

Clockwise from top left:

The summit of Snowdon (left) from Garnedd Ugain... Sunset over Y Lliwedd from wild camp... Crib Goch after leaving Gallt y Wenallt... Misty layers from the summit of Snowdon... Looking along the Crib Goch ridge between Snowdon and Garnedd Ugain... The 'new' Snowdon cafe

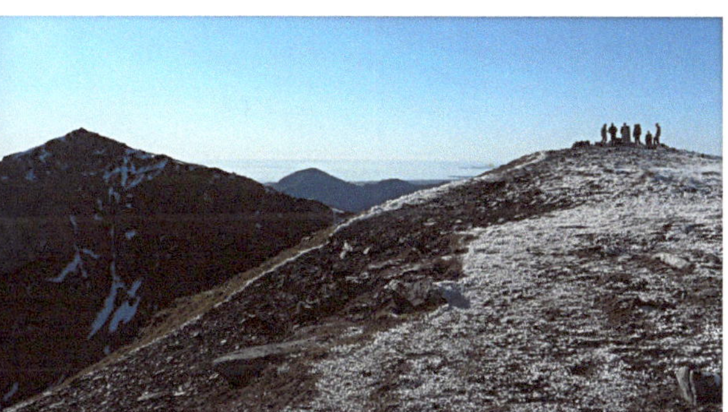

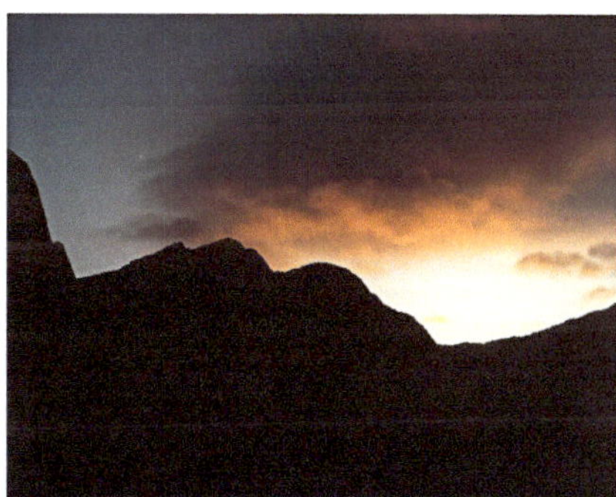

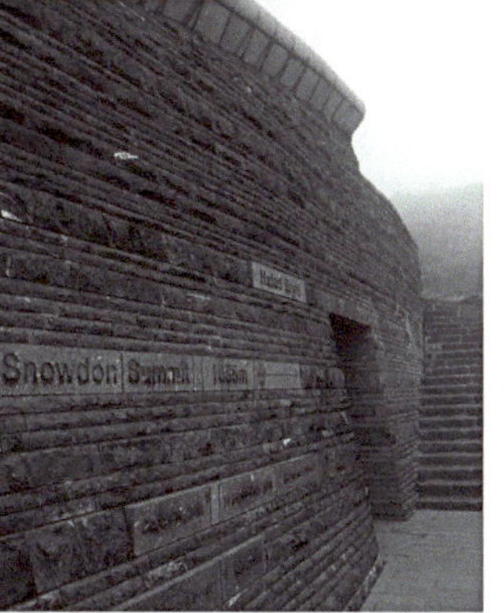

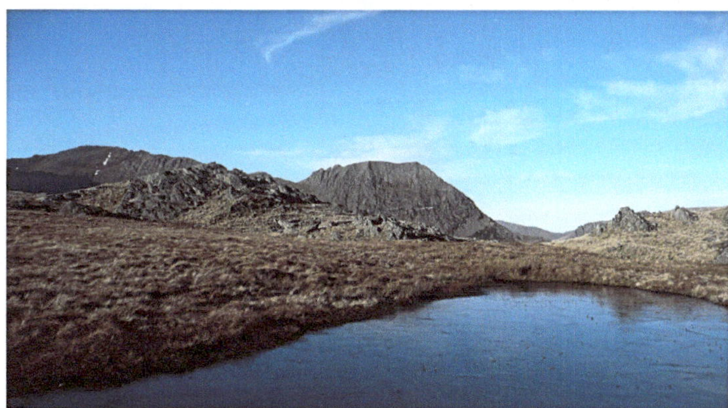

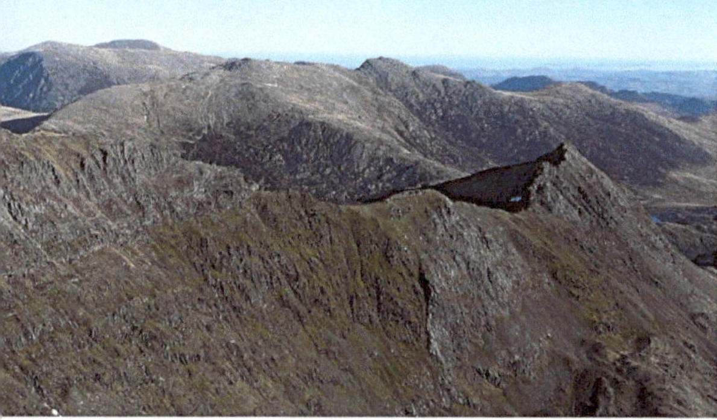

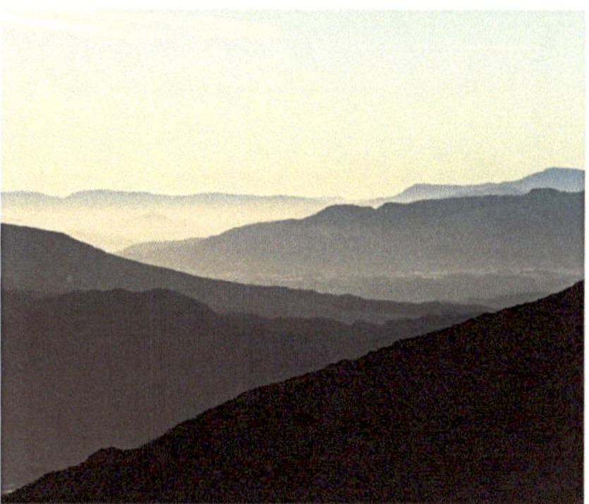

Route Description

1) From the Watkin path carpark on the A498 at Bethania (SH628507) take the Watkin path which starts in the woodland just across the road. Follow this attractive, wide path around a large loop to the left and then right for just over 1km. Towards the end of the woods a small path drops down to the stream on your right. Cross a bridge and then head in a north westerly direction whilst contouring the southern slopes of Y Lliwedd. If you are camping out tonight it's worth filling up your water bottles before gaining the high ground as this is your last chance. Towards the head of the valley the path peters out somewhat but aim for the skyline then the summit of Gallt y Wenallt.

Photo Location - Gallt y Wenallt

If you strike the broad ridge to the left of this summit it is worth taking a detour off to your right as this peak has steep north and easterly aspects offering unrivalled views down into the deep valley below and to the outlying peak of Moel Siabod.

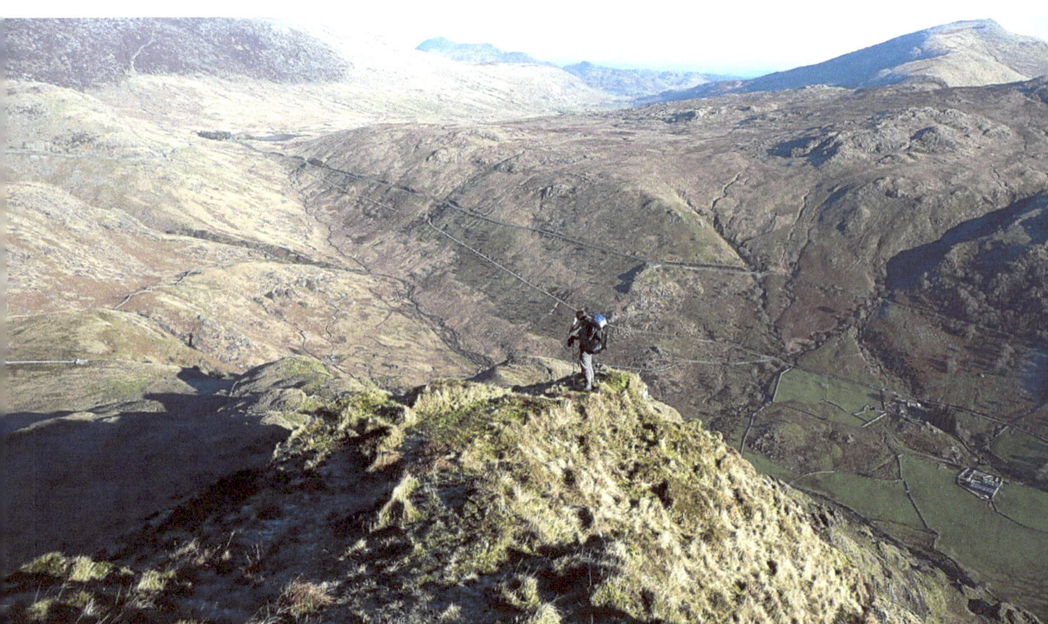

09.30 am 19th January – As we reached the summit the ground just dropped away at our feet, 500m down to the distant valley floor.

The route between Gallt y Wenallt and Y Lliwedd doesn't get many visitors and therefore there is no main path. However, by sticking to the northern side of this broad and meandering ridge you get ever more impressive views over to the wedge of narrow rock that makes up the legendary Crib Goch. Looking back over to the east, the rocky outcrops that you have just clambered around lead the eye along to the pyramidal peak of Moel Siabod. In effect this is a reverse view of the classic Snowdon horseshoe which is often shot from this peak.

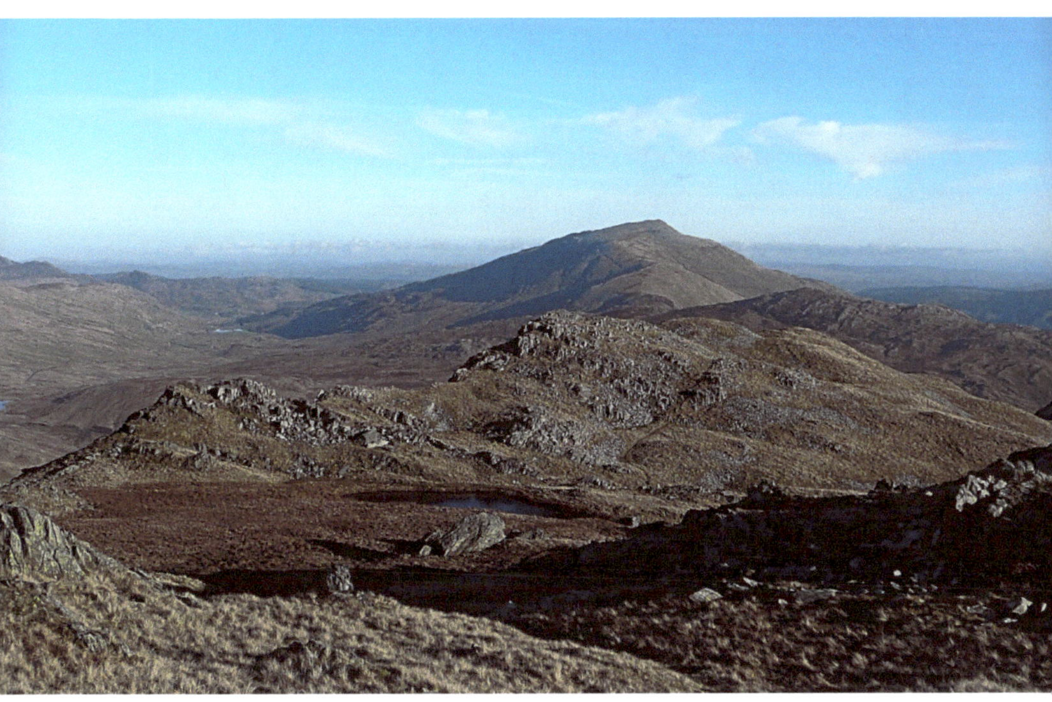

10.05 am 19th January – We spent some time exploring this rugged area before finding this elevated spot. It offered a grand position to take in our surroundings, especially looking down the fine valley that leads to Capel Curig.

If you also started this walk quite late in the day or have spent a good bit of time exploring this wild area then check out the ample wild camping spots on offer around here.

On making a late afternoon start to this route I selected a perfect wild camp spot on a flat piece of springy grass just before the steep climb started up towards the summit of Y Lliwedd. Being quite late in the day I was surprised to see two final walkers heading down from the southern end of the Snowdon horseshoe. Once they had descended I then had the mountains to myself until I reached the summit of Snowdon late the next morning. Watching the sun go down over Snowdon from this elevated camp was a memorable way to spend the evening.

2) Continue in a westerly direction, weaving your way along faint paths and use the steep drop to your right as a good navigational handrail. After passing a couple of small llyns, which make for excellent foreground interest, you soon reach the foot of Y Lliwedd's steep eastern ridge.

3) The climb up Y Lliwedd is relatively steep on a narrowing but non-technical ridge which makes the hard work seem somewhat more enjoyable. The mountain has three rocky summits, the last of which offers exciting views over to the rest of the route and a full 360 degree panorama. So it's worth spending some time here waiting for any changing light before heading down the rocky, but again not too hands on, western ridge of the mountain. This takes you to the surprisingly large pass, Bwlchy Saethau. If you're not in cloud you get a great perspective looking back over to the brooding cliffs of Y Lliwedd that you have just clambered above. Also you get a fine view down the length of the equally brooding waters of Llyn Llydaw far below.

4a) If you want to avoid climbing up to the summit of Snowdon or if the weather just isn't playing ball then a good option is to look for the Watkin Path that drops down to your left from the pass. By following this well managed path it will take you back to the carpark and is an interesting walk in its own right.

4) However, if conditions are good then climb the steep scree path in front of you, following a number of zigzags with a left or westward trend. This path brings you out a couple of hundred meters south of the summit of Snowdon so follow the last short climb to a well earned summit. If you are lucky and have timed it right (i.e.before the first train delivers its hoards) then you might just get the place to yourself with probably one of the most extensive views in the whole region.

Photo Location – Snowdon

It can be hard to decide what to take in first from the summit of Snowdon if and it is a big if, you are lucky to get a view from the top of this mercurial peak.

I have visited the summit many times although one of the most memorable was my first when, many years ago, a friend and I climbed the Watkin path on an extremely soggy Monday in February. We didn't get a single view once we were above 300m but we also didn't see a soul out on the mountain. On our descent I did get to see my first peregrine falcon as it streaked passed us, which was rather special.

However, the vista looking south east back to Y Lliwedd is rather striking as this rocky monster, that you have just traversed, appears almost alpine from here. Whilst the cliffs will be in shadow for most of the day this can add to the drama of the image as they encircle the interesting Llyn Llydaw below.

Looking south west you get extensive views all the way to the coast and sandwiched in between the south ridge of Snowdon, which you will soon be walking, Yr Aran and the fine Moelwyn range of hills. Far below in Cwm Llan the old spoil heaps litter the valley floor which not only add texture to the image but link you to this areas important historical past.

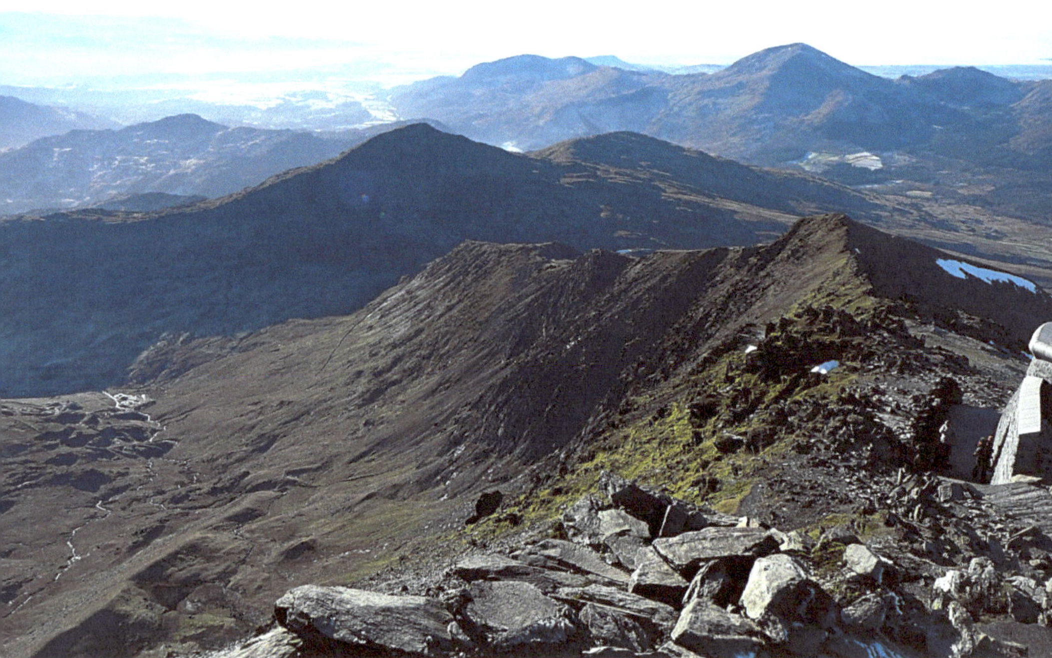

11.10 am 20th January – The much maligned but equally sublime summit of Snowdon was a joy to behold on this crisp winter morning. Having camped out at Bwlch Cwm Llan we were one of the first to reach the summit that day.

It is worth dropping down from the summit pile and carefully exploring the eastern edges to drink in those views. Talking of drinking, and taking shelter for that matter, you can't rely on the summit café being open all year round. If the trains aren't running, for example if the weather is grim, then the café won't be open.

5) Once you've finished with those extensive views then it's time to enjoy one of the finest airy ridges that doesn't require any scrambling skills. The south ridge of Snowdon is a real cracker and being narrow but easy angled it gives you a chance to look over to the Nantlle ridge to the west and into Cwm Llan below to the east. Ignore the split in the path to the right, which takes you to Rhyd Ddu, and follow the main south ridge spur which drops you down to the pass, Bwlch Cwm Llan. If you are seeking another wild camp spot there is a nice flat grassy area just off to the right of the pass above the quarry.

Photo Location - Bwlch Cwm Llan

Passes do not always offer the best views as their full panoramas are often hindered by surrounding slopes. However, this one seems to deliver one of the finest vantage points to take in the full glory of the wonderful Nantlle ridge and neighbouring Mynydd Mawr.

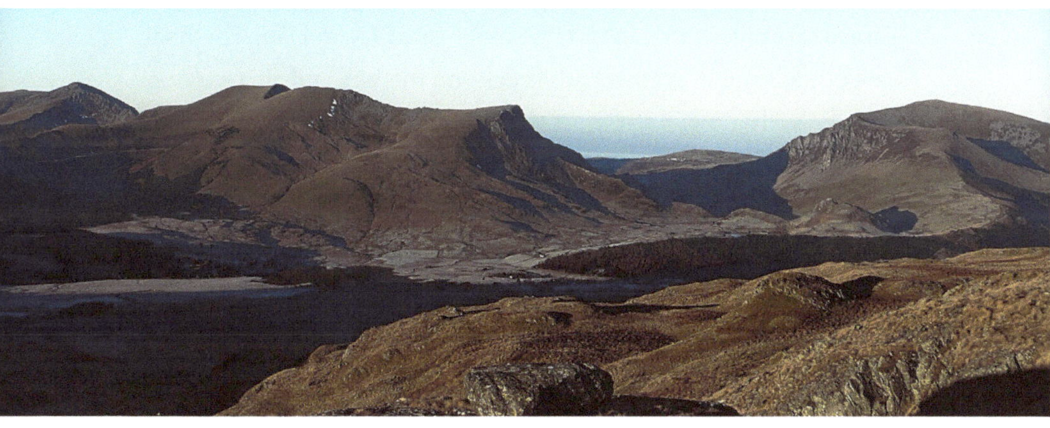

08.00 am 20th January - We had pitched up as the sun was dropping down over the horizon, beautifully silhouetting the Nantlle ridge across the valley. A cold, clear night meant it was a frosty start to the following morning. This provided ideal conditions to take in last night's sunset view. Two shoots for the price of one. Result.

The view is dominated by Y Garn's imposing northern ridge which is nicely balanced by the opposing crags that make up Mynydd Mawr's Craig Y Bera. Whilst there is a fair bit of forestry plantation in the area, the lower elevation of the viewpoint minimises the impact of these on the image.

6a) The quickest and easiest route from the pass is by taking the obvious path off to your left which quickly drops down into Cwm Llan and then picks up the Watkin path back to the road.

6) However, with a bit more effort a final climb to the summit of Yr Aran makes for a superb finale to the route. The ascent is quite steep, however, as the summit is an outlier to the main Snowdon massif it makes an excellent place to look straight back up the ridge you have just descended. As the ground drops away in all directions you also have a good chance of taking in some final far reaching views, whatever the time of day. From the top of Yr Aran descend by following the easier angled eastern ridge along a fine stone wall to a flat grassy plateau. From here, drop north, steeply into Cwm Llan. The final walk out along the Watkin path is easy on the legs and also easy on the eyes with a few small waterfalls to get in some long exposure water shoots before reaching the road at the trail head.

As is often the case on returning to civilisation after climbing Snowdon, the thick clag that had clung to the summit whilst I was there a few hours ago had now shifted. This made me even more determined to plan another trip as I'd discovered that this mountain had more than one side to its character.

1.4 The Dovey Hills – an Unexplored Gem

Focal Point – the stunning Cadair Idris from a number of equally wild and stunning viewpoints.

Route Summaries

Full route – starting from the pass at Ochr y Bwlch climb up to the fine viewpoint of Pen y Brynnfforchog before continuing on to Glasgwm. Head south above the cliffs of Craig Cywarch and traverse the grassy Y Gribin to Foel Benddin ridge. A steep descent brings you down to the valley floor where you start the steady climb to the cliffs of Craig Maesglase. The rolling ridge line then takes you over the summits of Maen Du, Craig Portas and Cribin Fawr before it drops back to the pass again.

23 km; 1590 m ascent

Shorter routes – a there and back taking in Pen y Brynnfforchog and Glasgwm

5 km; 420 m ascent

Or

A there and back to the cliffs of Craig Maesglase from Dinas Mawddwy

6.5 km; 570 m ascent

Whilst most of the route follows various fence lines, making navigation fairly straightforward, there are a number of steep ascents and descents on grassy hillsides.

You can start this walk from the pass Ochr y Bwlch as described below. This makes a lot of sense if you are starting later in the day and want to camp out on the northern half of the walk. However, you could equally start the walk in the village of Dinas Mawddwy.

Why Try this Route

A traverse of Cadair Idris should be on everyone's wish list as it has to be one of the finest hills in Wales. However, whilst on the hill itself you don't get the best perspective of this stunning group of summits. You need a bit of distance to allow you to fully appreciate its finery. This route gives you this distance and allows you to take in some of its finest viewpoints in some pretty wild settings. You also get to walk above some breathtaking cliffs where two waterfalls plunge down their precipitous slopes. If you also pack your tent you get the choice of some superb wild camps which put you in the right place to enjoy the golden hours.

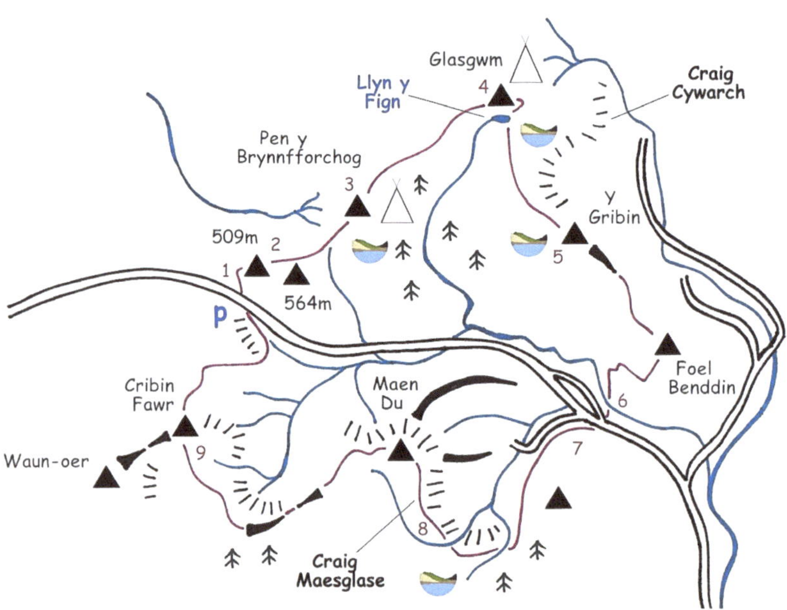

Clockwise from top left:

Descending from Maen Du with the distant Pumlumon and incoming rain... Sunset over the Rhinogs from Pen y Brynnfforchog... Sunrise over Rhobell Fawr from Pen y Brynnfforchog... The ridges of Cadair Idris on the ascent from Ochr y Bwlch... Pen y Brynnfforchog summit wild camp... The crystal clear waters of Llyn y Fign

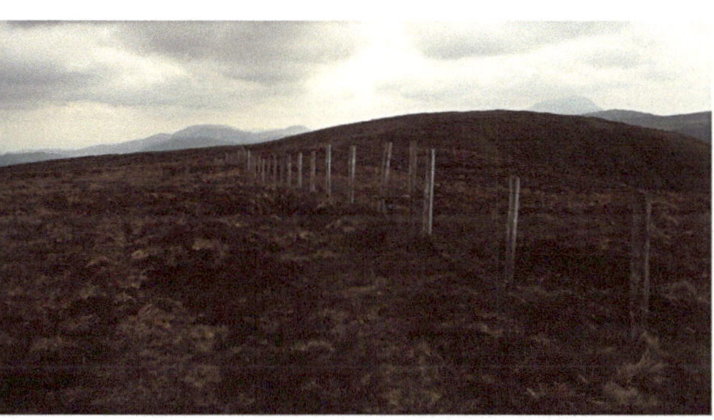

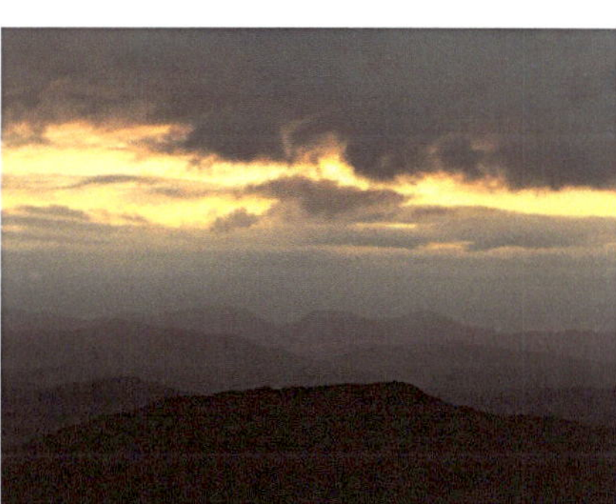

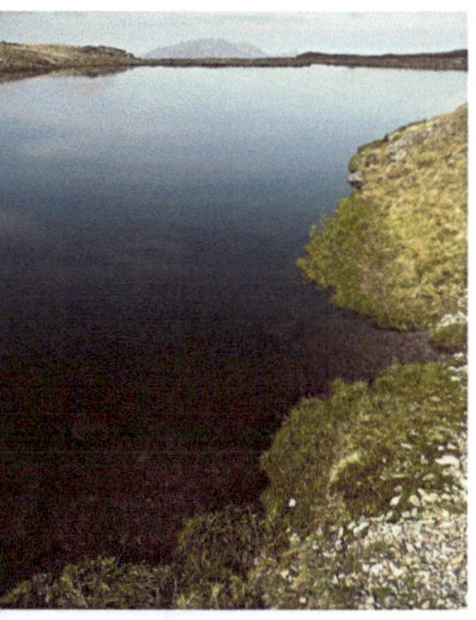

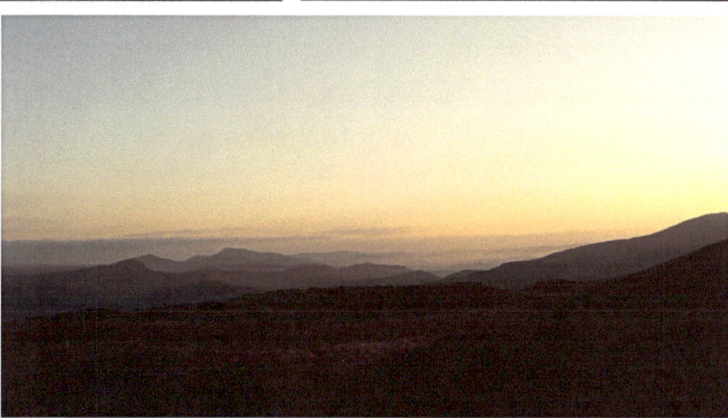

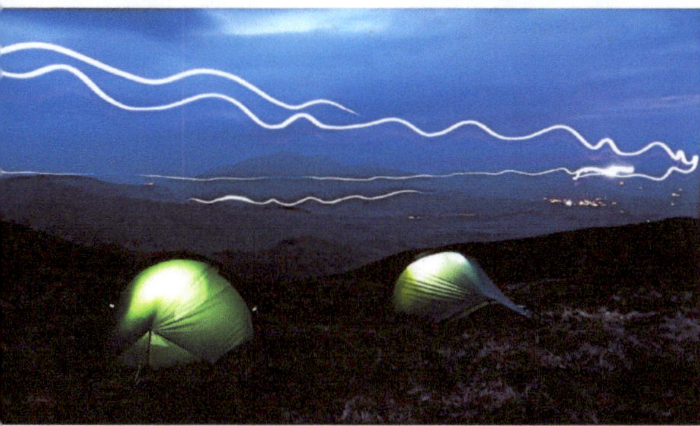

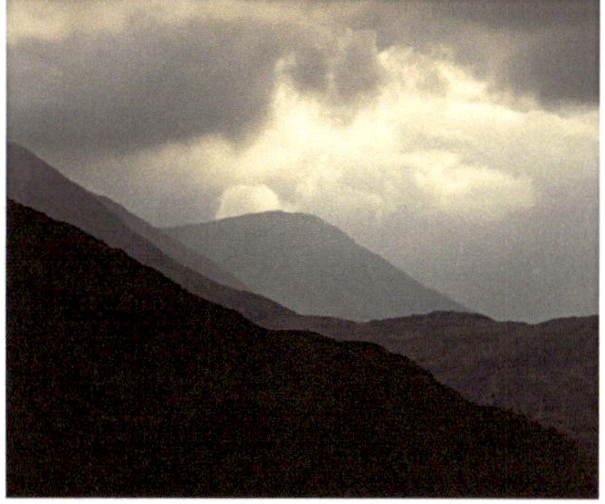

Route Description

1) From the carpark at the top of the Ochr y Bwlch pass on the A470 (SH 802170), cross the road, climb over the stile and start a really steep grassy climb following the fence to your left. This is a hard way to start a walk but as you climb the views start to open up above the Craig y Bwlch ridge opposite giving you plenty of reasons to stop and catch your breath. The serried ranks of Cadair Idris's multi topped range should have you reaching for the camera. Further west the sinuous curves of the Mawddach river lead their way out towards a distant sea. The first summit, no more than a rocky knobble (unnamed peak, spot height 509m) gives you your first taste of far reaching views north to the distant Rhinog ridgeline and beyond. This is a place to savour as most of the really hard work is done and the views from higher up only get better and better.

2) Leave the summit by following the fence in an easterly direction. Ignore the first ladder stile on your left and take the second one. Follow a faint grassy track that traverses below the hill (unnamed peak, spot height 564 m) on your right. You are aiming to pick up the fence line again at a broad pass to the north east. On rejoining the fence, follow it as it steadily climbs to the fine but no doubt little visited summit of Pen y Brynnfforchog.

Photo Location - Pen y Brynnfforchog

The additional height gained from the first summit helps put you at one of the best viewpoints of Cadair Idris with its layers of ridgelines rising up from the green valley floor. The distance to the summit of Cadair from here allows you to appreciate its full uninterrupted grandeur. To the west you can take in ever expansive views to the estuary as it meanders down to the sea. To the north west, the rolling ridgeline of the mighty Rhinog range makes for a striking vista. Further north, the shapely summit of Rhobell Fawr stands proud and forms a perfect focal point for a sunrise shoot. Both of these views benefit from multiple layers of lower hills which add depth to the image and often add contrasting shades. Sadly the forestry to your east does distract from the pristine nature of this viewpoint. However, the view south into the wild Afon Cerist valley, surrounded by the cliffs of Cribin Fawr and Craig Portas more than makes up for this. It also helps to whet the appetite as you can trace out the route's southern stretches from here. In fact the hills you can see from here just go to show that there is more to Snowdonia than just the classic northern summits. There's a lifetimes exploring to be had round here..

There are numerous wild camp spots around the summit, especially just a few meters north west down from the summit ridge. There are also some slightly more sheltered camp spots to the north before you reach the forest.

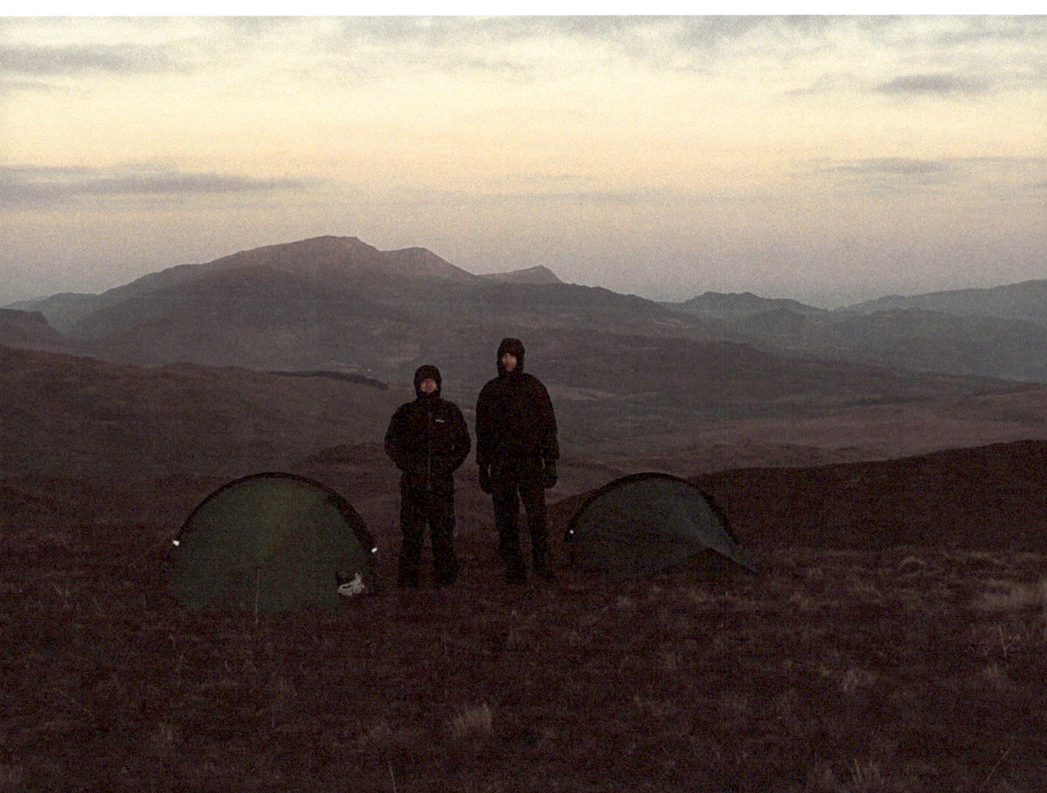

05.30 am 15th May - Waking up to the sound of a cuckoo and the skylarks taking to the skies broke the silence of a very peaceful night. It might have been very early in the morning and pretty chilly, but it was worth Simon and me getting out of bed for.

3) On leaving the summit cross a ladder stile and head north aiming for the top left of the forestry enclosure. On dropping down to the fence that runs alongside the trees you pass a small llyn. As you reach a fence junction near some rocky outcrops, clamber over a ladder stile. A faint path skirts the right hand side of a shallow bowl, keeping around 50-100m to the left of the treeline. Cross another ladder stile about 200m up from the forest and follow the fence line past a large quartz outcrop. The path climbs up through rocks and as the angle eases cross another ladder stile before you reach the rather fine summit of Glasgwm.

Photo Location – Glasgwm and Llyn y Fign

On examining a map of Glasgwm or even looking at its heavily forested southern slopes you could be forgiven to disregard it as a stunning photographic viewpoint. However, as soon as you step foot onto its summit you start to appreciate its rather fine qualities. The first of these is of course the nearby Llyn y Fign which is a beautifully shaped strip of water. The crystal clear water forms a stunning foreground to the distant Dovey and Cadair ranges. Depending on the conditions a water level shoot can result in some excellent images. A calm day gives you the chance to look for reflections and also to peer into the depths of the lake. More choppy conditions and a darker sky can add some drama to the image.

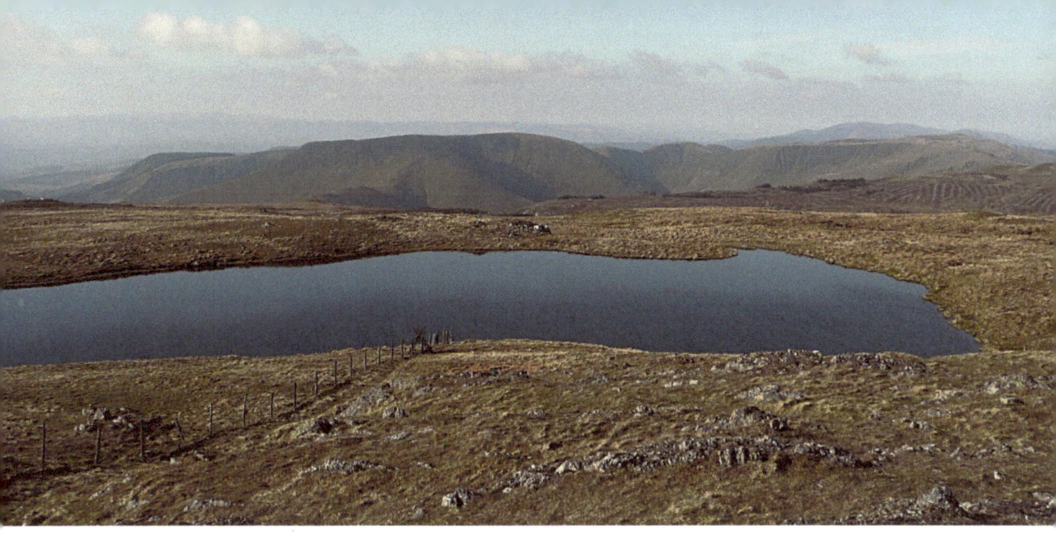

09.20 am 15th May – Despite following a number of fences to get there, the summit of Glasgwm felt pretty remote and was a delight in the early morning light.

To the north the rather smaller but equally shapely waters of Llyn Bach add real value to the view over to the main Aran hills.

There are numerous wild camp locations around the summit area, especially between the summit and Llyn Bach. This truly is a sublime location.

4) From the summit, if you haven't already made a visit drop down to Llyn y Fign by crossing a ladder stile. At the eastern end of the lake pick up a faint path that heads south, aiming for a rocky outcrop. From alongside the outcrop drop diagonally down to a fence on the right. Follow the fence line down and as the drop starts to steepen keep an eye out on your left for the cliffs of Craig Cywarch.

Photo Location - Craig Cywarch

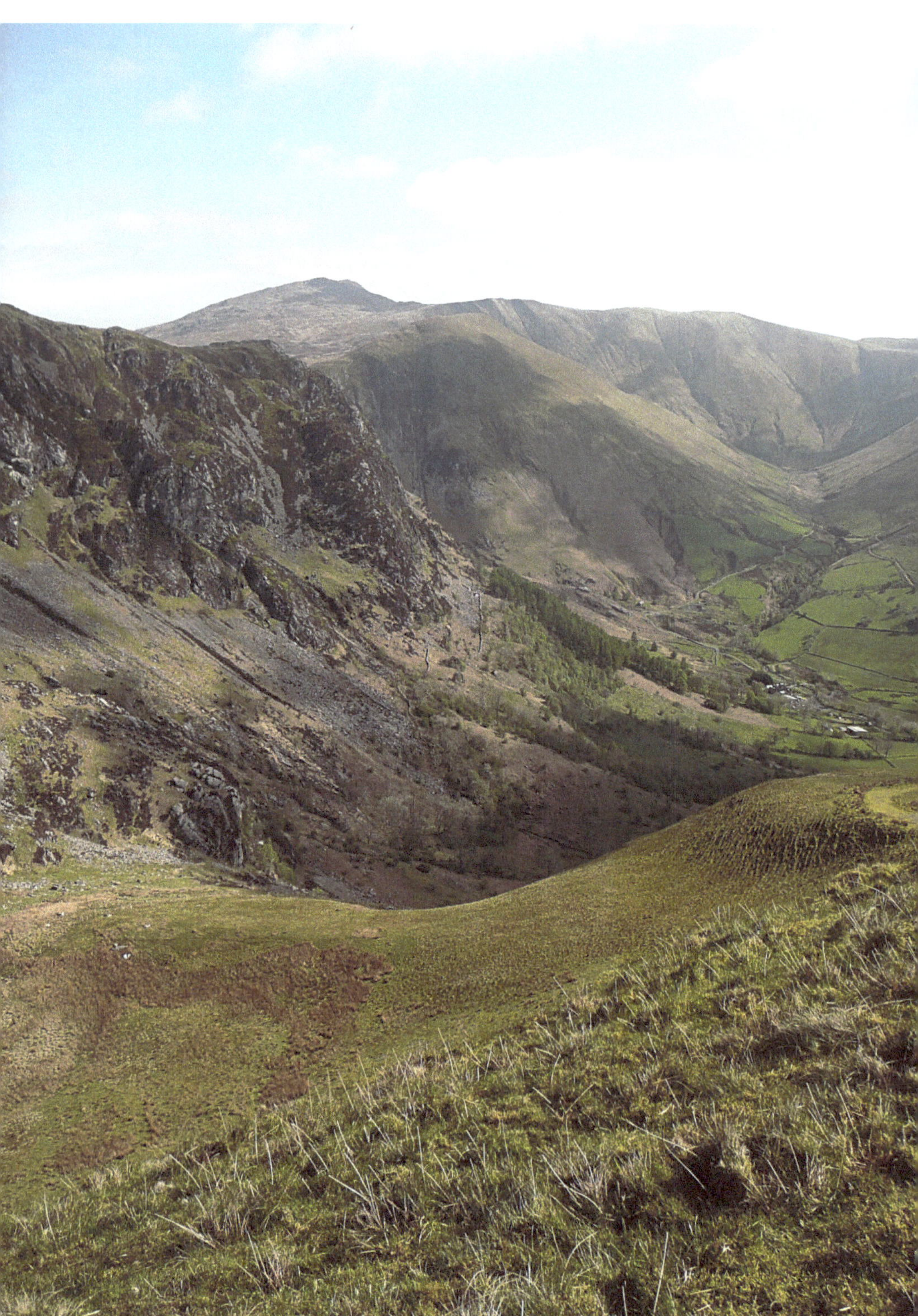

10.40 am 15th May – The cliffs of Craig Cywarch reminded me of my time in the Howgills above Cautley Spout. Also, seeing the distant summit of Aran Fawddwy took me back to an amazing walk with my old dog Millie one snowy winter.

There are numerous vantage points along the top of these cliffs which allow you to shoot them from various angles. Being east facing they are best shot in the morning as the light picks out their craggy nature and the different tones of the vegetation. This is a classic glacial valley which has the interesting contrast of lush green pastures that merge into the scree lined slopes above.

For future route planning, note the standard way up to the main Aran hills: A great walk starts from this valley and heads up between the end of the cliffs and the shapely dome of Gwaun y Llwyni. The highest summit of the Aran range, Aran Fawddwy, can be clearly seen poking above the cliff line. Encircling the upper reaches of the valley below are the peaks of Drysgol and Pen yr Allt uchaf which make up the standard return route around the Arans.

5) Cross a stile and follow the fence up and over the grassy top of Y Gribin, following the ridge down towards a pass. Just before reaching the pass, cross the fence to the right before climbing the steep grassy slopes of Foel Benddin.

On our descent of Foel Benddin we were treated to our own private air show by the RAF. First some trainer jets ambled through the valley then a series of Euro Fighters tore past banking right in front of us to make the tight turn.

From the top of this rather flat and featureless hill head in a south westerly direction down a broad ridge, keeping the gorse well to your left. Cross a stile and head on down to a gate. Go through the gate and pick up a track that heads diagonally down the hillside towards Dolobran. Just before Dolobran turn left and contour round the lower slopes of Foel Benddin. This track leads you to a junction. From here, a good track leads left, leading you down to the village of Dinas Mawddwy where there is a pub and café. However, this is a there and back detour of 2.5 km.

6) To avoid the detour to the village turn right on a track over a small river then around to the left onto a minor road. Follow this down to the main A470 road. Turn right along the main road for 100m before crossing over to pick up a minor road that leads into the Nant Maeglase valley.

7) Follow this minor road as it steadily climbs up through a farm for just under 1km. Before the road drops down to the stream to your right take the track in front of you and go through the gate. This track contours you slowly up into the valley. As you reach the end of the wooded area on your left go over a ladder stile to enter open access land. As you edge your way up into this valley the two waterfalls dropping down the Craig Maesglase cliffs spur you on. Skirting to the left around the bog in front of you, make your way to the ruined buildings at the head of the valley. From here the climbing starts in earnest but something rather special is waiting for you to make all the hard work worthwhile. Pick up the path that steeply climbs the grassy face in front of you either taking the zig zags off to the right or the more direct path in front. Both paths bring you out on a small pass where you head up to the right before reaching the forestry. The path winds its way up through heathery slopes, crossing the feeder stream of the first waterfall. As the gradient finally starts to ease above this stream, bear right along the top of the magnificent cliff edge. As you start to drop down towards the feeder stream for the second waterfall the view along the top of these cliffs really start to open up for you.

Photo Location - Craig Maesglase

It is worth stopping well before you reach the stream crossing as the undulating cliff line makes for an interesting composition with the sweeping grassy slopes dropping away into the valley below.

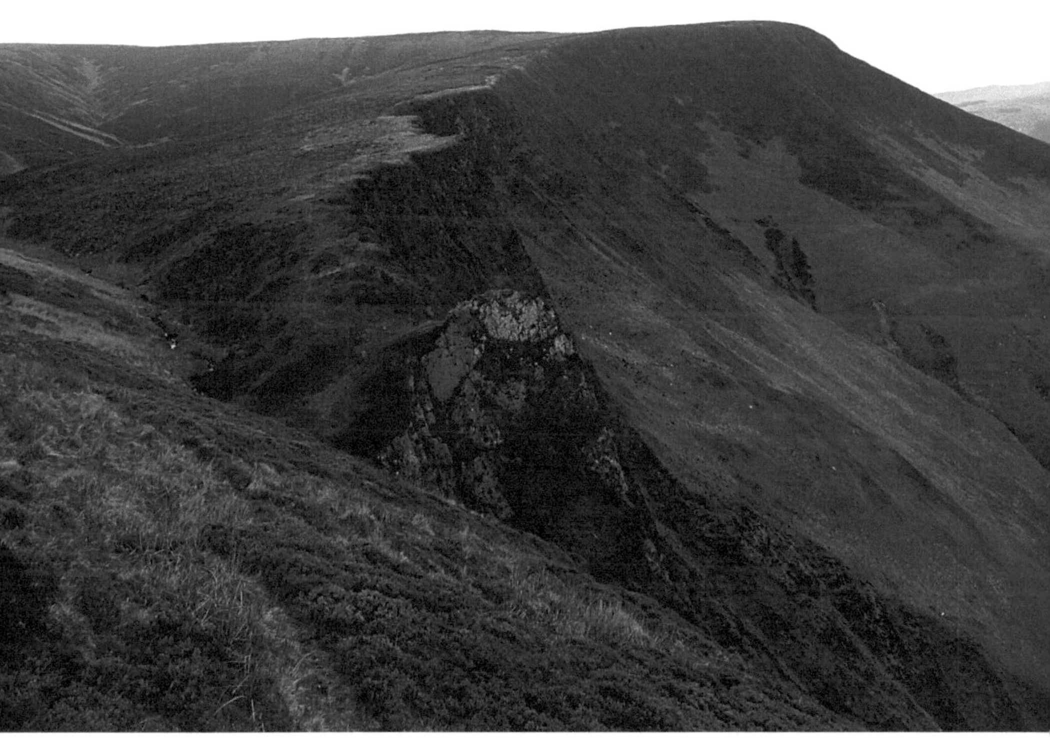

14.50 pm 15th May – Despite the approaching rain clouds this was a fantastic spot to enjoy the wilderness of the Dovey Hills.

Also note the rocky outcrop that stands proud of the escarpment. This is an amazing natural promontory from which, with a bit of a head for heights, you can stand and take in a great view of the Maesglase falls. So head down to cross the stream and clamber up to the rocky outcrop.

8) From the viewpoint follow the top of the escarpment as it winds its way up to the summit of Maesglase where the cliffs swing round to the north west and the main summit Maen Du. This summit is slightly disappointing in its outlook, however it does offer an interesting view over to a number of Mid Wales' finest peaks which includes a distant Pumlumon. Here you pick up a fence line again, so cross the stile and follow the fence for 500m. As the fence kinks off to the left, then right, you can cut the corner, heading out across the open moor, quite a novelty on this walk, on a faint path. As you pick up the fence line again you start to follow the top of a relatively narrow ridge. Follow the path as it leads you over two shortish climbs above the Craig Portas cliffs. Drop down into a pass before a bit of a slog up the last real climb of the day. The fence leads you all the way to the summit of Cribin Fawr crossing a large peat bog which takes some negotiating.

9) This summit offers some fine views of Cadair Idris again. However, if time and energy permits, an out and back detour to the summit of Waun Oer can be made from here. Either way, for the route home from here, cross the stile and turn right following the fence as it ambles its way towards the quarries around the top of Cribin Fach. Here you have a choice for your final descent back to the pass. The shortest, most direct route is to continue following the fence as it drops steeply down Craig y Bwlch. A slightly longer, and easier on the knees route is to pick up the old quarry path that heads east down and around the hillside. To do this, just before the final rocky outcrop next to the quarry, cross the fence and drop down the slowly descending track to your right. As you round the ridge the path contours left down the hillside towards the pass. As you near the car park the ground starts to steepen, however, a reasonable path weaves its way down to the flat field in front of you. Cross through a gap in the fence and head diagonally across the field to a stile. Go over the stile, then over a ladder stile to get you back into the car park at the top of the pass.

We had timed our 24 hour trip to almost perfectly match the fine weather window. Sadly the rain caught us on the last mile back which did little to dampen our spirits. One fine mini adventure in a rather special, little visited corner of Wales.

On a Visit to the Area Why Not Also Check Out These Coastal Options

1.5 The Isle of Anglesey and the Lleyn Peninsula

Why Try These Routes

Sometimes the weather in the Welsh mountains can be, shall we say, somewhat challenging to the landscape photographer. Ok this is an understatement and probably on days like these you are unlikely to want to head out into the hills with your camera. However, on more borderline days when you are already in the area but not sure if you want to commit to a full day in the mountains these coastal locations can be just as rewarding. In fact this combination of rolling hills that overlook some of the UK's most stunning, wild beaches should be seen as more than just a plan B option.

Clockwise from top left:

Looking towards the central Snowdonian hills, Newborough beach... Newborough beach on Anglesey looking towards Llanddwyn Island... The Yr Eifl range from Newborough beach... Porth Ysgo from Mynydd Penarfynydd on the Lleyn... Sunset from the summit of Moel y Gest... Centre : Moel y Gest from Black Sands beach

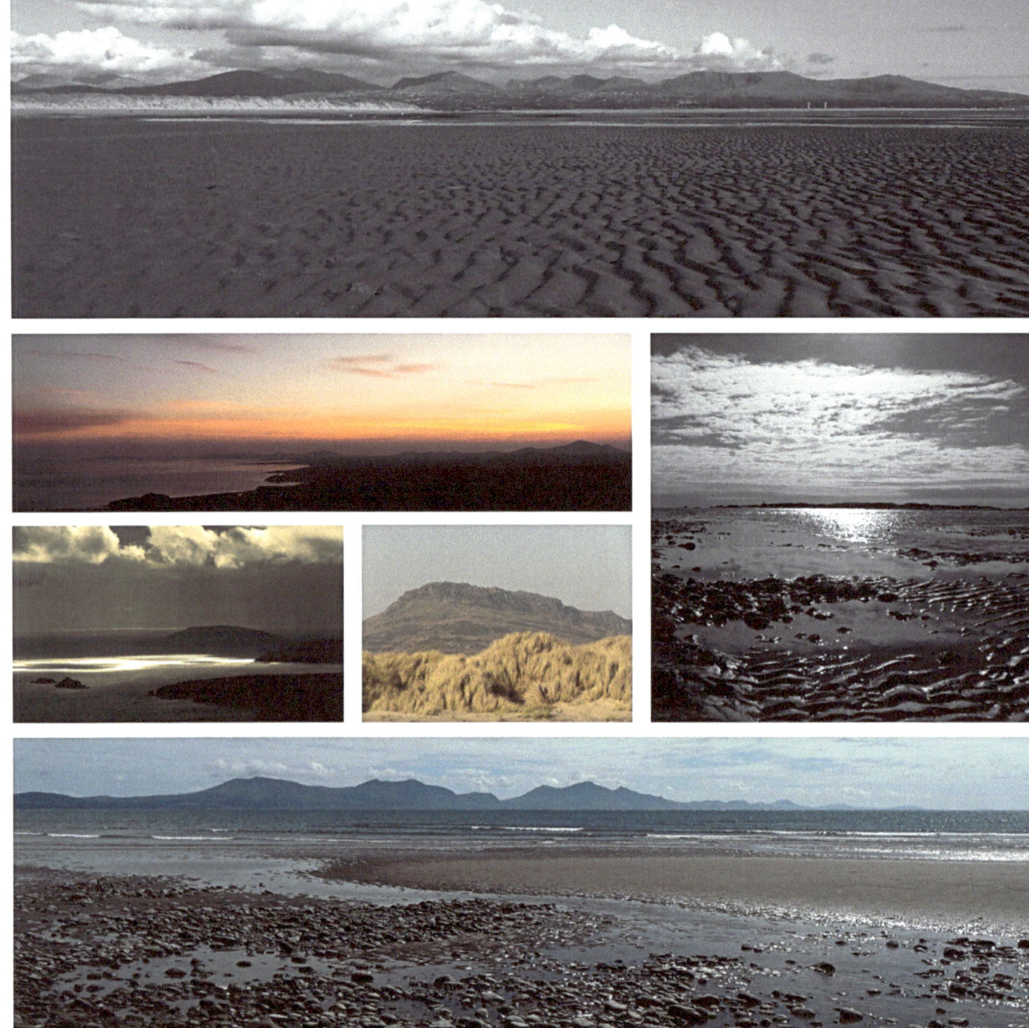

The Isle of Anglesey

From the dramatic cliffs of Gogarth near Holyhead Mountain to the tidal stretches of the Menai Straits, Anglesey has a varied and hugely photogenic coastline.

Newborough Beach

One of my Anglesey highlights is the simply sublime Newborough beach which overlooks Llanddwyn Bay (parking at SH 405634). This south west facing sandy beach is huge, especially when the tide is out and delivers a stunning panorama. Therefore it has something to offer the photographer at pretty much any time of day. The lighthouse on Llanddwyn island is an obvious classic. However, from this beach you also get to appreciate the full Snowdonia panorama from a sea level vantage point.

As I clambered to the top of the dunes the wind hit me full in the face. I was still reeling from this onslaught when I started to take in my surroundings. Golden sand stretching off for miles in each direction and some of my favourite hills seen from a rather new and exciting perspective.

Looking directly out across the bay, the outline of the Lleyn hills should not only have you reaching for the camera but also reaching for the map as well. This diminutive range of hills not only looks stunning but demands to be explored. Looking east, you can take in Snowdonia's southern skyline from the Nantlle range to Snowdon and its outliers.

Mynydd Bodafon

We once hired a holiday cottage at the foot of Mynydd Bodafon. For every night we were there I went out to explore this mini mountain of a hill to catch the sunset. At 178m it is hardly a challenging hike to the top, however, the view from the trig point offers a roll call of all the Snowdonian ranges. There are not many places that you can take in the panorama of the Carnedds to the Lleyn hills with everything in between.

First visits to a new location are always exciting but on reaching this little summit I knew I'd found somewhere rather special.

There is a small car park at SH 470852 where a path winds its way to the top up the western ridge. With sunsets out over Holyhead and stunning views over the excellent Lligwy bay it is worth spending some time exploring this rocky outcrop.

The Lleyn Peninsula

The Lleyn Peninsula is a rugged strip of land that juts out into the Irish Sea. Its entire length is dotted with numerous rocky hills, many of which have stone age forts, standing stones and cairns littering their summits. It might take a bit of effort getting here but you'll be glad you did. Being a relatively narrow strip of land these summits deliver excellent sea views which are a delight to shoot in all sorts of weather.

Mynydd Penarfynydd

This short, rocky ridgeline stands at the western end of the fantastically named Hell's Mouth beach. From the village of Rhiw (SH 225 277) head south west down a minor, dead end road and pick up the path that traverses to the top of Mynydd Penarfynydd. From here there are dramatic views west over Porth Ysgo to a distant Bardsey Island. A path along the ridgeline leads in a north easterly direction and is a joy to explore.

The rain shower had just cleared as I made my way to the top and sunlight was streaming between the dark clouds. Bright patches of steel grey sea were lit up making for a superb shoot.

Moel y Gest

This is another fine example of a pocket rocket hill which offers ridiculously good views from a summit of very modest height. However, although it might only be 262m high the final climb to the top is quite rocky thereby requiring some enjoyable easy scrambling. This walk takes the most direct route up but you could easily start from Porthmadog or even the beach at Black Sands. As the minor road turns sharply right at SH542392 go about ten paces up a concrete drive before heading off left on a faint path. This winds up through some trees alongside a house. It doesn't really look like the path that is marked on the map but on checking with the owners of the house I found out that it is the public right of way. Go straight over a track, through a 5 bar gate and follow the fence line on your right. Go through the next gate and follow a path that winds steeply uphill passed a farm on your left until you reach a good track. Turn right onto this track and follow it as it gently climbs for around 400m. Just before you reach the next building go through a gate on your left and follow a path along a wall for 300m. At the wall junction turn left for 50m then follow it right at the next turn. Ignore a gate to your right and take the path that traverses left and then right up through the gorse. On reaching a stone wall head left uphill. Just before the wall turns left cross it on a makeshift wooden stile. Turn left along the wall to the right angled turn, following it for another 50m. From here you leave the handrail of the wall and start a rock and heather scramble up to the summit. After passing a large boulder climb up the heathered slopes towards a steep rockface. Just before this wall of rock turn right up a heathery gully which leads to the top.

I was a bit late starting out on this walk so the race was on to reach the summit before sunset. On topping out, whilst I was trying to get my breath back, the view did little to get my heart rate down.

This summit is a wonderful place to savour at any time of the day as it delivers a full 360 degree panorama that the higher hills of Snowdonia would be rightly jealous of. As you are only 2km from the coast you get a far reaching vista along the southern Lleyn coastline taking in everything from Criccieth castle to the distant sweeping headland at Abersoch. Looking northwest and the glorious Lleyn hills start the dramatic undulating skyline. To the north the Nantlle ridge and the large brooding bulk Moel Hebog fills your viewfinder. You can even see the top half of Snowdon before turning to the north east where the horizon is dominated by the wild summits of the Moelwyns. From here it is easy to see why the pointy summit of Cnicht is nicknamed the Matterhorn of North Wales. Looking south east and south across the complex estuarine coastline at your feet your eyes are naturally drawn to the distant Rhinogs which completes a roll call of southern Snowdonia's finest.

These views are enhanced by the fact that Moel y Gest is surrounded, on pretty much all sides, by low lying flat estuaries. Also as the ground drops away steeply from the rocky summit this means you get uninterrupted views of some rather fine scenery. You get a lot of bang for your buck from a visit to this little peak by the sea.

The Brecon Beacons

The Brecon Beacons are made up of three main hill ranges. The Black Mountains in the east are dominated by the wonderful Waun Fach horseshoe walk. The central Brecons are where the highest peaks of Pen y Fan and Corn Du rise up out of a steep escarpment with ridges radiating off in all directions. Both of these two ranges offer excellent and challenging walking, however, for photographic potential it is hard to beat the Black Mountain group in the west of the National Park.

2.1 The Black Mountain – a tale of two llyns

The Black Mountain, which is actually a range of hills in the less popular western end of the Brecon Beacons, can be over looked. This area, including Fan Brycheiniog, is often seen as the poor relation to their higher, brasher neighbours Pen-y-Fan, Cribyn and Corn Du. However, don't let this put you off as the Black Mountain range offer some of the most photogenic landscapes in southern Britain. The Brecon Beacons are well known for their fine escarpments and the Fan Brycheiniog group, also known as the Camarthan Fan, make one of the most dramatic. Stretching for over eight kilometres, these towering red sandstone cliffs make for a stunning walk in their own right. However, to get the most out of a visit you have to seek out some of their hidden treasures and also gain some distance to capture the scale of this wonderful area.

Focal Point – the escarpment links up a number of viewpoints both on the ridge itself, below the cliffs with two stunning llyns (lakes) and from a few more remote locations.

Route Summaries

Full route – starting from Bwlch Cerrig Duon an optional ascent of Moel Feity can be made on the way to Llyn y Fan Fawr. After taking in numerous viewpoints around the area, an ascent of Fan Foel's northern ridge brings you out onto the escarpment. From here drop down to a pass before climbing up to Bannau Sir Gaer then Waun Lefrith. Return by following the path below the cliffs back to Llyn y Fan Fawr and then down to the road.

19 km; 570 m ascent

An extension can be made to take in a viewpoint to the north of Fan Foel

adds 4 km; 390 m ascent

Shorter route – A there and back to Llyn y Fan Fawr.

10 km; 120 m ascent

Why Try this Route

The Camarthan Fan escarpment is an area of high ground that links up a number of summits. Each of the summits offers elevated viewpoints over the surrounding wild rolling moors and to the two glacial lakes that nestle below the dramatic cliffs. This route not only gets you up to these viewpoints but also gives you access to two fantastic lakeside shoots. There are also two optional route extensions which put some distance between yourself and the cliffs so that you get the chance to capture the full panoramas on offer.

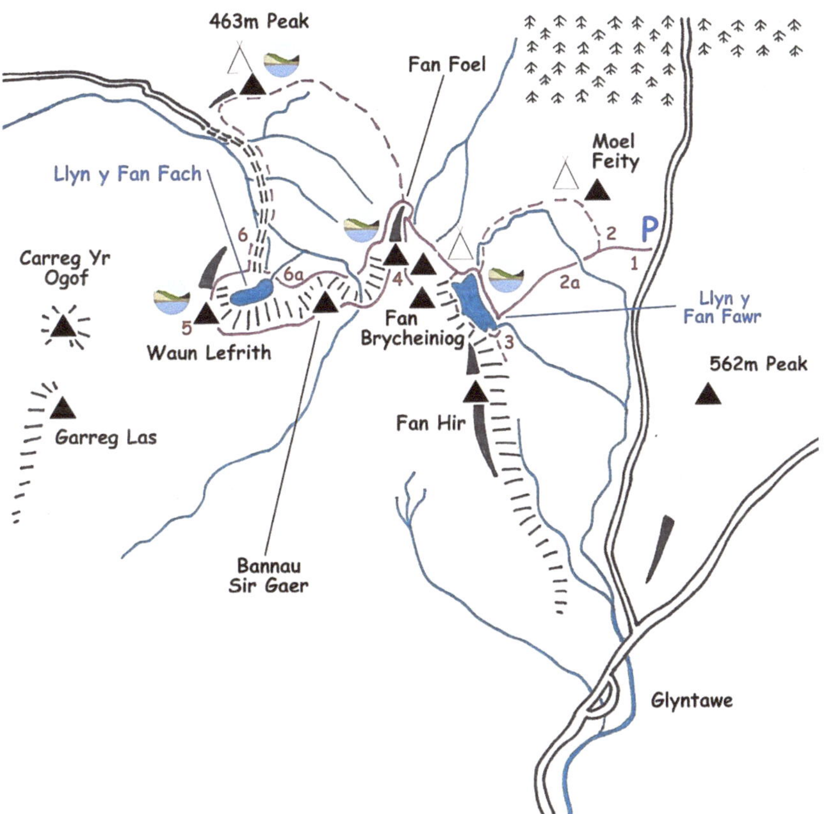

Clockwise from top left :

Bannau Sir Gaer from Fan Foel... The small beach at the northern end of Llyn y Fan Fawr...The wild camp at Llyn y Fan Fawr... Fan Brycheiniog from the ascent of Fan Foel...The view from Waun Lefrith...Llyn y Fan Fach from Waun Lefrith

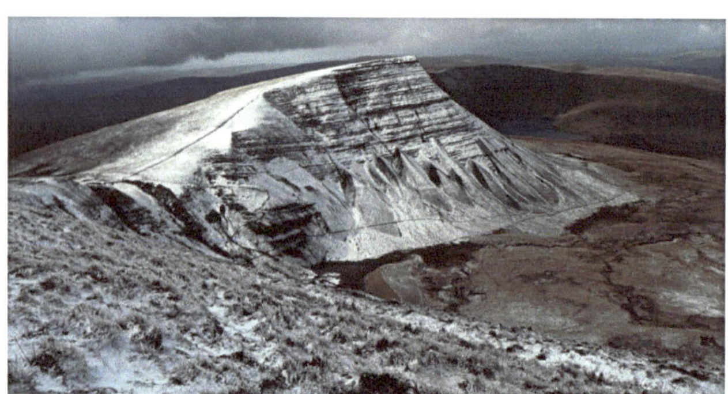

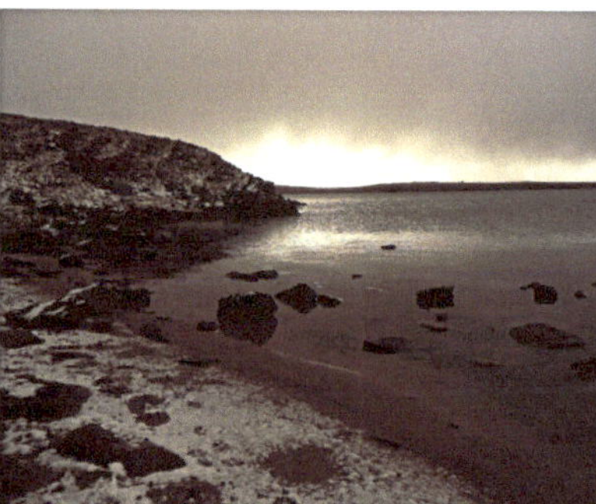

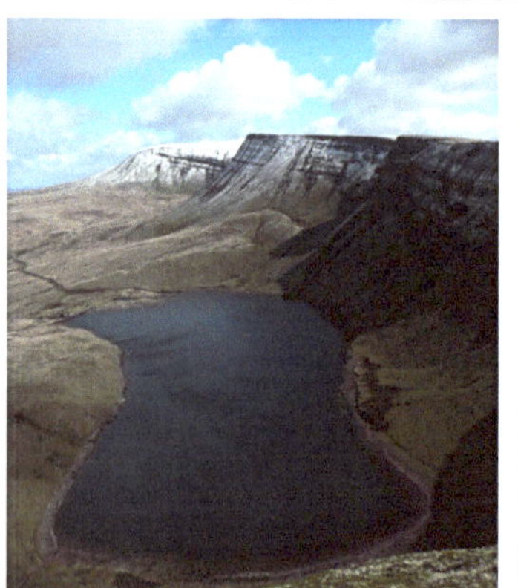

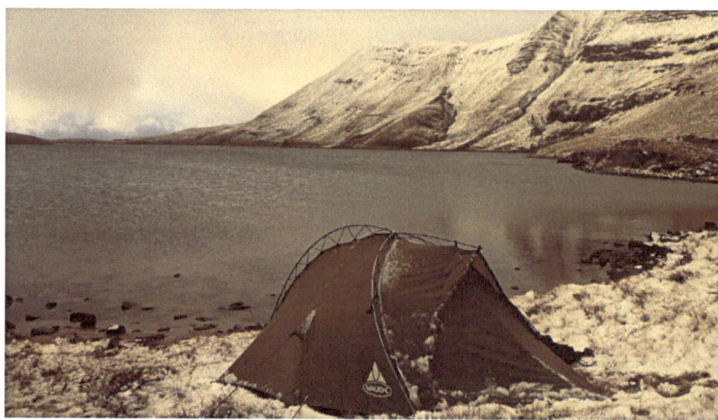

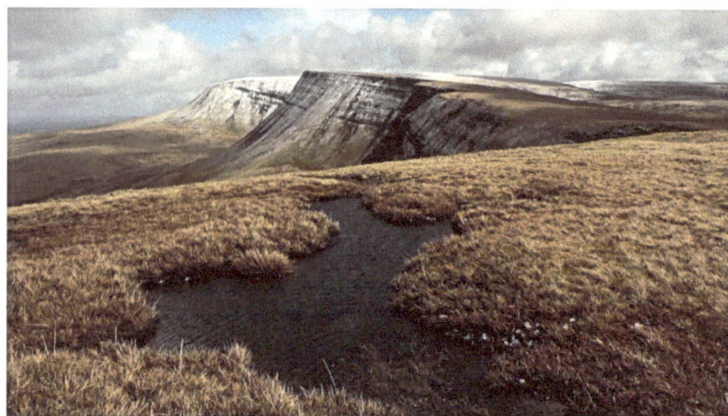

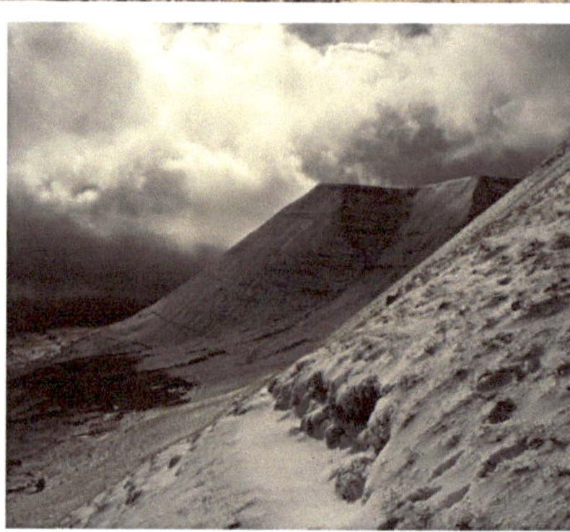

Route Description

1) Starting from the roadside parking area (SN 855223) just below Bwlch Cerrig Duon you get a reasonable view of the escarpment to whet the appetite of things to come. A track, then path, heads off in a south west direction, crossing three small streams that run down the flanks of Moel Feity. This rounded lump of a hill, whilst not very inspiring in itself, does offer a fine elevated viewpoint over to Fan Brycheiniog.

2) To take in this viewpoint follow the third stream up towards the summit plateau. There are a few small llyns south of the summit that make for an interesting foreground. As the summit is so flat it is worth heading over to its south western side where the slope steepens. This gives you more depth to your images. This area also makes for a good wild camp if you are arriving late in the day as the eastwards facing cliffs capture the morning's sunrise. Sadly this peak, along with others in the Brecons, was the site of a World War 2 plane crash. Whilst there isn't much in the way of wreckage, there is a small memorial which is a poignant reminder of this turbulent time.

After a bit of night navigation around the slopes of Moel Feity we pitched up on a good grassy spot. However in the morning we woke up to a good dusting of snow on the high ground which despite the lack of a sunrise made for an interesting start to the day.

From the slopes of Moel Feity head in a south westerly direction over pathless terrain, crossing a boggy area and pick up a stream which leads you up towards Llyn y Fan Fawr via the source of the river Tawe. You only get to see the lake as you reach its eastern shores as it is nestled in a shallow bowl below the cliffs.

2a) If you don't take the detour over Moel Feity continue to follow the path south westwards down and then steadily upwards until you arrive at the shores of Llyn y Fan Fawr.

On reaching Llyn y Fan Fawr the weather was far from ideal. The surrounding cliffs were hidden by a thick grey clag and the occasional shower of sleet came strafing across the water. However, there were a few breaks in the cloud. I knew that I would return here later in the day and I was optimistic that the weather would improve.

Photo Location – Llyn y Fan Fawr

The area around the lake and its surrounds has huge photographic and wild camping potential so it is worth spending some time here to take in all that it offers.

A circuit of the lake is a good place to start. The southern end has two beaches separated by a small elevated headland which are useful viewpoints to shoot down the length of the lake. The curve of Fan Foel's northern ridge acts as a backdrop with the streams and shorelines as lead in lines. From here, another fine viewpoint can be sought out by picking up a faint path that heads south from the lake over the rise and down along the bottom of the cliff line above you. This there and back walk of around 500m down from the lake gives you a great perspective of the Fan Hir escarpment with its striking geometric lines. Heading back up to the lake you can take in either or both sides of the shoreline with the light conditions probably making the decision for you. However, you will be returning past the lake later in the day which allows you to take it all in again under a different light.

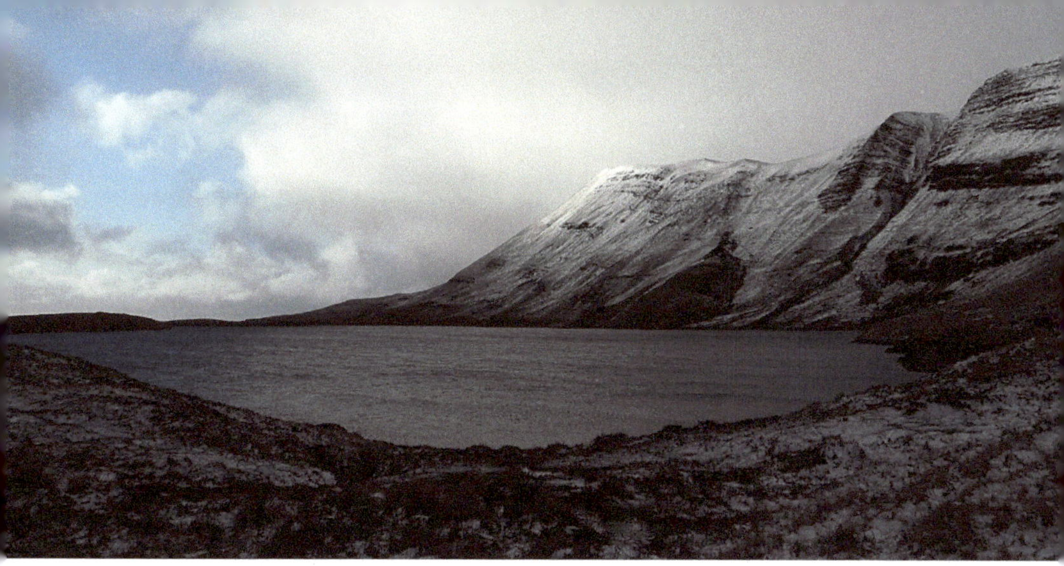

6.40am 23rd March - The white, snow plastered cliffs finally emerged from the cloud to reveal what I had been waiting for and boy was it worth the rather chilly wait.

If the cliffs below Fan Brycheiniog are well lit then the eastern shore is probably your best bet. However if the sun is still low to the east or has passed overhead then visit the western shoreline first There is a reasonable path that winds its way along this side of the lake a few meters above the shoreline.

Towards the northern end of the lake you get an excellent view over the water to the distant flat topped peaks of Pen y Fan and Corn Du. Before you reach a small feeder stream there is a tiny llyn that adds interest to the foreground. Crossing the stream, which is a useful water source if you are camping here, you can see a perfect little beach that is nestled in a bay at the northern end of the lake. This is a superb place to wild camp as it offers some shelter and superlative views right on your doorstep.

3) Once you've finished enjoying the delights of this area you are faced with a route choice. The standard walkers route ascends the cliffs from the southern end of the lake up a steep, stony path. This climb is a bit tedious. A more enjoyable, photogenic route can be found from the opposite end of the lake. From the small beach on the north side pick up a path that climbs northwestwards up the grassy slopes in front of you. The path traverses around the steep ridge that sweeps down from Twr y Fan Foel and into a small cwm (valley). With a derelict stone sheepfold in front of you pick up the path that heads round the left side of the cwm towards Fan Foel's northern ridge. Be sure to look over your shoulder along this section as the view back to the Twr y Fan Foel ridge is superb. On gaining this broad grassy ridge turn left. This might be a steep climb but it gives you access to some stupendous views.

On reaching the ridge the heavy grey cloud started to dissipate to reveal some blue sky. It was hard work kicking steps into the snowy ridge but summit fever was starting to take hold. I was keen to get to the top as I knew there was something special waiting for me.

4) On reaching the high ground, a there and back detour south east to the summit of Fan Brycheiniog not only bags you the areas highest but also gives you a chance to visit the airy top of Twr y Fan Foel. The former also has one of the few basic summit shelters on this walk, which is extremely useful on a cold, windy day.

Photo Location – Fan Foel

The flat topped summit of Twr y Fan Foel with its stark, angular ridges make for excellent images on the ascent of Fan Foel. The sweep of the ridgeline at your feet adds to the drama of the shot. On gaining the flatter ground above, this view takes on a whole new perspective as the summits rise above the surrounding bleak plateau. However, on heading over to the western edge of the escarpment there is a real show stopper of a view waiting for you. Bannau Sir Gaer has to be one of the most striking summits in Wales and is a delight to shoot from this angle. The heavily layered cliffs sweep dramatically down to the textured valley floor. Add to this the compositional aids of the ridgeline that leads from your feet to the focal point and a backdrop of Llyn y Fan Fach nestled below the cliffs of Waun Lefrith. This really is a special location and one that keeps on giving so follow the top of the cliffs south westwards down to the pass, Bwlch Blaen-Twrch. You are now at the same height as the striations on the cliffs opposite which makes for a stunning image.

10.05 am 22nd March - Feeling like I'd struck gold.

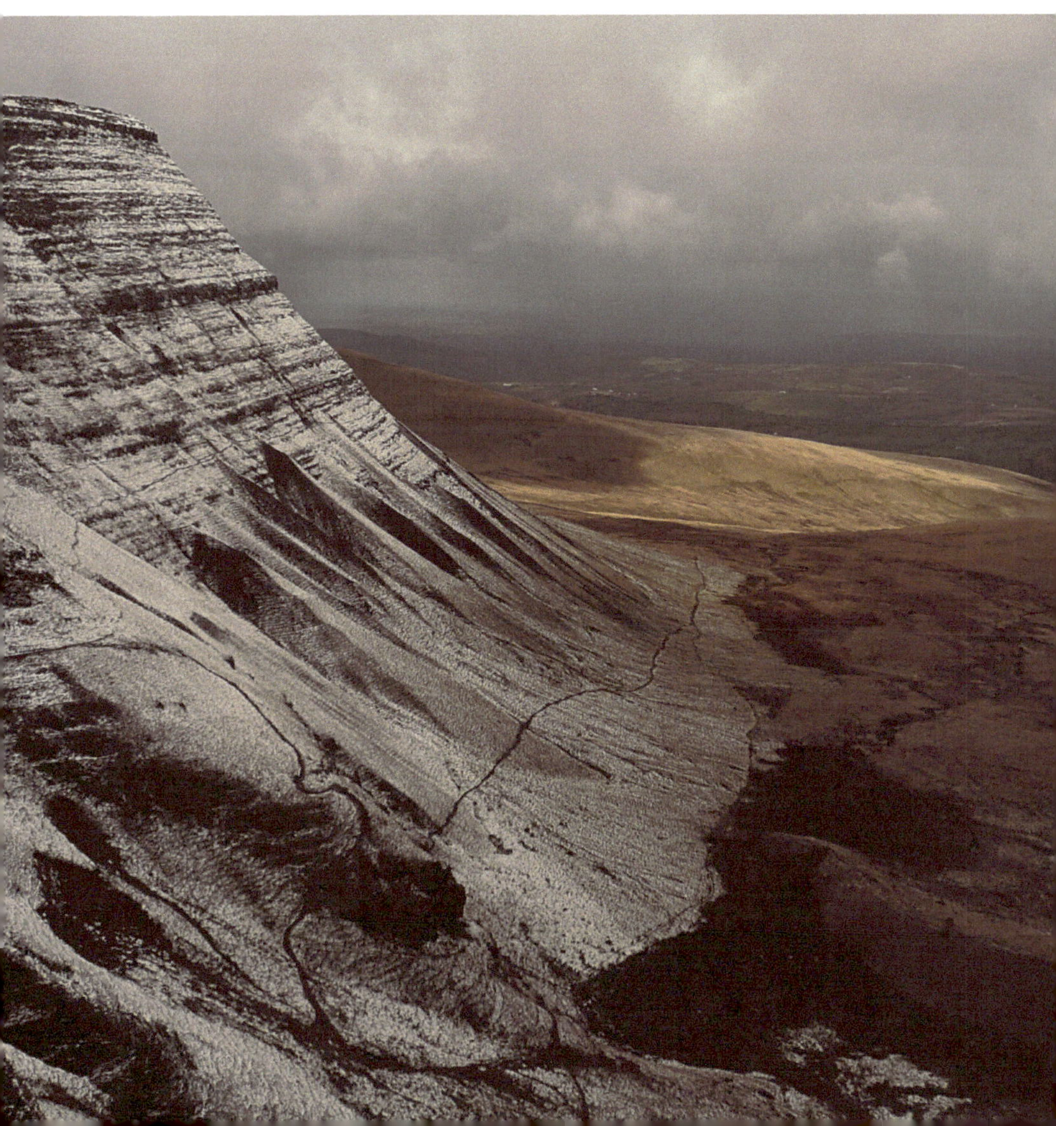

I'd stood at this spot several times before, the last of which was with some friends in truly terrible conditions. We knew that the stupendous view was out there, hidden by thick grey clag, but we were not to be lucky that day. Returning some months later, at the tail end of winter, I hit the jackpot. A fine dusting of snow accentuated every feature on the cliffs opposite making for a hugely enjoyable shoot.

On reaching the pass you ford a stream and are faced with a climb of around 100m up the grassy flanks of Bannau Sir Gaer (or sometimes called Picws Du) that looks worse than it actually is. If you really don't fancy it you can escape in either direction. The path off to the left leads you down the stream into the wild hinterland of the Black Mountain. This is an interesting return route if you started at Glyntawe although the paths on the ground are not as clear as they are marked on the map. If you turn right at the pass, a path zigzags its way down to the open ground below the cliffs, which the main route picks up on later.

However, if you have the time and energy, trudge your way up to the top of Bannau Sir Gaer where there are more treats on offer and some easier walking. From the summit you gain a fine perspective westwards along the cliffs to Llyn y Fan Fach. As the walking underfoot is now flat and easy going this allows you to fully focus on your photography, which is handy as there is a lot to shoot. Be sure to look in both directions along the escarpment as there are a number of excellent viewpoints. For example, on the gentle descent from Bannau Sir Gaer the ridge curves around slightly at Cwar-du-mawr GR806216. This enables you to look back along the cliffs to the flat topped summit on which you were standing on only minutes before. So enjoy this section as it leads you round to your next summit, Waun Lefrith.

Photo Location – Waun Lefrith

The summit itself is a bit disappointing to look at as it is quite flat and boggy. However, as it forms the end of the Fan Brycheiniog escarpment it is in a prime location that offers far reaching panoramic views. Sticking to the top of the cliffs your eye will be drawn east back along the route you have travelled. As you work your way along the escarpment and start to lose some height the view down the length of Llyn y Fan Fach opens up with Bannau Sir Gaer taking centre stage in the background. Moving slightly away from the edge of the cliffs there are a number of small llyns that make for interesting compositions. This is also a fine spot to admire the view north which is made up of some wild open moorland and lush green pastures.

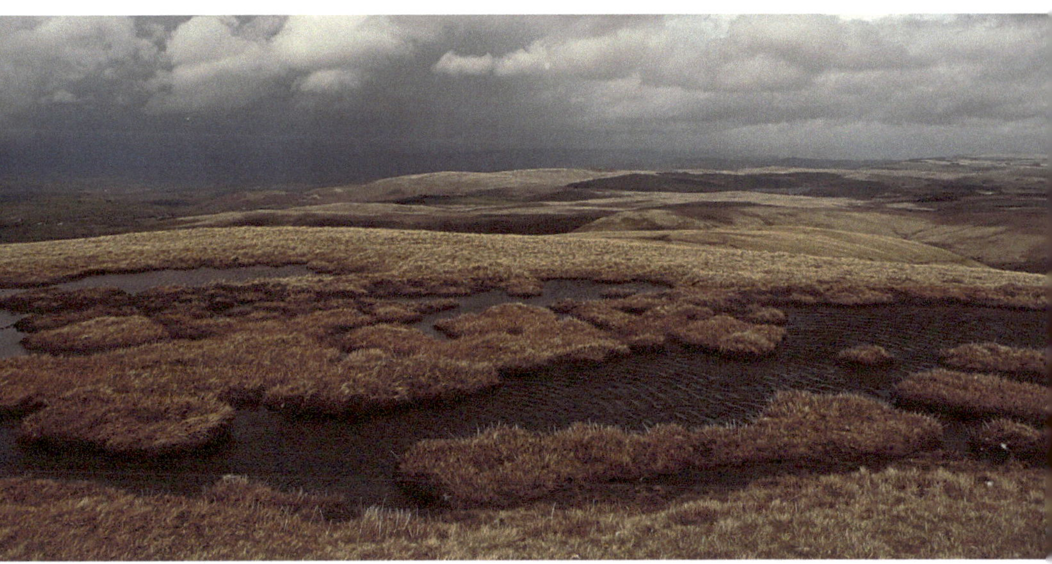

11.20am 23rd March - Pain and pleasure : I knew the next hail shower was rapidly approaching but at least it added to the drama of the shoot

Looking westwards you look out over an area of rocky hills that are little visited but make for some excellent wild camping trips in their own right. This also marks a geological boundary as the red sandstone that forms the escarpment gives way to limestone scenery to the south and west. Far off on the edge of this high ground the rather stunning remains of Carreg Cennan castle stands proud on its natural fortress of rock (if you have time it is worth driving round to this rather excellent castle).

5) You are now faced with another route choice. One way is to retrace your steps back along the escarpment which allows you to enjoy the elevated viewpoints under no doubt different lighting conditions. If you do this, instead of dropping down the north ridge of Fan Foel, follow the edge over to the fine summit of Fan Brycheiniog and down to Bwlch-y-Giedd, where you can descend to the southern shores of Llyn y Fan Fawr.

Otherwise drop down from Waun Lefrith on the path that hugs the top of the cliffs and follow the spur that leads you steeply down to the shores of Llyn y Fan Fach. This Llyn is steeped in local folklore and is known as the 'Magic Lake' due to the following legend:

A long time ago a local farmer's lad called Rhiwallon saw a beautiful lady rise out of the waters of the llyn. He immediately fell in love and asked for her hand in marriage. She agreed but warned Rhiwallon that he should never strike her with iron. Sadly he did and the mysterious lady vanished back into the waters of the Llyn never to be seen again. Fortunately she did teach their son all about medicine and he became the first in a long line of local healers known as the 'Physicians of Myddfai'. In fact this area has been linked to a doctoral presence that stretches back over 600 years. Whether you believe the story or not it truly is a magical place.

From the dam over the outflow of the lake you are now faced with another route choice.

6) **Route extension:** If you have time, energy and a desire to photograph the escarpment, from a more distant viewpoint then this loop is a good idea. Follow the broad track northwards from the lake down along the Afon Sawddle which after 2km or so brings you to a small car park at the start of a minor road (this route is often used as a way in to the hills). From the right hand side of the car park, traverse up through open ground, aiming for the top of a fenced off area above a farm. Follow a faint path that leads you below a thicket of gorse bushes and brings you to the base of a broad ridge rising steeply to your right. Start climbing up this wide ridge, zigzagging your own way up. You'll soon reach the flatter ground of the hill top that has no name, just a 463m spot height marked on the map.

Photo Location – 463m Hill

On reaching this broad summit work your way north eastwards where you'll reach a small llyn. From here you can appreciate one of the few view points that allow you to capture the north facing escarpment, especially in late afternoon light. This is also a good wild camping area, although you will have to bring your own water or head down to collect it from the running streams below. From the summit area follow the broad ridge over to the remains of a stone circle GR809244, which despite being a bit vague on the ground adds to your foreground.

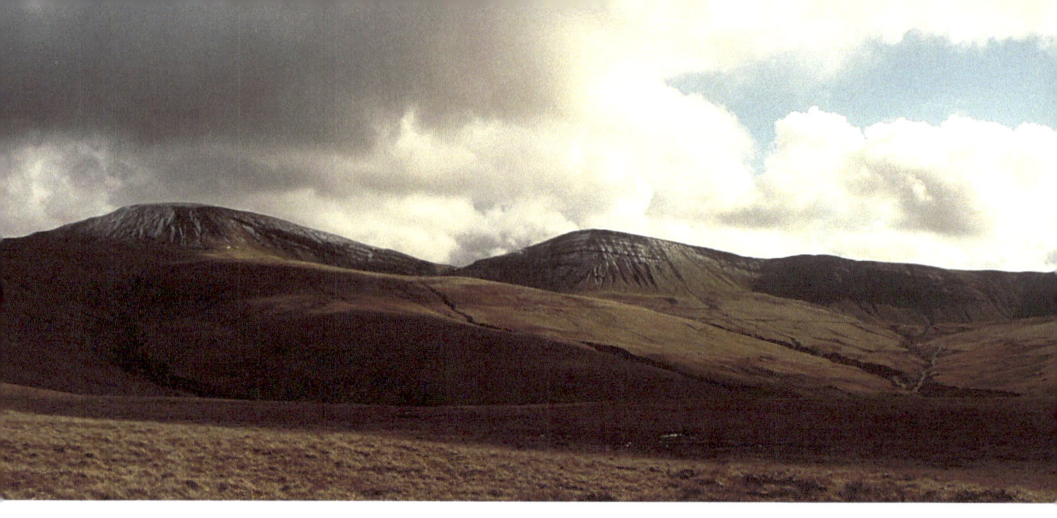

1.40 pm 23rd March - This was a great spot to sit down, enjoy the panorama and to just simply experience the solitude of the place.

Head across largely pathless terrain in a south easterly, then southern direction, aiming for the foot of the Fan Foel ridge that you climbed earlier.

6a) The more direct route from the dam takes you along the bottom of the escarpment which allows you get up close with these majestic cliffs. There are a number of paths that work their way eastwards over this wild, rolling, open moorland. After passing below Bannau Sir Gaer you reach the wide cwm below the pass of Pant y Bwlch. Traverse below Fan Foel on a path that maintains your height just above the valley bottom. As you round the 'nose' of the north ridge of Fan Foel, you regain the path that you took from Llyn y Fan Fawr earlier. So retrace your steps back to the llyn where you'll no doubt want to re-shoot the area in some late afternoon light. In fact, why not spend the night camped out next to the shores to fully enjoy this amazing area.

I pitched the tent just meters from the beach and set to work getting a brew on. It was a fine spot to spend the evening with the setting sun lighting up the clouds and hills to the east over the tranquil, clear waters of the lake. I awoke the next morning not to the sound of rain but snow falling on the tent. The skies were still quite grey and laden with cloud, however, the view down the length of the lake more than made up for the chilly start.

By revisiting this superb location at a different time of day you get a good chance to shoot it under a range of lighting conditions. So, if you have time you can make a full tour of the shoreline or head to some of the superb little beaches at either end of the lake. When it's time to leave head to the southern tip of the llyn and pick up a path that leads off towards the north east. If you are parked at the upper car parking area be sure you don't end up dropping down on a more easterly path as this will bring you out a good way down the road from where your car is. By heading back on this upper path, which is often faint in areas, you also give yourself a chance to climb the slopes of Moel Feity. This is pathless terrain but the views back over to Fan Brycheiniog are worthy of the detour. Either way you should be returning with full memory cards and with an appreciation for this fantastic area.

At times during the trip I, and probably my dog, had questioned my sanity – heading out onto a dark, rain swept hillside to camp might have seemed a little bit daft. However, some patience and hard work paid off with one of my most rewarding trips to this fantastic area.

On a Visit to the Area Why Not Also Check Out this Location

2.2 Mynydd Troed – a Little Hill with Big Views

Why Try this Route

The summit of Mynydd Troed offers elevated views of the surrounding countryside which includes a shapely lake, patchwork fields and a rolling range of hills. This short route gives you a quick 'hill fix' offering excellent views for relatively little effort. Being of a lower level it also makes for a good poor weather, or Plan B, alternative where you can still get some excellent results from any breaks in the cloud. If combined with a trip to the Black Mountains, this is a good walk either on arrival or just before leaving the area, when time is short.

Clockwise from top left :

Looking down Cwm Sorgwm, early in the climb... Cwm Sorgwm from nearing the summit... Lake Llangors on the ascent... Looking west from the summit... Middle – the view north from the summit

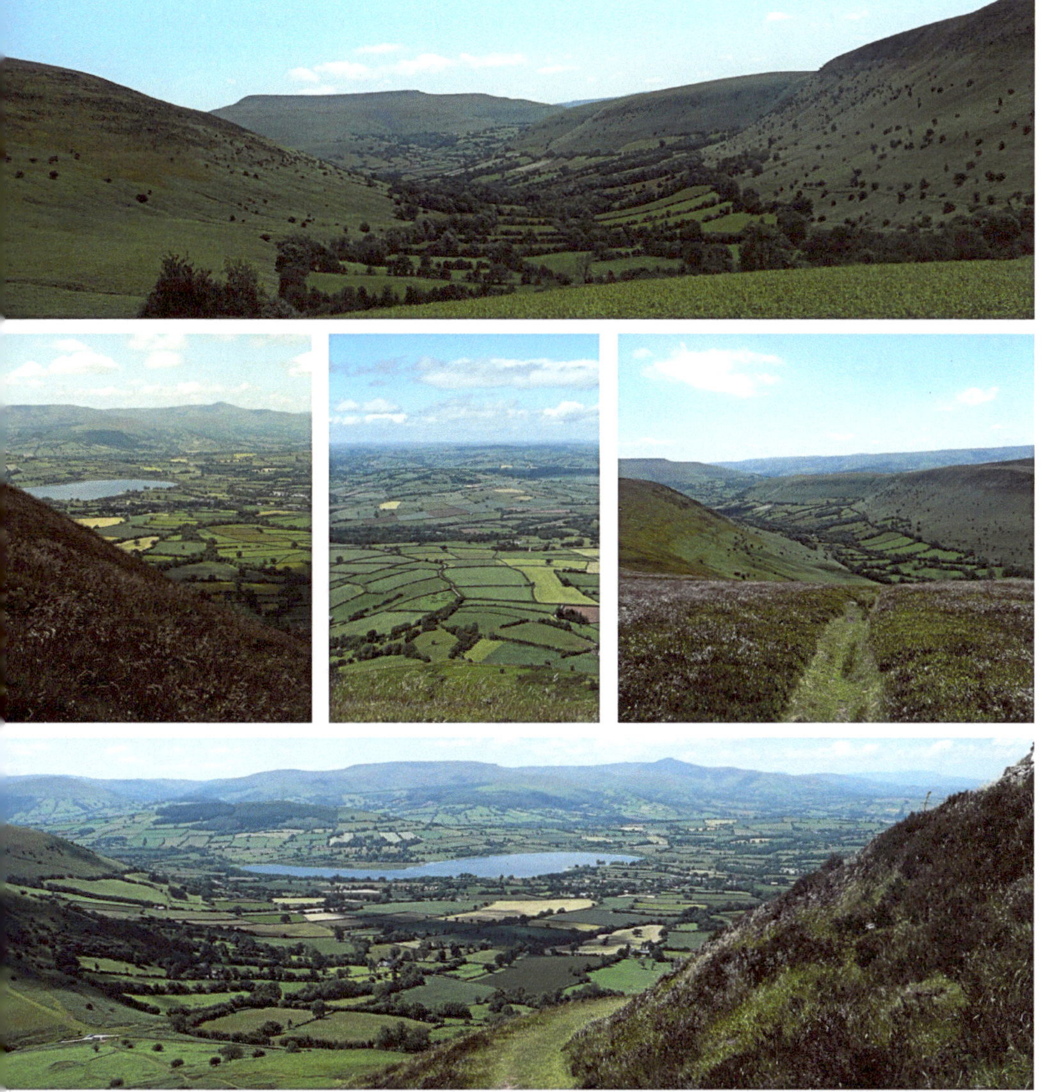

There is a small area for parking at the pass on the minor road that leads between Llangors and the A479, at GR SO 160283. Head north eastwards from the pass up a grassy track.

As you begin the climb the view south east down Cwm Sorgwm starts to open up and is especially fine in late Spring when the range of greenery is at it's most vibrant. The ferns make for a full foreground whilst the lush valley floor leads off to the flat topped summit of Pen Allt-mawr.

Seeing the slopes of Pen Allt-mawr under such clear blue skies was a real joy. I had visited this area many times, including several with a remarkable chap called Larry Coe. He inspired a lot of walkers in his time, organising numerous walking trips all over the UK and was a genuine character. His ashes were scattered from this hill, one of his favourites, so this beautiful view always makes me think of him and the amazing trips he took us on.

Just before the ridge steepens for the final push there is a split in the paths. The main path splits off left and leads you just below the ridgeline all the way to the summit. It is a steady climb but one that gives you ever expanding views; Llangors lake in the middle ground, surrounded by a patchwork of fields and the distant high ground of the central Brecons acting as a backdrop. The path you have just climbed makes a good lead in line for the image. Keep a look out for the wild ponies that are often on these slopes as they add real character to the area.

As the gradient starts to ease and you reach the summit plateau a full 360 degree panorama stretches off in all directions. This is a great place to explore and also just to sit and take in your spectacular surroundings.

By following the edge of the steep slopes around the summit area you get superb, elevated perspectives over the surrounding countryside. On reaching the northern edge, the patchwork of fields stretches off to the horizon giving you a reminder of how rural and unspoilt Mid Wales really is. Moving round to the north eastern facing slopes and you're looking down to the interesting remains of Castell Dinas and the delightful ridge of Y Grib that leads to the areas highest ground, the brooding boggy plateau of Waun Fach.

Looking over to the Waun Fach range brought back memories of one of Larry's trips. My good friend Chris and I had made an early start on a rather wintery romp round these hills. It was a long day so we needed our head torches to get us back. Fortunately Larry and the rest of the group were waiting for us at the pub.

Once you've finished enjoying the full panorama, the easiest way back is to retrace your steps. Alternatively you can head down the south eastern ridge of Mynydd Troed and pick up the blunt ridge and rather steep descent to the valley floor at SO176275. However, this is hard going, especially if the ferns are tall and is also largely pathless until you reach the bridleway at SO176269.

The views from this little summit will keep you smiling for some time and hopefully for once the rewards will be greater than the effort expended in obtaining them.

The Lake District

The Lake District is probably one of the most renowned areas for practicing landscape photography due its array of stunning lakes and tarns nestling in lush green valleys which themselves are surrounded by craggy mountains. It is quite literally the stuff of pure poetry. You might think that it's all been shot before. However, for the adventurous photographer who wild camps out in the hills there are unique experiences waiting to be captured. The area is well suited to summit camps with its numerous peripheral peaks that give a fresh, elevated perspective on this glorious landscape.

3.1 The Southern Shores and Hills of Ullswater

Focal Point – both high and low level viewpoints along Ullswaters southern shores

Route Summaries

Full route – the summit of Hallin Fell followed by a short but beautiful section along the southern edge of Ullswater, then an ascent of Place Fell by its pathless northern flanks.

12.5km; 635m ascent

Shorter route – a short up and back the pocket rocket hill that is Hallin Fell.

3.5 km; 160m ascent

Why Try this Route

Hallin Fell is a fine example of a type of hill called a pocket rocket – a summit that gives far more in return than the effort expended in getting to its top. A climb of less than 200m leads you to this classy summit with its extensive views down the northern stretches of Ullswater. A steep descent leads you to a beautiful woodland walk alongside the lake's shores with its intricate little beaches. The ascent of Place Fell via its northern flanks gives access to some far reaching viewpoints that are well off the beaten track and the summit itself is a great place to wild camp. The summit has numerous small tarns which offer interesting foreground to the neighbouring High Street and Helvellyn ranges.

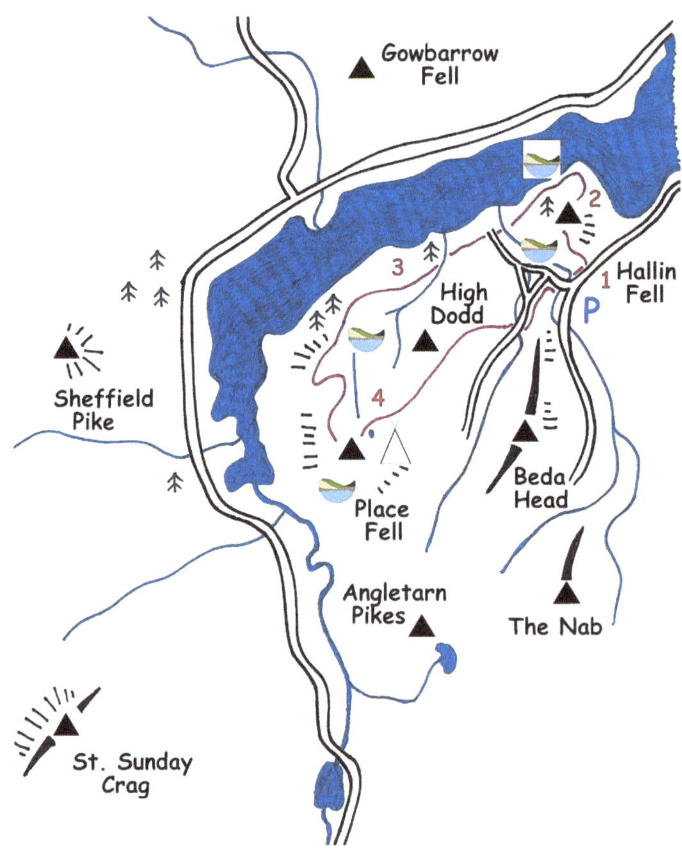

Clockwise from top left:

The view north down Ullswater from Low Birk Fell... Looking west from Hallin Fell... David enjoying a sunrise shoot from the camp on Hallin Fell... A misty Boredale from the summit of Hallin Fell... Early morning light on Ullswater... Unnamed tarn near Hart Crag, Place Fell

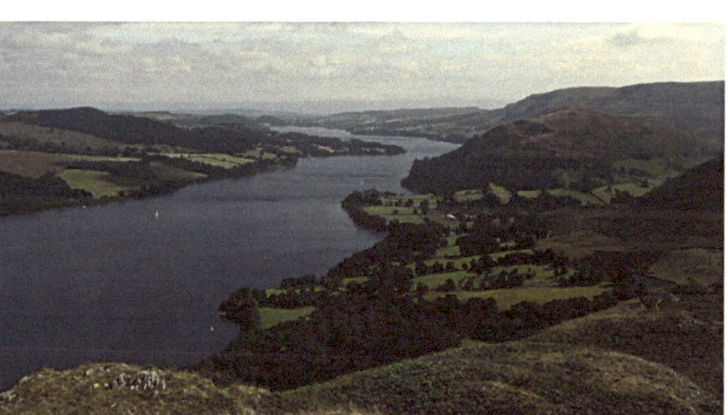

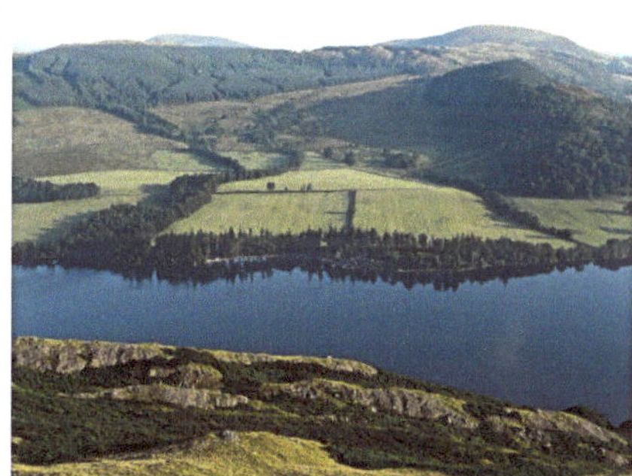

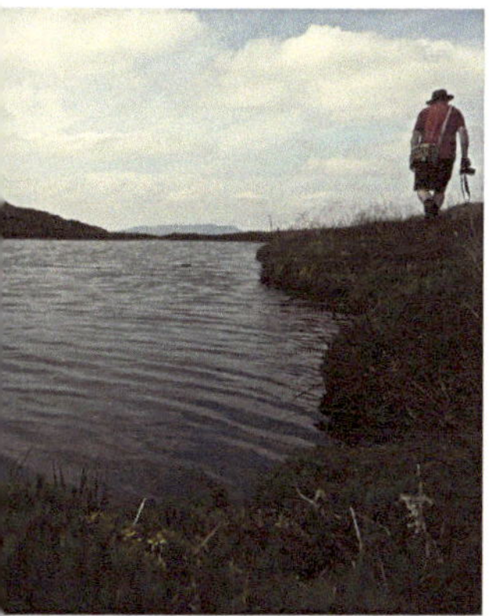

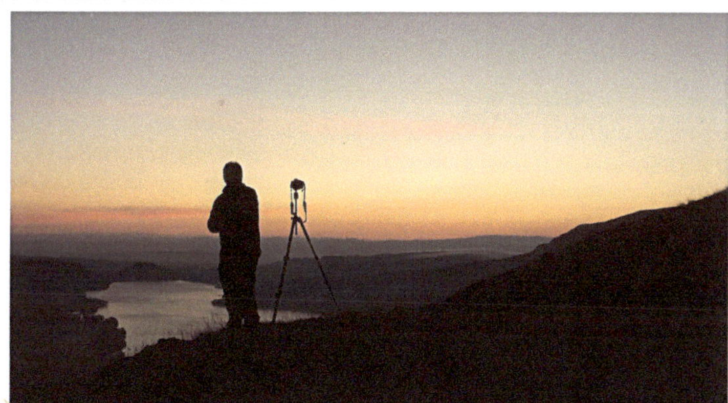

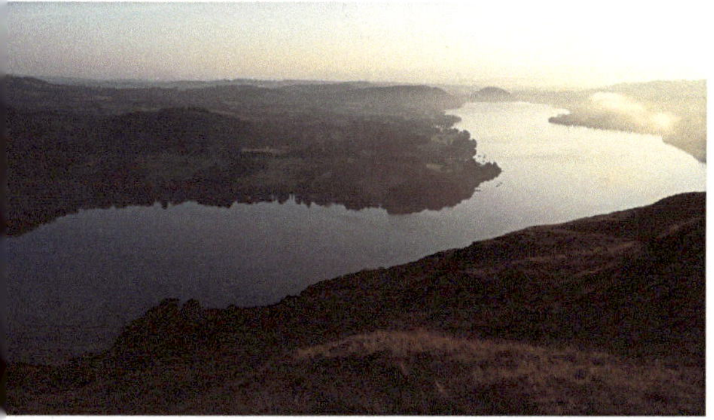

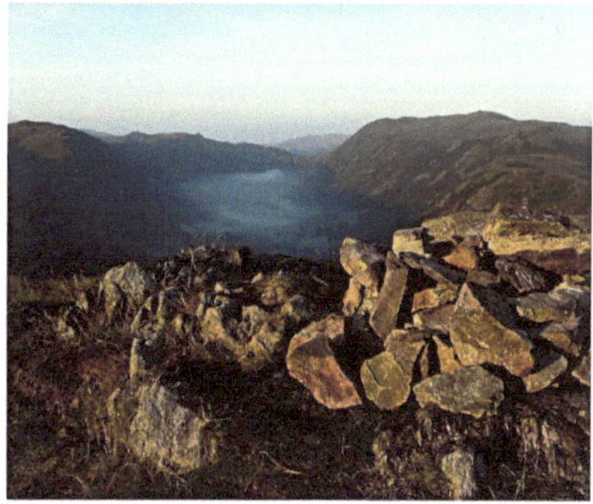

Route Description

1) The easiest place to tackle Hallin Fell and to start this walk is the small car park at the top of the pass next to the church in Martindale GR NY435191. This might feel like cheating a bit as you're driving up to 230m and the summit of Hallin Fell is only 388m in height. However there's plenty of legwork to do later and whilst the climb is short, it starts straight from the car park. So, cross the road and go north up a grassy path that heads straight for the top. This is quite a brutal way to begin a walk but the views from the top far outweigh the effort. Hallin Fell can be a popular walk with families as it is a relatively easy peak to bag so it can be worth timing the start to your walk if you want the summit to yourself.

After a late meet at the Sun Inn at Pooley Bridge it was time to make some final packing decisions and head off into the dark. It was a short sharp walk to the summit wild camp on top of Hallin Fell. With clear skies forecast for early next morning I'd reasoned that our efforts would return uninhibited views from our elevated view point. I woke before my alarm went off with a start. I had a feeling that the dawn would be good and after a quick peek out of the tent I couldn't get my boots on fast enough.

Photo Location – the Summit of Hallin Fell

It is worth exploring around the periphery of this summit as you get some of the best views from the rocky outcrops that surround the large cairned top. The obvious attraction is the view down the length of Ullswater's northern stretch which is especially fine at dawn. However, there are fine views off to the north west which capture the layers of rock bands on the flanks of the hill below you, a strip of the lake and then fine grassy tree-lined fields on the opposite shore. Also, by heading to the south western edge of the summit area you can create fine images of the classic Lakeland valleys that surround the shapely Beda Head.

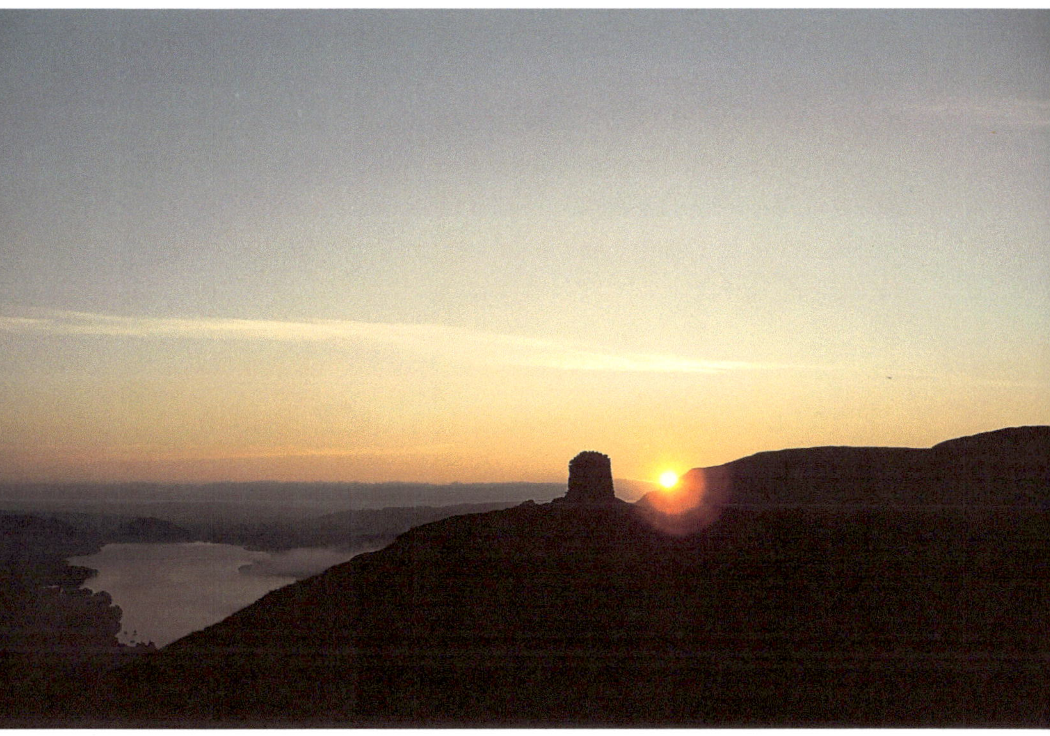

05.10am 11th August – This was David's first wild camp and what a great introduction to the joys of waking up in the hills.

There are in fact numerous flat and grassy areas to pitch up around the summit and what a place it is to take in a dawn shoot. You could of course make the walk up in the pre-dawn dark but this summit is a great introduction to the joys of wild camping.

After spending a glorious hour or so taking shots of the sunrise we enjoyed a brew and some breakfast whilst taking in our surroundings. On packing away our gear it was time to head down to capture the lake at shore level.

2) When you've had your fill of these fine views, pick up a small path that drops steeply in a north easterly direction down to the shores of the lake. This brings you down to the shoreline a couple of hundred meters to the east of Hallinhag wood. If steep grassy paths are not your thing then retrace your outward steps back towards the car park before contouring around Hallin Fell's eastern flanks. When you reach the shoreline, head in an anti-clockwise direction along the lakeside path.

Photo Locations – Lakeside Beaches

Just before you enter the woodland be sure to check out a small rocky promontory that offers an interesting view down the lake.

07.30am 11th August – A serene Ullswater stretched out in front of us from this prow shaped, rocky promontory

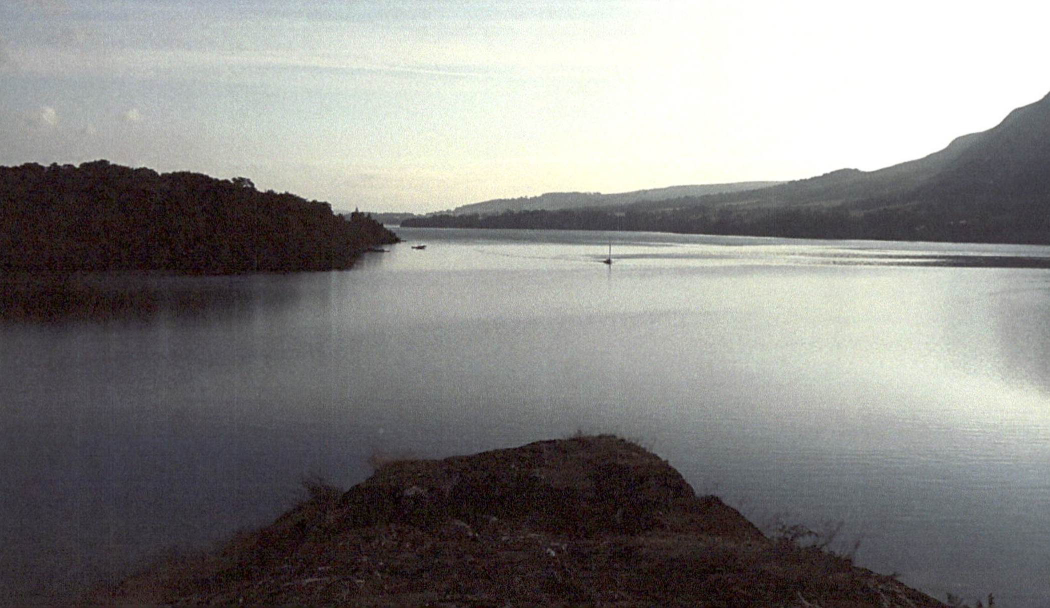

If the Ullswater steamer boat service is running, this is a fine spot to capture it as it comes round the headland.

There are further stunning beaches and vistas to explore along the shoreline path so enjoy this fine section of the route. This lakeside access allows you to get creative with your images, especially when the water is calm.

As the path leaves the woods at Sandwick Bay follow the main track towards the tiny hamlets of Sandwick and Beckside.

As you cross the bridge, turn left up the minor road for a hundred meters before taking a bridleway off to the right. Keep on this track until you cross Scalehow Beck over another bridge.

3) You can start an adventurous, although fortunately, scenic ascent from here picking a line up the steep but non-technical eastern ridge that brings you out onto Low Birk Fell.

After quite a leisurely morning it was time to gain some altitude again and although the ascent was quite steep and pathless the views started to open up again. One of the great things about being out in the hills on a photography trip is that you have to take your time and stop to check out the view.

Photo Location – Low Birk Fell to Birk Fell

From the summit cairn, head westwards over to the steep slopes that drop down to the shoreline and enjoy a number of airy viewpoints along the escarpment edge, following it to Kilbert How.

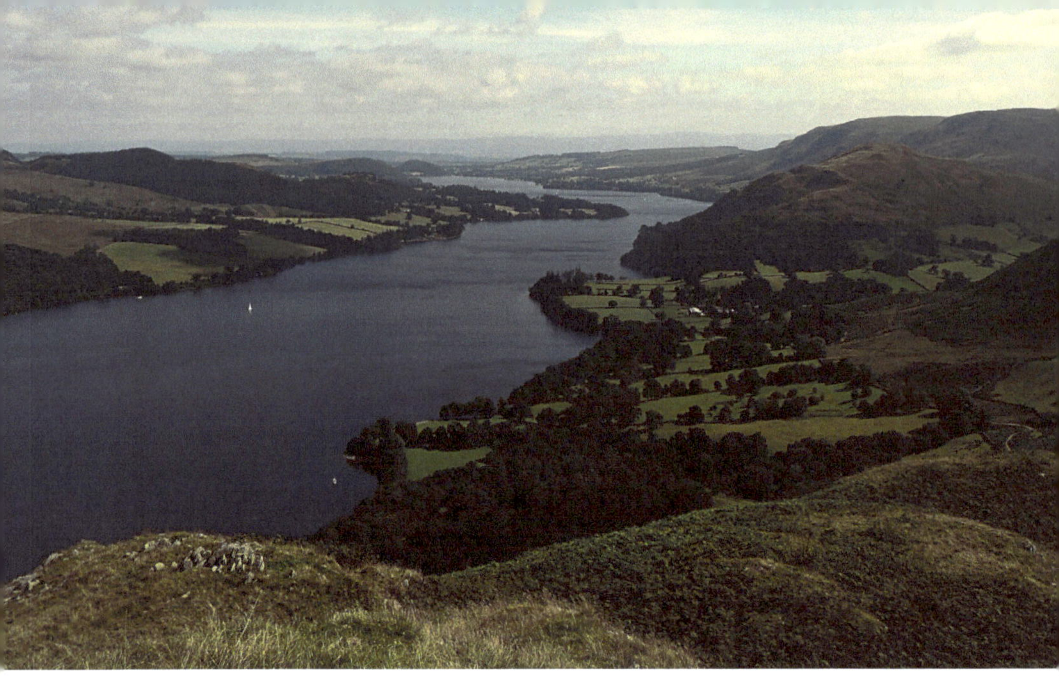

09.40am 11th August - On reaching the first summit on the ridge it was time for another brew and appreciate the peace and quiet you can experience in this little visited area (we didn't see a soul until we reached Place Fell).

From this outcrop you start to get ever expanding views over the middle section of Ullswater and the stunning Helvellyn range of hills to the west.

To ascend Birk Fell, first head east from Kilbert How to pick up the north eastern ridge that climbs steadily over classic Lake District open fellside. A further elevated viewpoint can be found from the second cairn over the ever steeper crags of Birkfell Earth. From this minor summit head south, south east along a broad plateau before picking up your first real path since leaving the lake side. The path winds its way southwards towards Place Fell, your final ascent of the day.

More steady climbing and photo stops brought us to our high point of the day and whilst the clarity of the sky was failing, the opportunities to shoot were everywhere.

Photo Location – the Summit of Place Fell

The summit of Place Fell is a wonderful area to explore with fantastic views westwards over Patterdale which is surrounded by the Helvellyn range of hills.

15.40pm 11th August - The view from our wild camp, complete with a rocky sofa and a ringside view of Helvellyn

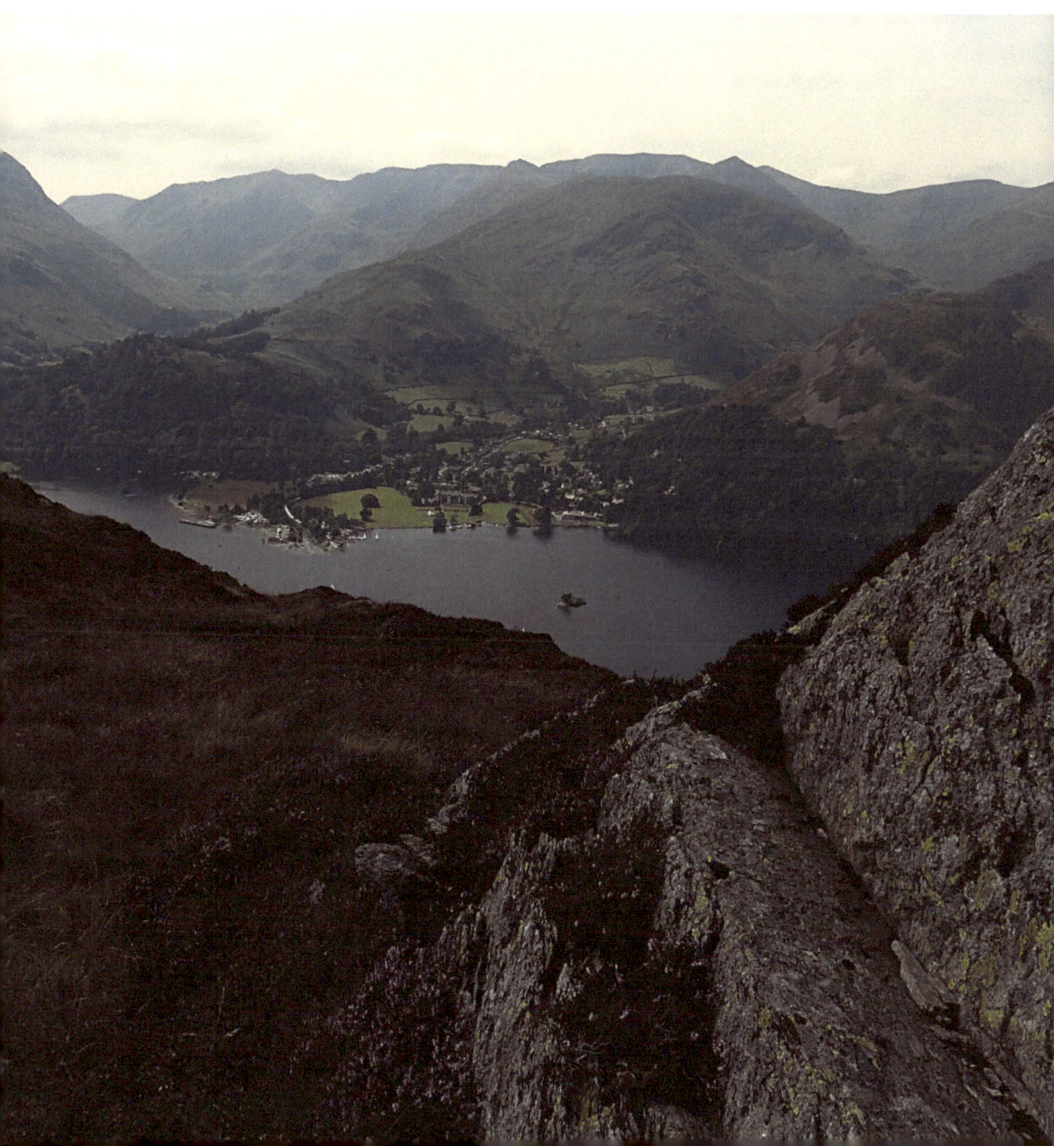

There are also numerous small mountain tarns with various distant backgrounds that make for fascinating shoots. The main tarn is about 200m along the path that descends north east from the summit. It is worth making your way around the whole tarn to take in all of its interesting aspects.

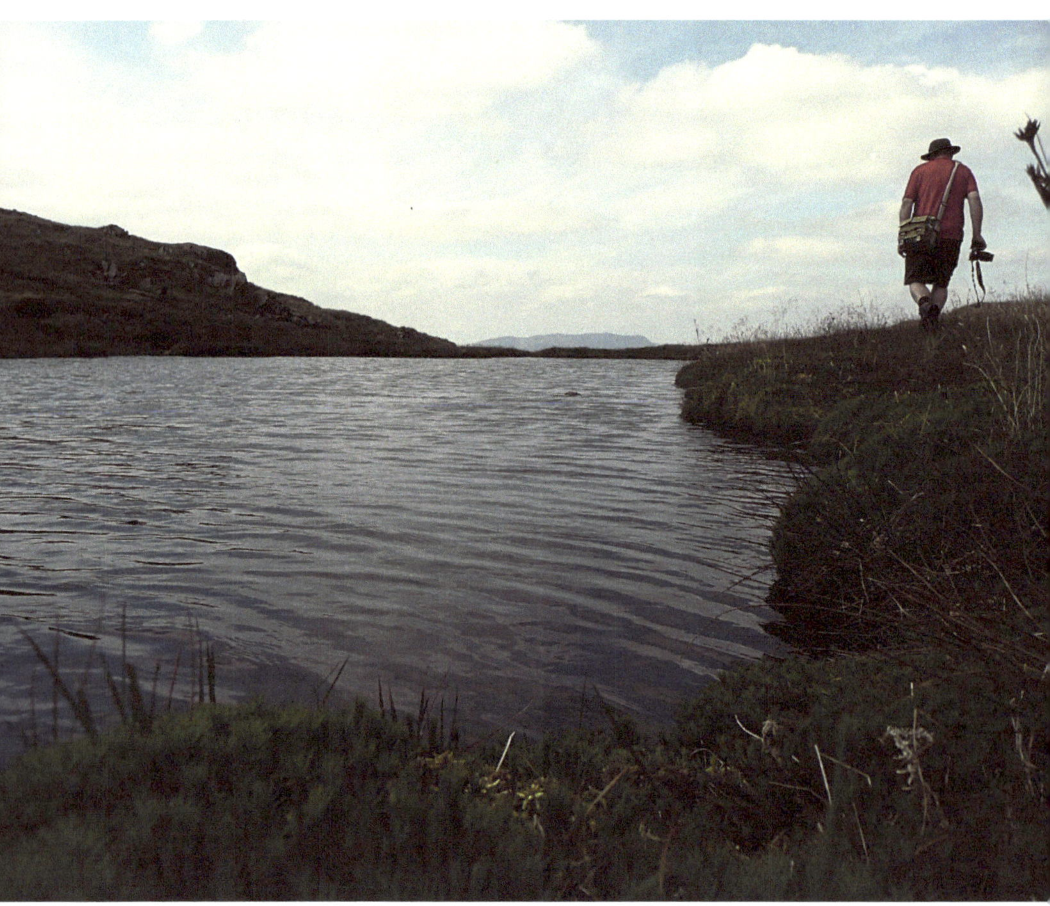

16.50am 11th August –From the 360 degree views over distant ridges, to classic mountain tarns it was a great place to spend some time. As the afternoon was rapidly disappearing, along with the handful of people attracted to the summit, David and I decided to pitch our tents just a few metres below the summit cairn.

Place Fell also makes a superb summit to wild camp on with a range of options peppered around the area below the summit rocks.

The hill haze had set in which meant any sunset would not be forthcoming but it was a mild and calm evening making it pleasant to sit out, cook some tea and chat before hitting the sack.

If you fancy extending your time on the hill a couple of relatively easy add ons can be taken in from the summit of Place Fell: Angle Tarn and Beda Head. From the summit of Place Fell take a good path that heads south down to Boredale Hause. A there and back can be walked over to Angletarn Pikes and Angle Tarn. On returning to the pass, a bridleway can be taken up onto the ridge over Beda Head, picking up a path along the ridge down to Winter Crag. Pick up the path that heads east into Howe Grain valley where the road will lead you north back to the car park.

4) The easiest and most direct route off the summit is to take the path that heads along Hart Crag. This route offers a relatively easy, gradual descent which allows you to take in a distant Hallin Fell. After about half a kilometre from the summit drop down to a broad, boggy pass called Low Moss. Continue in a north easterly direction below the outlying summit of High Dodd as the path contours quite steeply towards the valley floor. Just before you reach the field boundary pick up a path that heads towards an old farm building then crosses the stream over a stone slab bridge. On reaching the road turn left and after a further 250m take the right hand fork at an interesting old signpost. The road then bends round to the right above Howegrain Beck, crossing a bridge before taking a left fork which rises steeply past the fine hamlet of Martindale. The climb might be steep but it is soon over and as the path levels out you suddenly realise you are back at the church.

On waking early, a quick peek out of the tent confirmed what we'd been expecting-more cloud and no sunrise for us. The compensation was the chance to roll back into bed and get another couple of hours sleep. After a leisurely breakfast we struck camp and were heading back down long before anyone had started making the climb up.

3.2 A Walk of Two Ranges, Coniston and Langdale by the Backdoor

Focal Point – Tilberthwaite quarry, the distant Scafell fells, Red Tarn and of course the glorious Langdale. This route packs it all in.

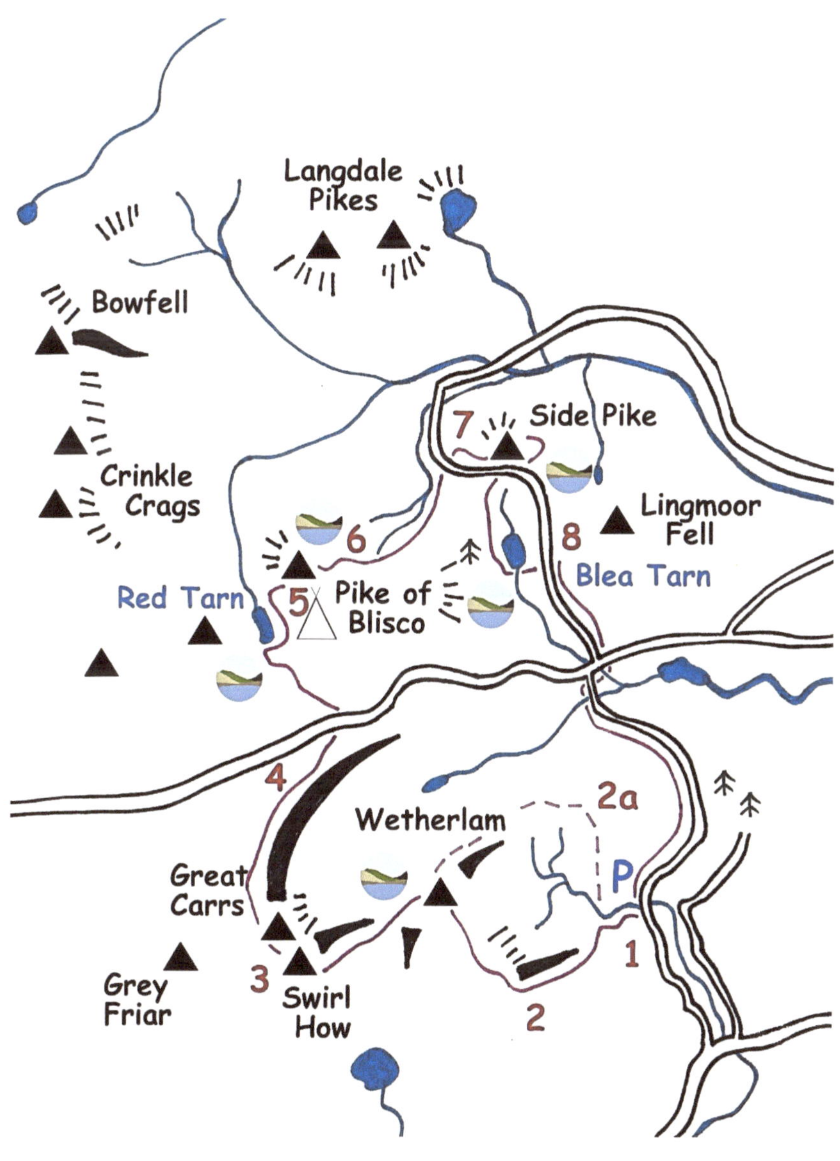

Route Summaries

Full route – an ascent of the eastern Coniston fells via Tilberthwaite Gill, followed by a sneaky route into the Langdale area including the wild Red Tarn and the stunning view point of the Pike of Blisco.

20 km; 1190m ascent

Shorter route – the full route can easily be cut into sections. A short trip to Tilberthwaite quarry and Tilberthwaite Gill make an excellent option, especially in poorer light.

2km; 145m ascent

Why Try this Route

This route accesses the classic and rightly popular Coniston and Langdale Fells by less visited but equally stunning paths. There is a lot of evidence of mining in this area which doesn't always go hand in hand with dramatic photography, however, the disused quarry near Tilberthwaite Gill is a fascinating place. A couple of very low grade but enjoyable scrambles lead you to the stunning peaks of Wetherlam and Great Carrs which offer extensive views over to the central Scafell range. The next objective, Red Tarn, is a wild but accessible place offering a stunning shoot towards the shapely Bowfell. This is followed by an ascent of the Pike of Blisco which gives you elevated views down the Langdale valley and a full 360 degree vista of the surrounding area. And if this isn't enough you can top it off with a trip to Side Pike which overlooks the sublime Langdale Pikes and on to the classic Blea Tarn.

Clockwise from top left:

Crinkle Crags and Bow Fell over Red Tarn... Simon on a summit shoot, Pike of Blisco... Taking in the beauty of Red Tarn... Getting wet feet, lakeside shoot, Red Tarn... The Langdale Pikes from Blea Tarn... Centre: The Scafells from Wetherlam

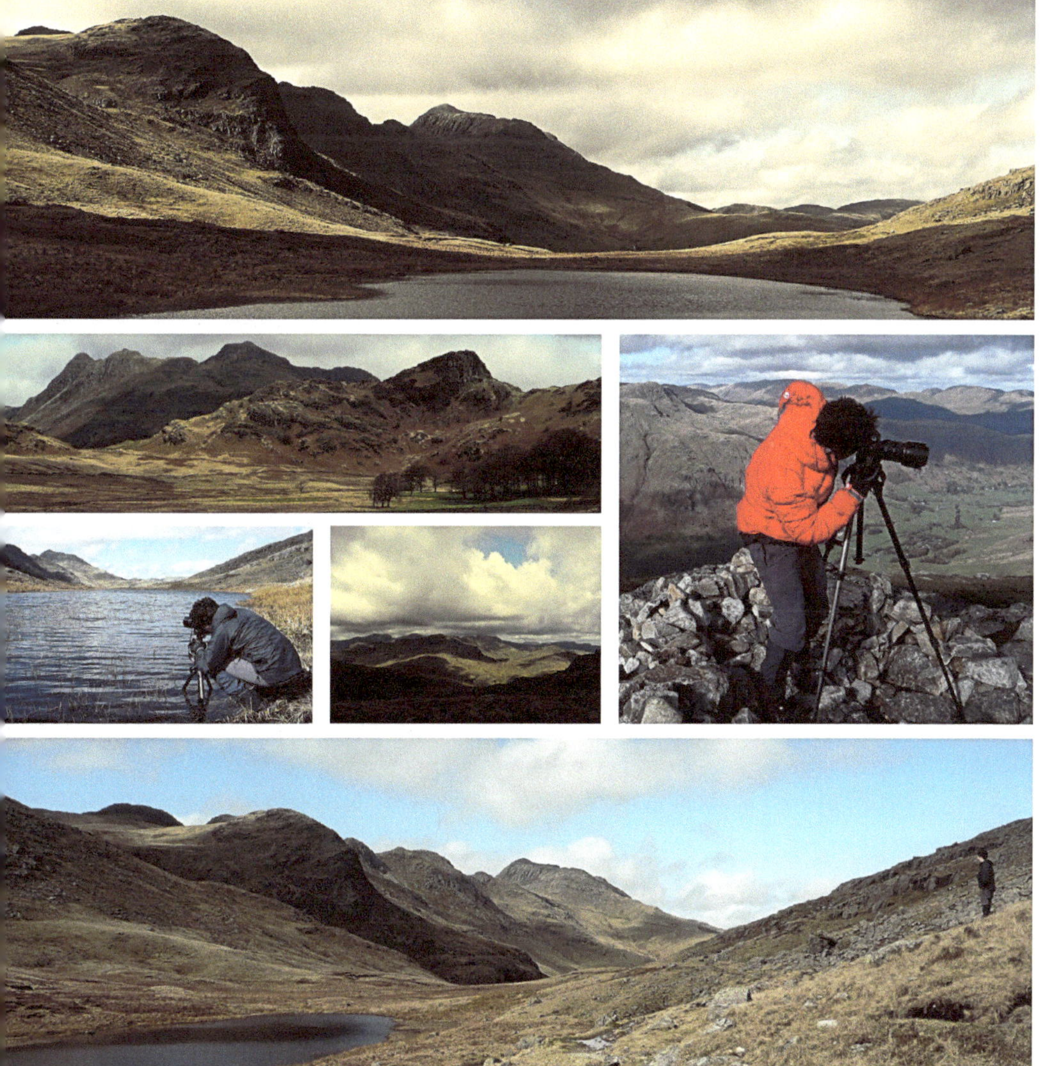

Route Description

1) Starting at the car park (NY 306010) where Yewdale Beck crosses the minor road, take the path that heads up the southern side of the beck heading for Tilberthwaite Gill. The climb is fairly steep but after about 200m there is a large disused quarry on the left that is well worth an exploration. The sides are extremely steep so take care, however, there are a number of easy access points into the quarry and some good viewpoints at the top end of the quarry next to the main path.

We were welcome of a breather on this short sharp ascent and the view down the disused quarry proved a timely distraction.

Once you've finished at the quarry continue up the path where you have a choice – to carry on up the higher southern path above the gill or drop down into the gill, cross the footbridge and head up the northern side. Either route is a joy so take your pick. They both meet up at the top of the steep sided valley where you are faced with a somewhat bigger choice.

Your next target is the fine summit of Wetherlam and it can be reached by either of its two fine 'edges'.

2) The most adventurous and direct ascent is via Steel Edge, the start of which is a couple of hundred meters north west from the meeting of the paths. There are faint paths that wind ever steeper up Steel Edge avoiding most of the rocks until the ridge narrows towards the top. There are no serious rock steps to negotiate although there is a rough scree path on the last section of the edge. Fortunately there are some far reaching views over to the south and east as you climb upwards which takes your mind off the hard work at hand. At the

top of Steel Edge turn right up the broad south ridge of Wetherlam that takes you to its summit. There is a good path that ambles up the middle of this ridge, however, good views can be found above the steep cliffs to your right.

2a) The alternative route to the summit of Wetherlam heads north from the meeting of the paths at the top of Tilberthwaite Gill. A wide path meanders below the outcrops of Blake Rigg and then turns left below Hawk Rigg before contouring up to Birk Fell Hawse (a pass). Your views start to open up as you climb the ridge, Wetherlam Edge, in front of you.

Either route brings you out on the fine summit of Wetherlam.

Photo Locations – Wetherlam to Swirl How

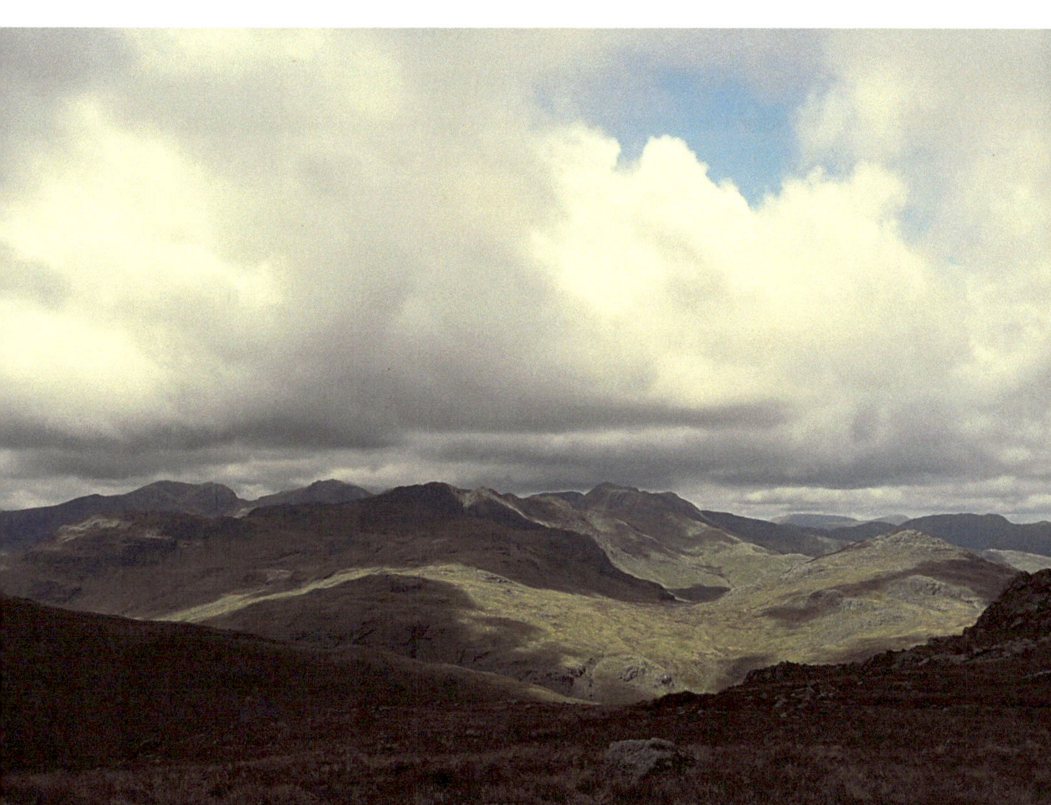

11.10am 14th May - Along the whole section, from Wetherlam to Swirl How, we got extensive views over to the brooding Central Fells to the north and also to much of the rest of the route to come.

Wetherlam is an outlier of the main Coniston fells, which means you get extensive views over a good portion of the Lake District. This along with the ridge linking the next summit, Swirl How, gives you far reaching views over to the central Lakeland fells. The line up of some of the highest peaks in England from the brooding Scafells to the mighty Bowfell is a joy to capture from these parts.

On leaving the summit, take care to pick up the path that heads off westwards over the broad Red Dell Head Moss before dropping down to the narrow pass at Swirl Hawse. The path starts to get a bit rockier as you ascend the interestingly named Prison Band. Whilst this sounds a bit tough, the ridge is a real joy to walk and soon brings you to the stunning summit of Swirl How.

3) From the summit of Swirl How follow the path that skirts the top of the cliffs to your right, heading west and then north, to the last summit of your Coniston round, Great Carrs. This is a good place to take stock of your route so far and of what's to come so find a good spot to take it all in. Head north, dropping down over the minor bump of Little Carrs and onto the arcing ridge of Wet Side Edge. Fortunately the 'wet' refers to the fact that the edge is a watershed with major streams heading off on both sides. If you are running out of time or don't fancy camping out tonight you can follow the edge all the way down into Greendale valley. There are a number of options back to Tilberthwaite but for the easiest drop down the last steep section and take the left hand path that leads to Fell Foot. Turn right as you reach the road and then take the first track on the right that skirts round Little Langdale Tarn.

4) If you want to stay out for longer keep an eye out for a faint path that drops down to the top of Wrynose Pass as the edge starts to open up to your left. The steepish path drops nicely down to the top of the pass where there are often a few parked cars. Cross the road and pick up a good path that climbs the right hand side of the open valley.

If you are wild camping tonight it is worth filling up your water bottles from the streams just across from the pass.

The climb is never too steep but it does seem to drag on for a while. However your reward is a fine one. As the path levels out you get your first glimpse of the glorious Red Tarn which is in a wild but accessible setting.

Photo Location – Red Tarn

Whilst the shoreline is usually pretty damp, a water level shoot makes for some interesting images.

15.45pm 8th May - Getting your feet wet for a good cause. Si going to great lengths to get the shot in the bag

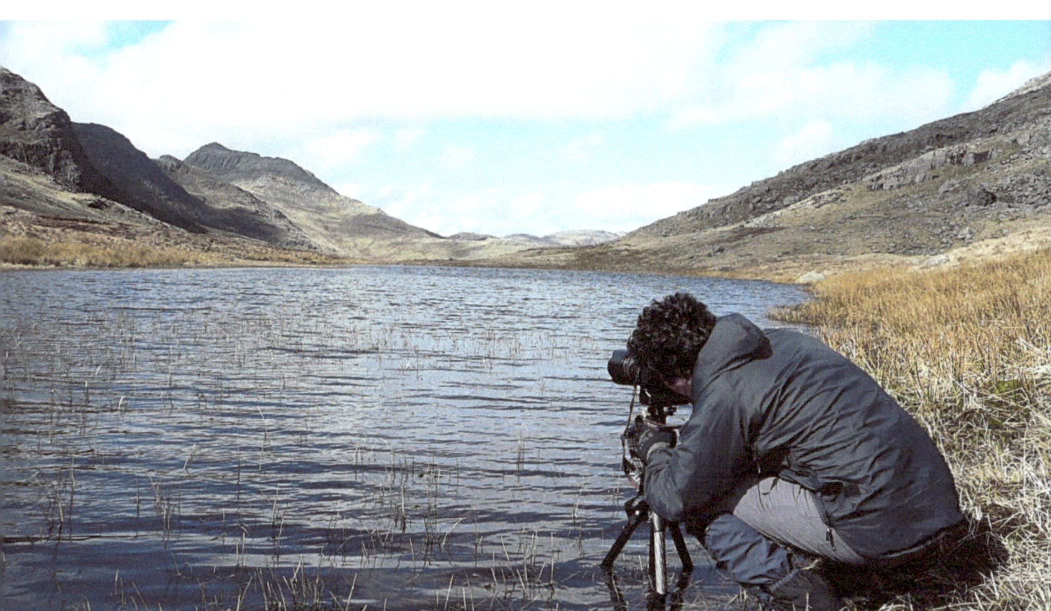

Be sure to also position yourself just above the eastern shoreline as this gives you a fine elevated perspective with the scoop of the valley in front of you and a fuller panorama of the hills to the northwest.

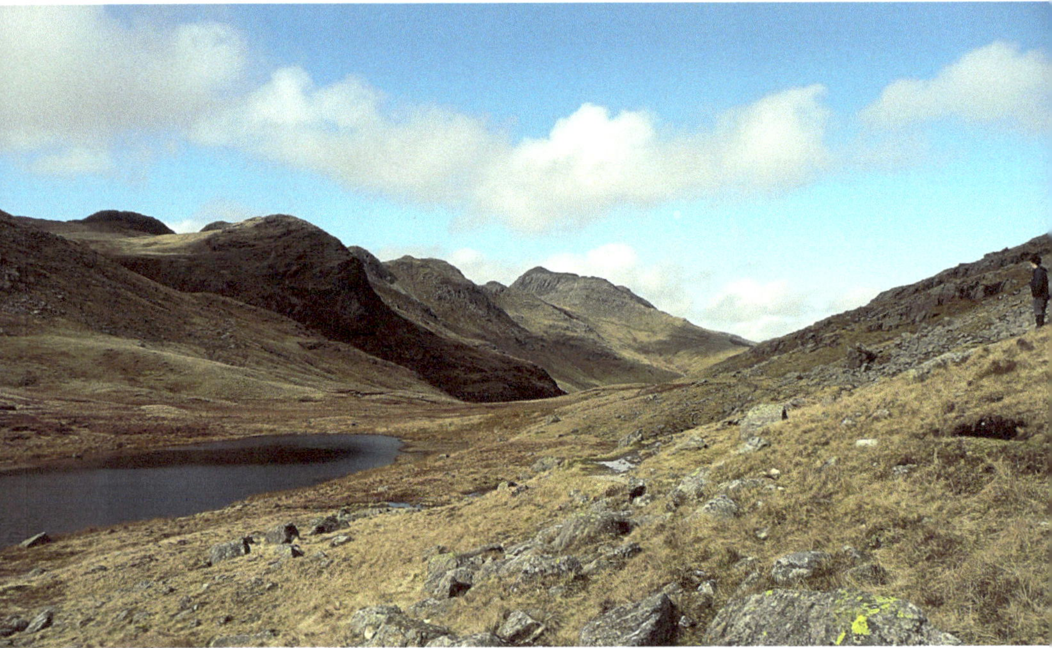

16.05pm 8th May - The views down Red Tarn from just above its southern end were fantastic with some of the finest hills in the Lakes as a stunning back drop. Crinkle Crags looking formidably crinkly and craggy and the huge bulk of Bowfell acting as a fine bookend.

You can wild camp around the tarn and in fact there are often a few people doing so. However, it can be a bit of a wind funnel as there is limited shelter.

If waterfalls are your thing, and especially if you don't fancy the climb up the Pike of Blisco, a detour can be made by heading north into Oxendale. About 1km from Red Tarn you'll reach a rocky knoll, Brown Howe. The waterfall that tumbles down Browney Gill is a real cracker. If you are avoiding the Pike of Blisco, continue down the good path that leads you to the upper reaches of the Great Langdale valley where you can climb up the road to Blea Tarn.

5) If you fancy a spot to yourself and don't mind making one last climb, head past the tarn and seek out a path that heads up to the right. This might seem a harsh way to finish your day but the summit of the Pike of Blisco is one of the finest in the area.

Photo Location – The Pike of Blisco

As it stands out, isolated from the main Langdale hills, this peak offers unimpeded views in all directions so it's often difficult to know where to point your camera first. The Langdale Pikes across the valley certainly shout out to attract your attention. Their pointy, rock crowned summits spill scree and streams down to their heathered flanks before they, in turn, merge with the valley floor and its seemingly timeless pastures.

18.35pm 8th May - The beautiful lush sweep of the Great Langdale valley opened up before us with its intricate stone walled field boundaries leading to steep fellside.

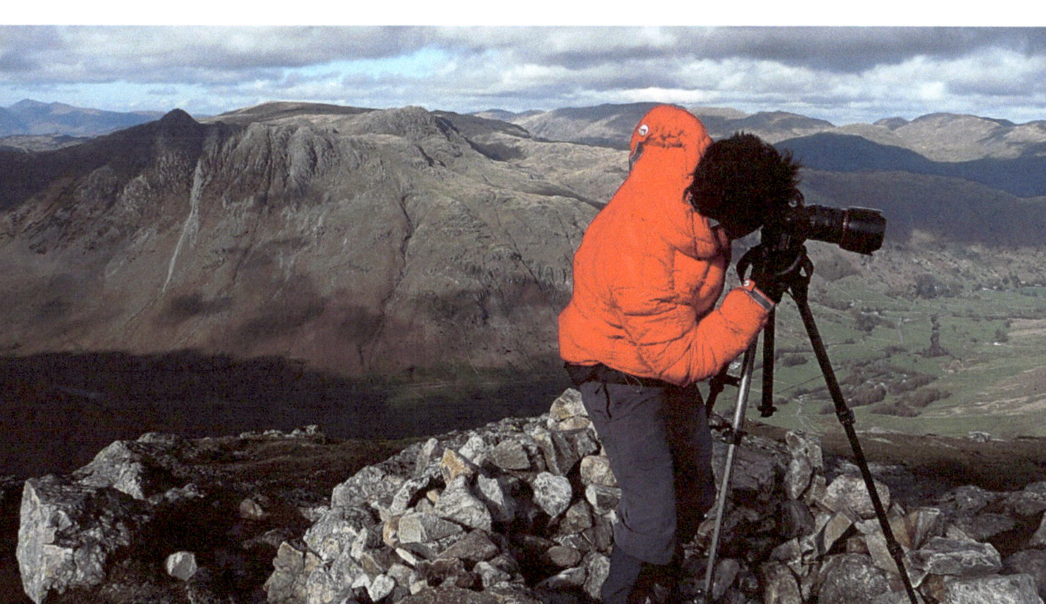

However, the Coniston Fells, which you travelled over earlier, are also worthy of your attention with the broad curve of Wet Side Edge forming an excellent middle ground. As there is so much to take in, this makes it an ideal place to camp out at and whilst the Pike is fairly pointy, there are a number of flat grassy areas just down from the summit in a south easterly direction. The only downside to such an elevated pitch is that it lacks a good water source nearby so if you haven't filled up earlier on you'll have a fair walk to get some.

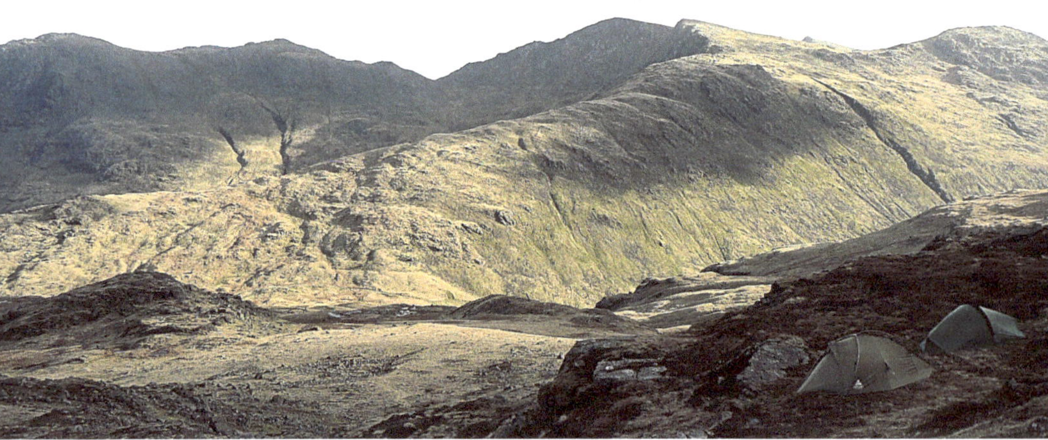

19.10pm 8th May - As time was getting on we pitched up for the night at a suitably sheltered spot near the summit. This gave us plenty of time to capture the moody skies gathering around the mountain tops. After a quick brew and some tasty grub we used up the remaining light to clamber around the rocky summit, getting in some final shots before turning in for the night.

6) On leaving the summit, pick up a faint path that meanders down the eastern flanks of the Pike. The going is fairly rocky at times but a reasonable path leads you down to a flatter section around Wrynose

Fell. The path then descends in a north easterly direction into a steep gully. A good path leads down to the road just below the pass on the Great Langdale side. On reaching the road turn right for the short climb up to the pass.

7) From the pass a visit to the summit of Side Pike is a must as it offers sublime views across the valley to the Langdale Pikes for very little effort. The ascent starts from the top of the pass, before the road dips down towards Blea Tarn, and picks its way over the rocky nobbles that make up Side Pike.

After an impromptu product shoot in a mountain stream, with the Langdale Pikes as a backdrop, we headed on down to the road and convinced ourselves that a short, sharp final uphill would be worth the effort.

Photo Location – Side Pike

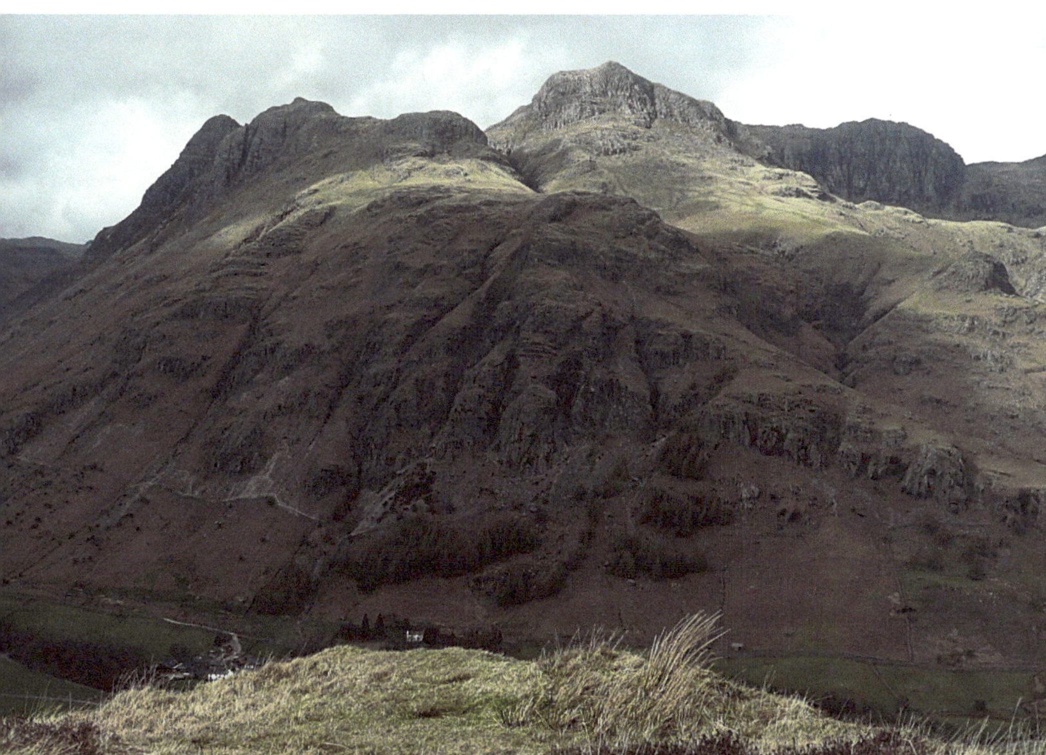

11.20pm 9th May - Side Pike, at only 360m, may be the lowest of the Langdale hills but it possibly possesses one of the areas best views. The route to the top is quite steep and can be made quite entertaining. We managed to get in a final bit of shutter action before a shower came in and called an end of play for the weekend.

Hills seldom offer such great photographic potential for such little effort but Side Pike certainly hits the spot. The beautiful Langdale Pikes are all stacked up in front of you with their rocky crags running down to the classic 'U' shaped valley that is at your feet.

After carefully dropping down from the last, slightly higher summit you'll end up on a broad shoulder. You can carry on eastwards over Lingmoor Fell which offers a slightly different perspective on the view across to the Langdale Pikes. However, if time or energy levels are running short then drop down south from the shoulder to reach the road again. Turn right along the road for a couple of hundred meters before picking up a good track that turns left and leads you alongside Blea Tarn.

Photo Location – Blea Tarn

The view from the southern end of Blea Tarn is a real classic and is probably one of the easiest Lake District view points with a car park only 250m away. So this is often a busy spot especially at dawn. However, it is a wonderful place to explore at any time of the day as long as the cloud isn't obliterating Langdales finest across the water. With plenty of foreground interest and the back drop of Side Pike and the Langdale Pikes vying for your attention it's worth spending some time here to enjoy any change in the light and shadow.

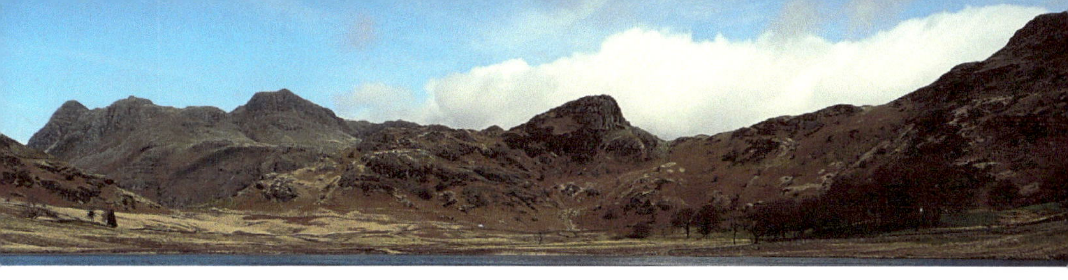

09.50pm 8th May - The rain quickly cleared as we reached the southern shores of Blea Tarn which gave us the perfect opportunity to shoot down the lake. Sometimes a location doesn't have to be hard won and whilst every man and his dog has pretty much shot the same images its still a great place to visit and savour.

8) Leave Blea Tarn by following the main path round its southern end and rejoin the road by the carpark. From here the easiest option is to follow the road south eastwards down to the Little Langdale/ Wrynose road. Turn right for 200m before taking a track on your left over Fell Foot Bridge. This track leads you round the southern edge of Little Langdale Tarn before picking up a right turn that leads you back to Tilberthwaite.

Two of the Lake District's mightiest ranges in one weekend is more than enough to leave you with tired legs but very happy memories.

3.3 Hopegill Head from the Wild North

Focal Point – The three main ridgelines that radiate from the summit of Hopegill Head ooze quality both in terms of their walking and photographic potential. On this route you can walk all three, allowing you to experience them from every angle.

Route Summaries

Full route – Leaving Low Lorton on minor roads and then footpaths you soon reach the climb onto the northern approach to Ladyside Pike. A short scramble brings you out on the summit of Hopegill Head. An extension can be made to Grisedale Pike as an out and back before continuing on to Whiteside. The descent is made via the northern ridge towards the outlying summit of Dodd. Dropping down to Hope Beck leads you to the road and a return via the outward paths.

18 km; 1160m ascent

Shorter route – The main route can be shortened by starting from the minor road near High Swinside Farm. Whilst it is hard to form a low level route incorporating the main summits, an exploration of Hope Beck and a there and back ascent to Dodd would make an excellent shorter day out.

10km; 370m ascent

Why Try this Route

The ridges that branch out from the fine summit of Hopegill Head not only make for superlative walking but also offer a number of excellent photographic opportunities. The very nature of being on a ridge means that you'll have, as a minimum, sweeping vistas to either side of you. On these ridges the views reach down into some glorious wild valleys and to some of the shapeliest peaks that the Lakes have on offer. You also have the satisfaction of being able to photograph what you have just walked and what you are about to experience underfoot. Whilst this route gets you into a beautiful area it does so by starting from the quieter northern approaches which means you'll probably enjoy much of the walk by yourselves.

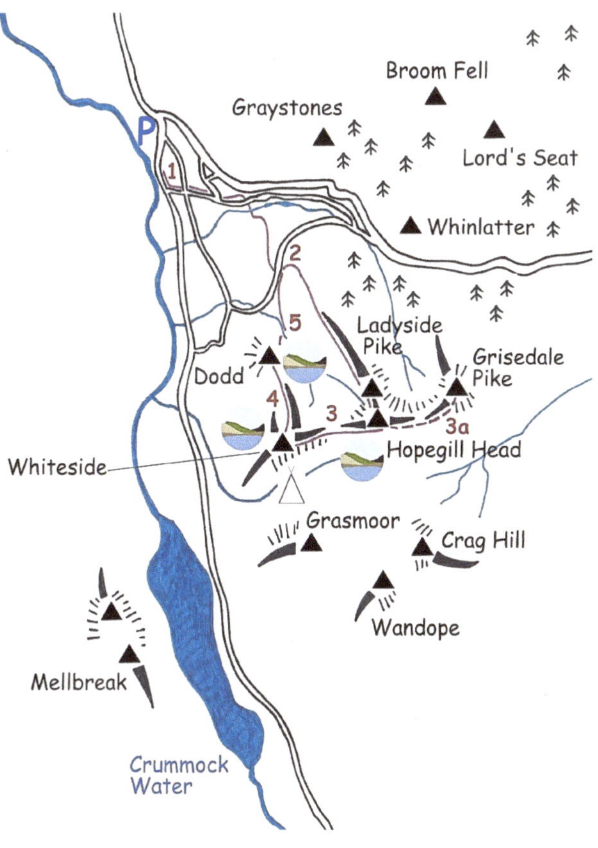

Clockwise from top left :

The view down Gasgale Gill to Mellbreak from Hopegill Head... Looking back to Grisedale Pike from Coledale Hause... Ladyside Pike from Hopegill Head... The view to Hopegill Head from Grisedale Pike... The Ladyside Pike ridge on route to Dodd... Hope Beck

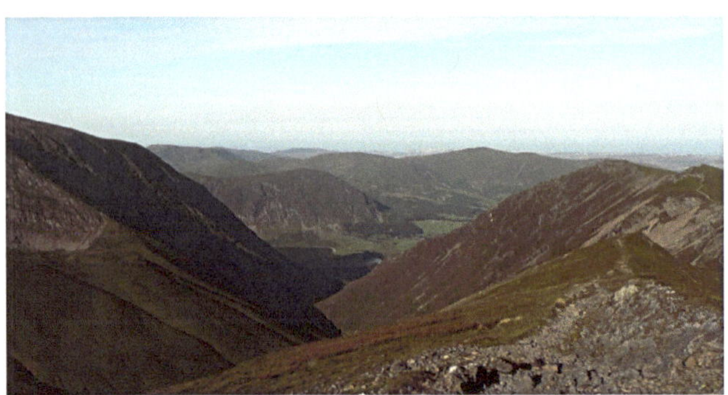

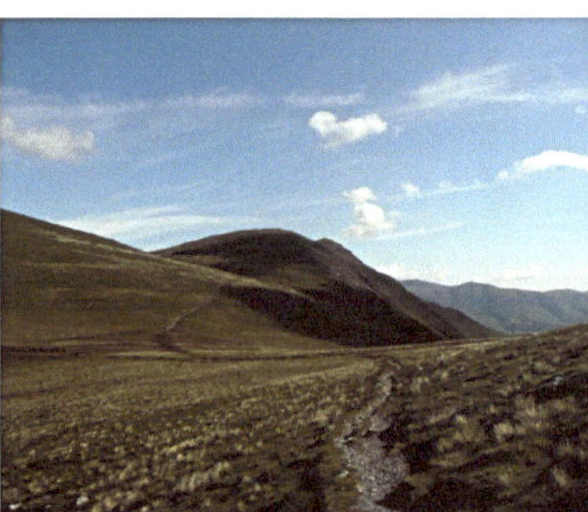

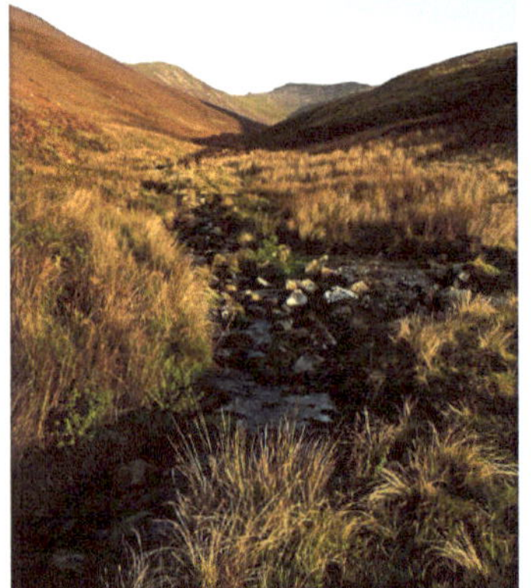

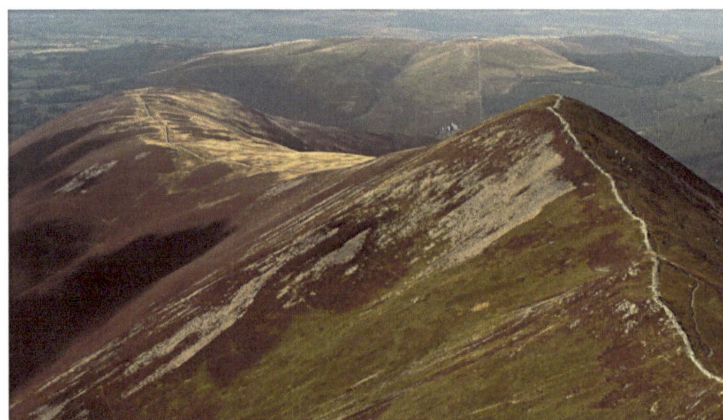

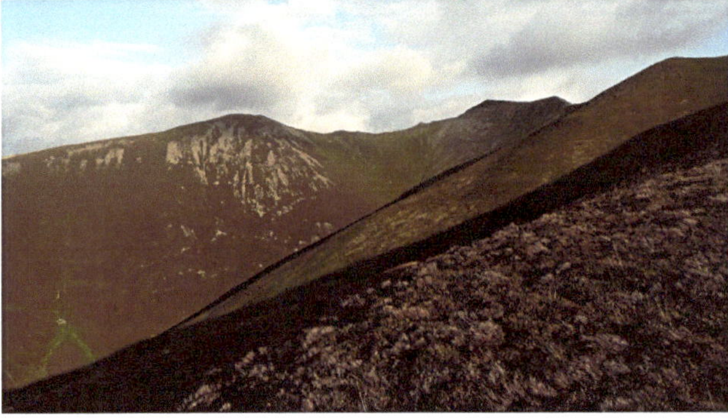

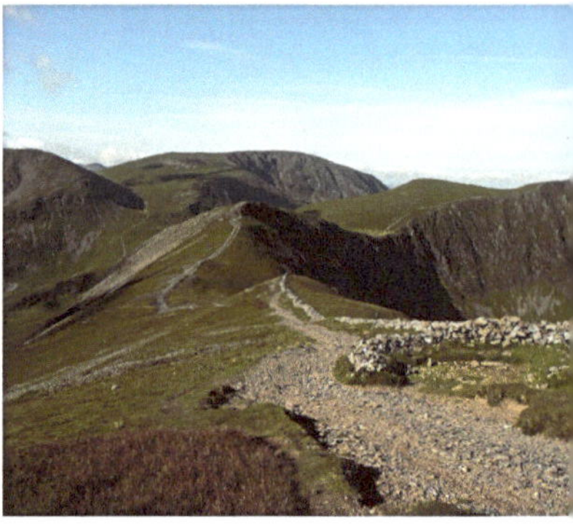

Route Description

1) You can start this walk from Low Lorton which is a good base from which to explore the area. It has a couple of campsites and an excellent pub, the Wheatsheaf Inn, which also acts as the local shop and cafe. Alternatively you can shorten the route by starting from a small layby near High Swinside Farm (see Point 2). From the pub, head south on the B5289 for 200m to a staggered crossroads and turn left.

The view south down Lorton Vale towards the double humped peak of Mellbreak made for a great start to the day in the early morning mist. I was already anticipating the delights of what was to come and this put a spring in my step.

Head straight over a second crossroads and pass a school on your right. Soon you are looking to pick up the second minor road on your right, signposted Scales and Boonbeck. Ignore the first footpath and as you start to climb the hill take the second footpath on your right that leaves the road through a metal swing gate. The path follows the edge of the field for around 200m before dropping down to another metal gate in front of a farm building. Head up the track on the left hand side of the buildings and as you pass the entrance to a house called Scales, the track turns sharply left. Just after this corner, pass through a large gate on your right that leads you up a stoney track. After a further 200m the track turns sharply to the right where it steadily climbs up to High Swinside Farm. Along this section the views really open up over the valley below, especially towards Mellbreak.

At the end of the track go through a five bar gate, heading round to the left of the house and then follow the track towards the road. After passing the last building you cross a cattle grid where you can break left over open ground to reach the road.

2) On reaching the road, head north. Just before the gate across the road look for a faint path that heads steeply up the slopes to your right. The path roughly follows the stone wall, although it is worth taking any zig zags to make it a little less lung busting. There's no getting away from the fact that this is a steep, and I mean steep, ascent. However, with every step you gain ever expanding views over the pastures below and to the slopes of the hills that stretch off to the south. This gives you ample excuse to stop, admire the view and allow your pulse rate to drop down to more sensible levels. Also, every step gets you closer to some really exciting ridgelines ahead. So stick with it and after 250m of climbing the gradient begins to ease. The path continues to follow the stonewall boundary which now leads you along a broad ridgeline.

Sadly on reaching the final push to the summit of Ladyside Pike we walked into some rather persistent hill fog. This hid not only the views we were seeking but also the chance to see the route to come; the cracking little scramble to Hopegill Head.

After some gentle climbing the gradient steepens and the ridge starts to narrow a little as you clamber onto the small top of Ladyside Pike where there is a large pile of stones marking the summit. Drop down from the summit to follow the ridge to a small pinnacle of rock. You can scramble directly over this obstacle or head round it on a path to your right. If you do go around it, join the ridgeline again as it reaches a small notch next to some sloping slabs. This is a dramatic position to be in with the imposing ridgeline rearing above you and a gully sweeping down the cliffs at your feet. Fear not however; as the route to the top is nowhere near as hard as you can make it. The easiest approach is by taking an open gully that climbs the slab, well to the right of the cliffs. There is no real exposure on this section as the slopes to the right aren't too steep. This short pull quickly brings you out onto the small rocky summit of Hopegill Head where the 360 degree views should have you reaching for your camera and a well earned break.

On revisiting Hopegill Head our patience paid off. The mist cleared to reveal breathtaking views. It was a delight to see the route we had walked earlier; however, the best was yet to come.

Photo Location – Hopegill Head

One of the main problems you'll encounter when you reach the summit is where to point your camera first. Looking back over your shoulder to the route you have just walked certainly grabs your attention. The slender ridgeline over Ladyside Pike is accentuated by the drystone wall that traces its apex. The flatter northern section of the ridge is enhanced by its slopes being cloaked in a good blanket of rich purple heather in Autumn. You also get an excellent backdrop of the Whinlatter peaks to one side which is nicely balanced by the lush green of Lorton Vale to the other.

07.45am 8th August – It might have been an early start from my high camp on Whiteside but to be on the summit of Hopegill Head at this time of the day was a real feast for the eyes.

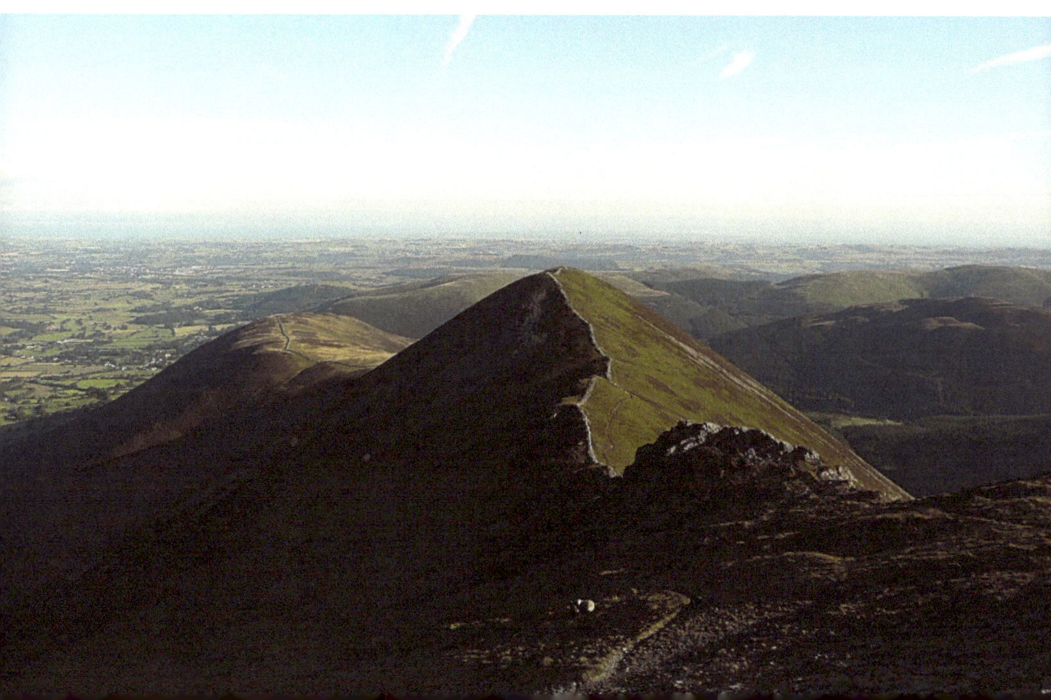

Looking east, the precipitous Hobcarton Crag attracts your eye as it carves a chunk out of the smooth moors. And to the south the hills that make up the other half of the classic Coledale horseshoe, Causey Pike, Crag Hill and the enormous bulk of Grasmoor make for a stunning skyline.

However, for me at least, the view to the west is what gets my pulse racing. The ridge that stretches off from Hopegill Head to the craggy slopes of a distant Whiteside not only make for excellent walking but also for immense photographic potential.

16.10pm 20th September - Liz, Andrew and Adrian heading off down the Whiteside ridge. I'd first seen this ridge when I walked the Coledale horseshoe almost 20 years previously. Finally I'd got round to traversing this brilliant route and it didn't let me down. The walking was always exciting but never too challenging that you couldn't stop and admire the breathtaking scenery.

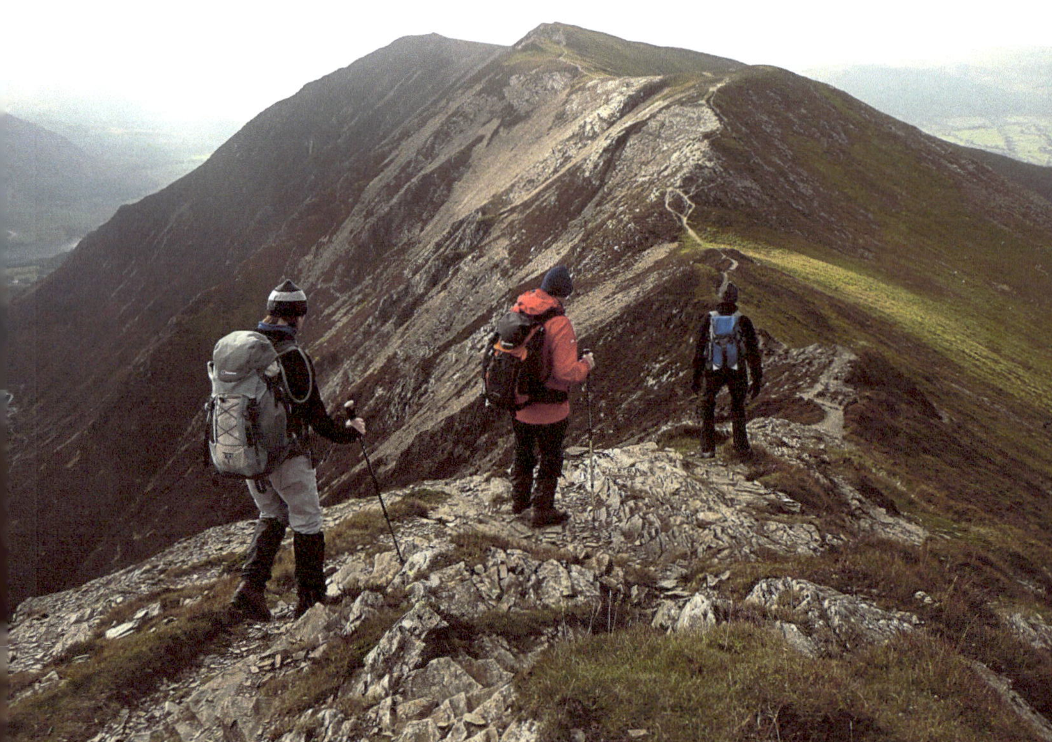

Hopegill Head is a meeting of paths so you have your first real route decision to make.

Route Extension

3a) A worthwhile diversion is to traverse along the top of the Hobcarton Crags to the east and head over to the shapely and well positioned summit of Grisedale Pike. A role call of Skiddaw, Blencathra, the Helvellyn range, the Newlands and the Coledale horsehoes is quite a list of superb hills to shoot from here. This outlying peak not only offers far reaching views over much of the northern peaks and lakes but it also allows you to peer into the impenetrable Hobcarton Crags. These cliffs sweep round to your earlier scramble up to Hopegilll Head which from this angle makes it look pretty epic.

Dropping down to the first pass between Hopegill Head and Grisedale Pike are a couple of tiny tarns that are perched at the top of Hobcarton Crags. They make an interesting foreground to the spectacular Ladyside ridge.

So, whether you just drop down to the col above Hobcarton Crags or follow the ridge all the way to Grisedale Pike, the best option on this diversion is to return via the outward route. A second visit to Hopegill Head is no bad thing either as the changing weather can give you fresh perspectives from this excellent vantage point.

3) When it is time to leave Hopegill Head, turn west along the roller coaster ridge that leads you to the summit of Whiteside. As you start to descend, the grey rock that makes up Whiteside's southern slopes makes this ridge take on almost alpine proportions compared to its relatively modest height.

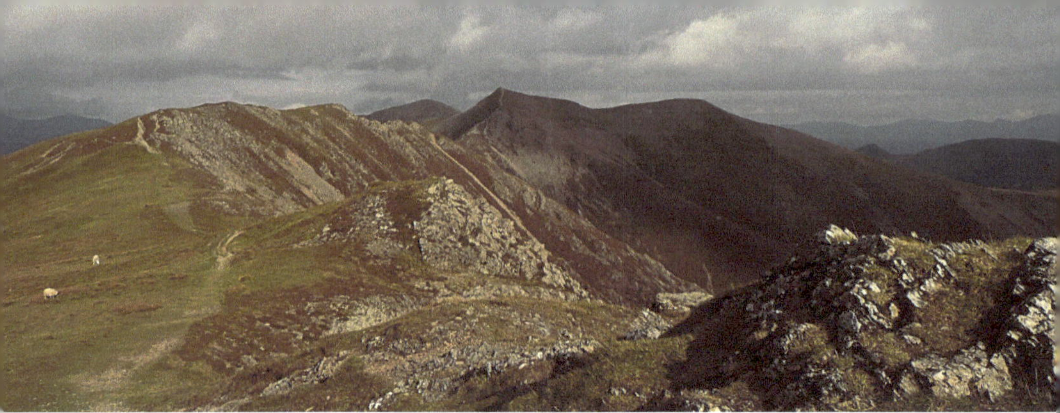

Photo Location - Whiteside Ridge and Summit

The route to the summit of Whiteside is pretty obvious with a good path heading due west just to the right of the steep drop. However there are a number of small outcrops that are worth exploring on your way to the summit. These give superb views down into the depths of Gasgale Gill that lies at the bottom of the rock, scree and heather that spill down the Gasgale Crags. The line that Liza Beck takes along the valley floor leads your eye nicely down to Crummock Water with a backdrop of Mellbreak. What is more, the slopes of Whiteside to the right and Grasmoor to the left book end this composition.

The ridge soon starts to both flatten and broaden out which allows an easy stroll to the final summit, marked 707m on a map. Stop here before the path you are on drops steeply down to the shores of Crummock Water, as our return route heads off in the other direction. This spot makes for a fitting final high viewpoint as you get to see the whole ridge sweeping back up to a very pointy looking Hopegill Head.

16.45pm 20th September - Only just over an hour ago these hills had been shrouded in mist, denying us any views. Now we were in for a glorious evening and we were still up high to fully enjoy it.

Turning the other way to face west the ground drops away steeply. This gives you an excellent vantage point over to the northern shores of Crummock Water. Again the scree strewn slopes of Mellbreak look fantastic from here as they spill down to the waters edge and into the green fields that surround the valley floor. From the summit you can drop down west for 100m to another flat grassy area that gives expansive and unimpeded views down to Mellbreak.

As the 707m summit has a flat grassy area just beyond the last rocks, with outstanding views in all directions, it makes it an excellent, if rather exposed wild camping location.

Having made the ascent in the dark the night before I spent a peaceful night 'recovering' in my tent, perched on a comfy bed of grass with a distant Liza Beck as my background soundtrack. I awoke to a crisp sunrise and with excited anticipation at the chance to explore the ridge before anyone else was likely to make it up here.

4) Our route off Whiteside is the north ridge that starts near the 719m summit on the main ridge. So back track around 300m eastwards before contouring around to the north where you'll pick up a faint path that leads you down a broad ridge.

As you lose height you look down onto the rounded hump of a hill at the end of the ridge; this is the little visited but rather splendid summit of Dodd.

Photo Location – Dodd and Hope Gill

The little hillock of Dodd and the ridge you are descending are amazing places to get a new perspective of the route you have travelled.

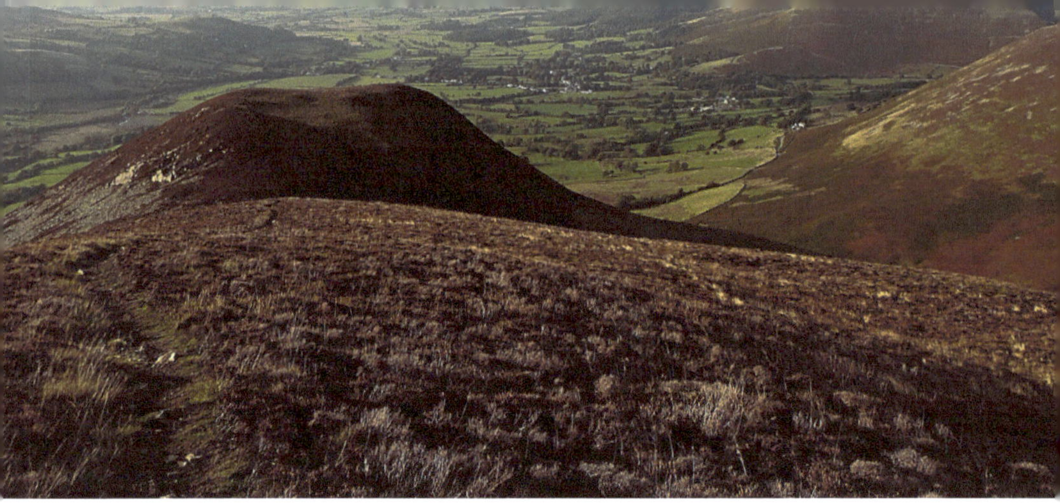

17.15pm 20th September – The descent down the heathered slopes in the early evening light was a real feast for the eyes. The shadows were lengthening and the autumnal colours were starting to shine through.

As a backdrop to this hill you can make out the village of Low Lorton. From here you can see how it is surrounded by the green pastures that you walked out through, and will return through soon.

Looking east you get an excellent view to the Ladyside ridge and the crags that you scrambled up earlier. This composition is somewhat aided by the sweeping slopes of, not only the ridge you are standing on, but also a second ridge that drops down into the valley below. A slightly more open composition of this view can be taken in by heading over to Dodd itself. At the end of the ridge, drop quite steeply into a small col where you face a scree slope in front of you. A direct assault of the scree can be made. Alternatively turn left at the col for 50m then take a right fork that heads up through a slope covered in slatey rock before picking up the ridge that winds to the top. Clamber over a rock band before a bit of heather bashing brings you out onto the first of two cairned tops. From the first top the view back over to Hopegill Head is sublime.

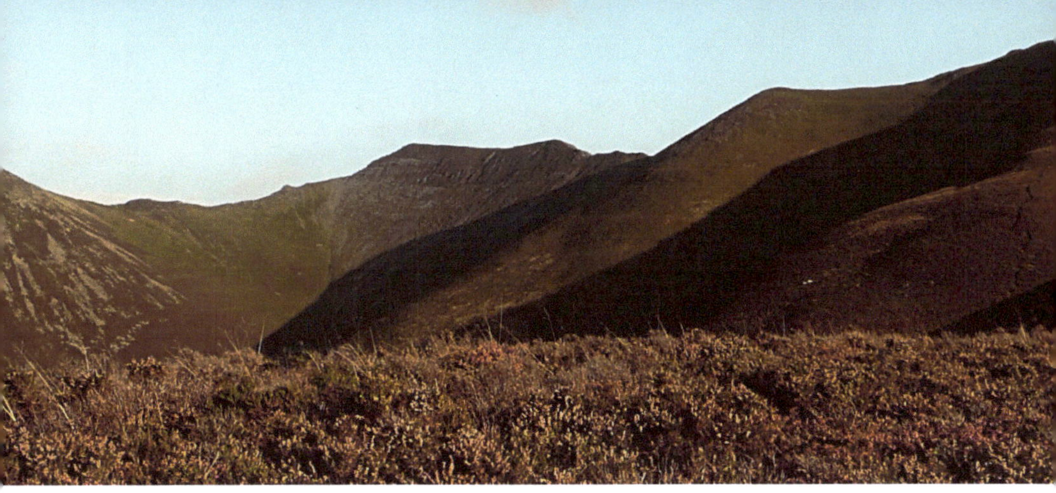

17.30pm 20th September – At 454m this hill is dwarfed by its higher neighbours. However, we felt on top of the world to be standing on this little summit where we could enjoy a hidden corner of the Lakes.

Heading over to the second top you feel like you are on a balcony that looks down onto the beautiful valley stretching out below your feet. The descent can be made by either heading down the eastern aspect of Dodd between the two summits, or backtracking to the col and picking up the path that heads north east. The latter, whilst being slightly longer is a bit easier on tired legs. Both routes converge at Hope Beck where there is a good path on its northern side. This requires making the only stream crossing of the whole route although this shouldn't cause any problems.

The view back upstream to the upper reaches of Hope Gill is a fitting end to a fine day on the hills.

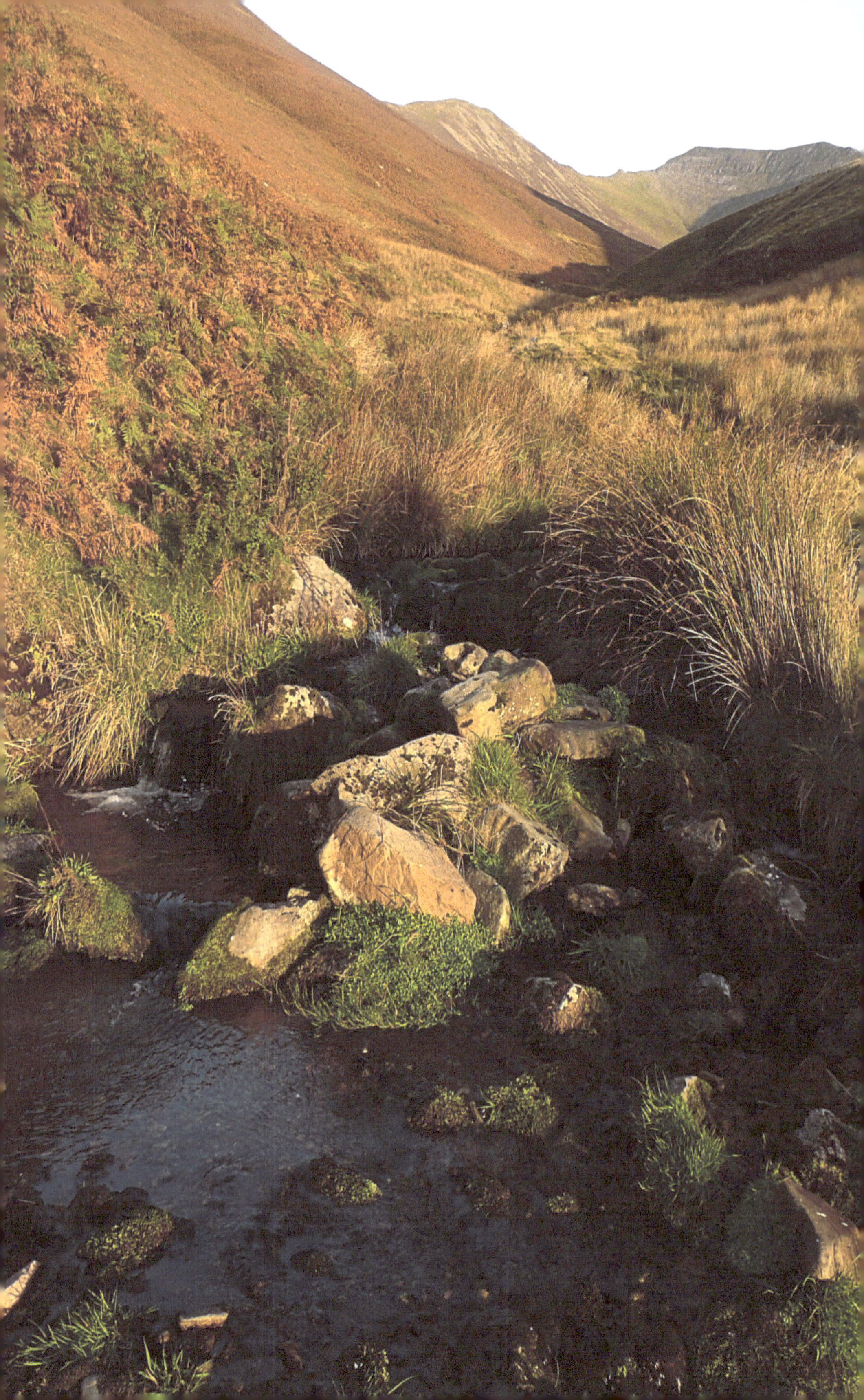

17.50pm 20th September – It's always a joy to take one final view of the high ground you've just explored before you return to civilisation. However, looking up this remote valley to such a glorious ridge, in such glorious light, was rather special.

5) On picking up the path on the north side of the stream turn left and follow it down to the minor road. From here you'll get one last view of Mellbreak over some beautiful pastures. Head north along the road for just short of 200m before you pick up the track to your left that takes you down to High Swinside Farm. You are now heading back along your outward route so follow the track down to Scales and then the minor roads to Low Lorton.

We returned to Low Lorton with tired legs and had worked up a bit of a thirst. Fortunately the pub was open which gave us a perfect opportunity to go in, enjoy a pint with friends and re-live an amazing day on the hills.

On a Visit to the Area Why Not Also Check Out These Locations

3.4 Far Flung Locations Around the Northern Lakes: Mellbreak, Barf and Great Calva

Why Try These Routes

These outlying hills are found around the periphery of the north western Lake District and form excellent vantage points from which to view their higher neighbours. Being set apart from the main hills they give a more sweeping perspective of some of the Lakes' grandest peaks; the Buttermere Fells, Skiddaw and Blencathra.

Clockwise from top left:

Great Calva rising above early morning mist... Liz and Andrew heading towards Lord's Seat, Barf in the background... Sunrise from Great Calva... The view to Skiddaw from Barf... Crummock Water and Buttermere from Mellbreak... Mellbreak from Rannerdale Knotts

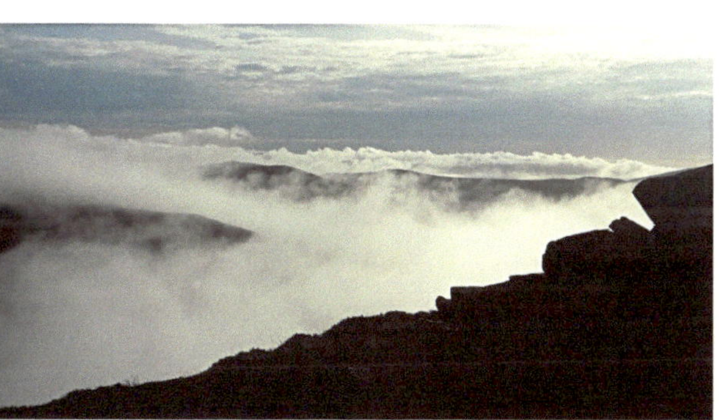

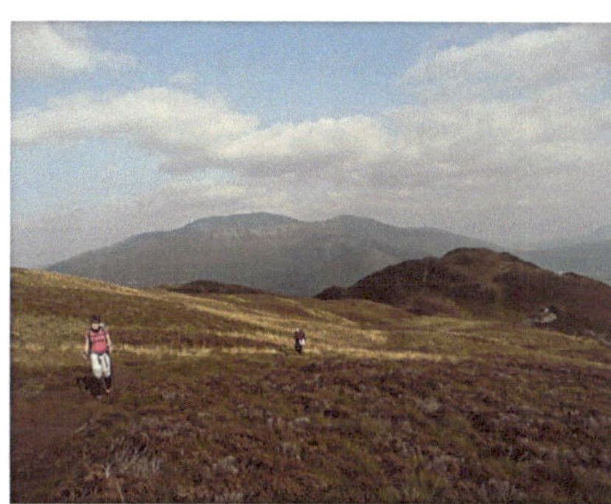

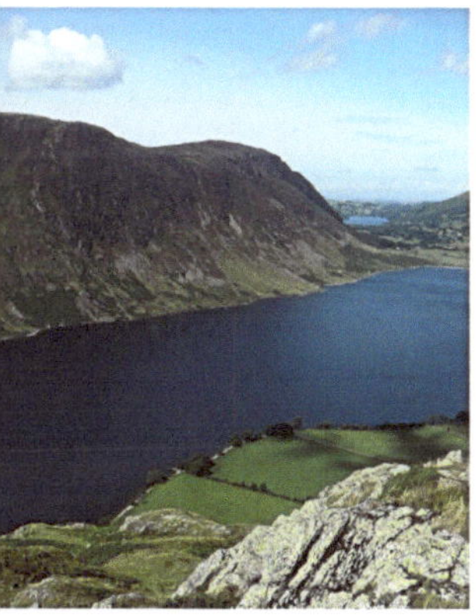

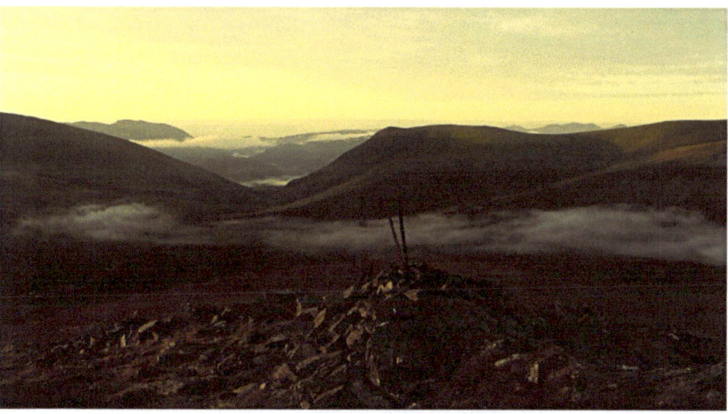

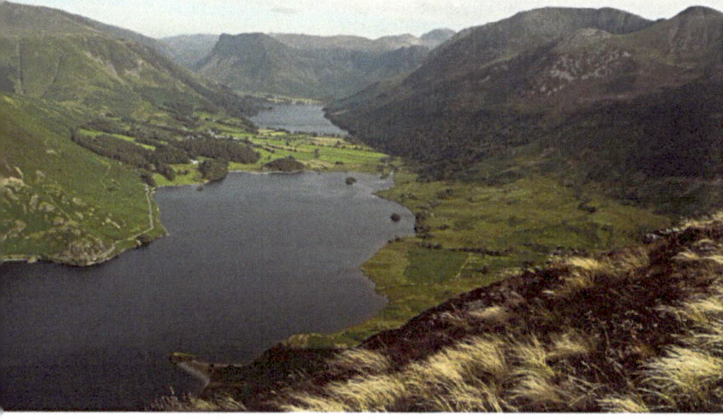

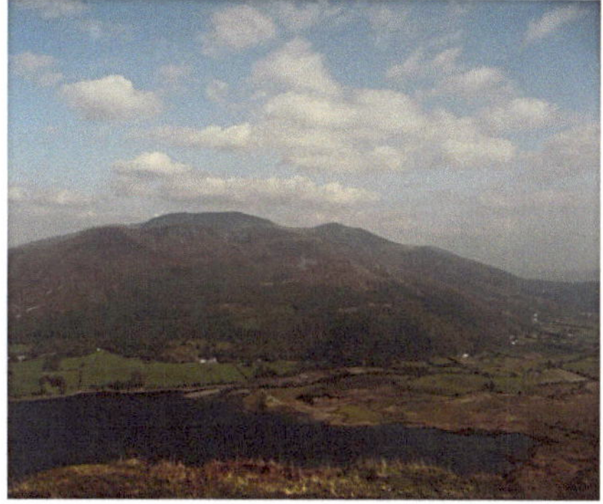

Mellbreak

This peak has two sides to its character. The upper reaches of the hill itself are quite uninspiring as they are largely made up of two rounded summits that hardly rise above a flat and boggy moorland. However, head off the path to peer over the precipitous cliffs on its eastern flanks and you'll soon be clamouring for your camera.

One of the finest routes up Mellbreak and one that is in contrast to its rather flat top, is the northern ridge that starts from the tiny hamlet of Loweswater. The route is quite 'exciting' as a path climbs scree, winds around rocks and takes you above a steep gully before delivering you out onto the northern 508m summit. It is steep going and has an adventurous feel but is not quite full on scrambling. Follow the main path south over open fell to reach the second, slightly higher 512m summit. From here head north east to the top of the cliffs and enjoy a bird's eye view down to Crummock Water and Buttermere far below. This is also a great place for a wild camp.

I pitched camp just meters from the cliff top and could peer down the length of Crummock Water and Buttermere from a rather special vantage point. These two fine lakes are encircled by some of the Lakes finest walking and also most shapely peaks.

The easiest way off Mellbreak is to continue along the main path that leads south from the second summit, however, there is an interesting alternative off to the west that leads you into the remote Mosedale valley. To do this back track slightly north towards the first summit. Just before you start to re-ascend, a faint path leads you down into the valley below. On reaching the valley, head south and then follow a path around the southern flanks of Mellbreak before reaching Crummock water. Whilst the shore line of Crummock is quite boggy, an exploration of its western side is a real joy as there are numerous small beaches, including the fine little spit at Low Ling Crag, from which to gain a water level perspective. You can follow the shoreline back to your start at Loweswater.

Barf

Ok, its name might be childishly amusing but this diminutive peak has much to offer the photographer as it stands at the top of fine steep cliffs that overlook the southern end of Bassenthwaite Lake and one of the flattest pieces of terra firma in the whole of the National Park; the section of marsh and River Derwent that links Bassenthwaite to the river's namesake, Derwent Water. The standard route is a steep slog up from The Swan Hotel, just off the A66. A more devious route that allows you to explore this area further starts from Darling How, just west of the Whinlatter Pass NY 181255. A good track leads you alongside Aiken Beck at NY 189262 . After crossing the beck a direct ascent of Broom Fell can be made to the north. A good path then leads to the rather fine peak of Lord's Seat which itself is a good vantage point. However, the best is yet to come. Follow the obvious path east down towards the grassy knobble that is Barf.

As we clambered up the flanks of Barf a bit of 'summit fever' took hold and spurred us upwards. We could sense the fine view waiting for us at the top and despite the heat haze it was pretty amazing.

The huge bulk of Skiddaw rises up above the rich textured Derwent valley as the river meanders its way up to Keswick. The easiest route back is to return via the same way, although you can drop down to the beck directly west from Lord's Seat.

Great Calva

Great Calva is one of a group of hills that form a wild area known as Back O' Skidda. This open moorland, on the northern side of Skiddaw and Blencathra, is quite a contrast to the main Lake District fells as it is made up of rolling, heathered hills, with few paths and even fewer visitors. It does have a distinctly remote feel to it with some big skies and even bigger views. Starting from the minor road at NY 249323, follow a good track that leads south east toward the Whitewater Dash waterfall. After climbing the main track above the waterfall take a faint path that leads you north east, steeply up to Little Calva. From this broad hill a fenceline can be followed east then south east to the shapelier Great Calva.

After spending a peaceful night camping on the summit of Great Calva I woke to find a band of mist hanging in the valley below me. This added to the drama of the sunrise and has to be up there as one of my top five wild camp experiences.

The view from the summit gives you a different perspective on the classic Lakeland peaks of Skiddaw and Blencathra where the eye is drawn towards the gap between these two sleeping giants. From here you can easily explore more of this fine wilderness or even make a sneaky ascent of Skiddaw from the north and return along the joy that is Longside Edge.

The Peak District

The Peak District is well known to landscape photographers because it offers relatively easy access to some wild rolling moors, dramatic gritstone edges and classic limestone scenery. However, there are still some hidden corners that don't see the usual footfall. This is mainly because there are few footpaths marked on the maps to give these places away, so they have kept below the radar of most photographers.

4.1 A Tale of Two Edges – Gardom's and Birchen

Focal Point – two contrasting gritstone edges, with Gardom's offering a more secluded, tree lined escarpment whilst Birchen has more open views. A number of historical links add both to the interest and photographic opportunities.

Route Summaries

Full route – a circuit that includes both Gardom's and Birchen edges

5.5 km; 160m ascent

Route extension 1

After Gardom's Edge a visit to Wellington's Monument, Eagle Stone and Baslow Edge can be easily be added.

6.5km, 110m ascent

Route extension 2

From the carpark a short, there and back, can be made to Chatsworth Edge

2.5km, 30m ascent

Shorter routes – either edge can be tackled by itself in a more linear fashion

Why Try this Route

Gardom's can be regarded as one of the Peaks more esoteric gritstone edges being tucked away in a heavily wooded valley. However, to explore this rocky outcrop is a real delight as it has plenty to keep you interested and you'll usually have it all to yourself. Birchen Edge on the other hand has more extensive views over the southern Dark Peak, is a good place to photograph climbers in action and take in some fascinating links to our maritime history (even if we are about as far from the sea as is possible in the UK).

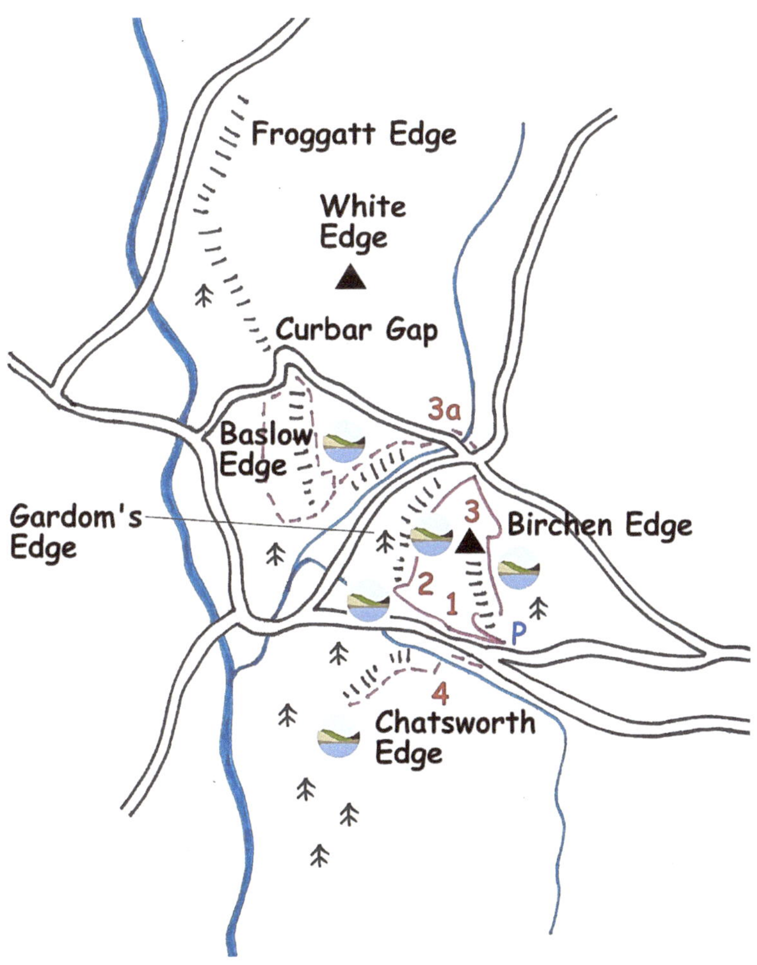

Clockwise from top left:

The view from the northern end of Gardom's Edge... Sunset over Nelson's Monument... One of The Three Ships : Victory ... Nelson's Monument in winter...The view from the mid section of Gardom's Edge... Birchen Edge

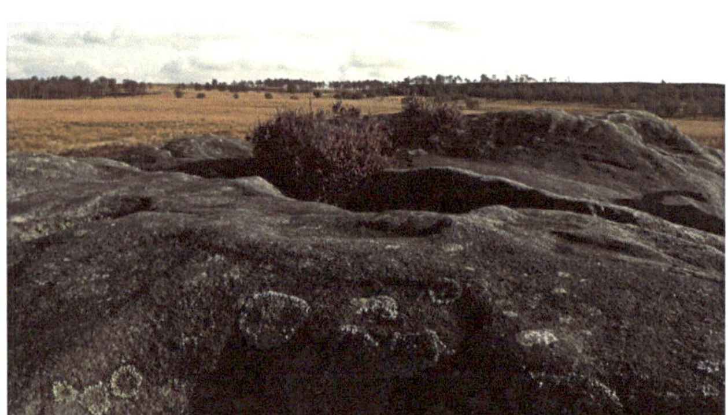

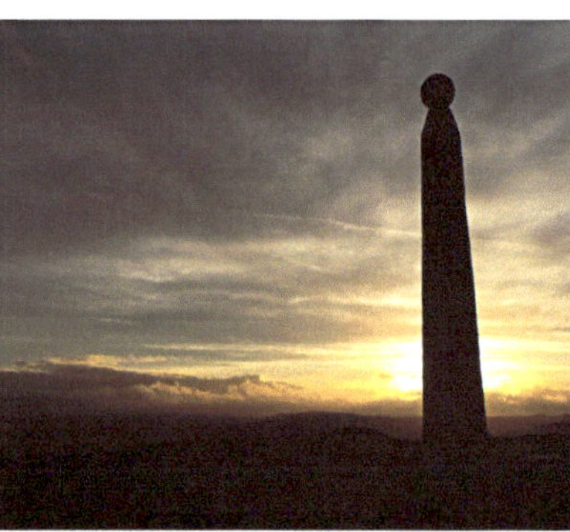

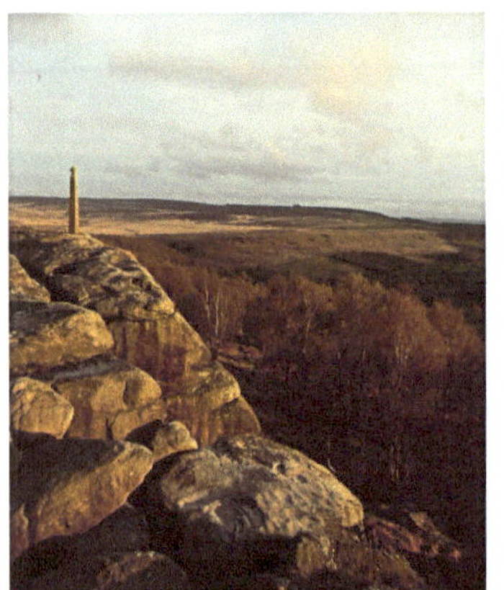

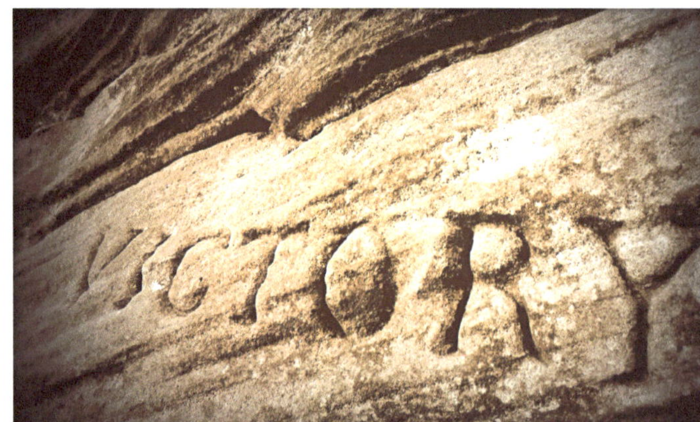

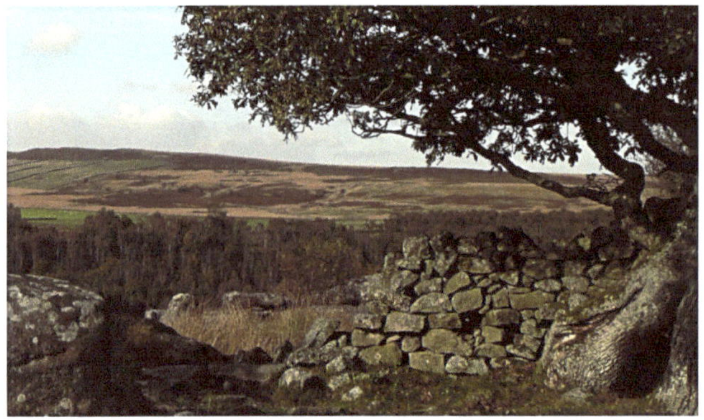

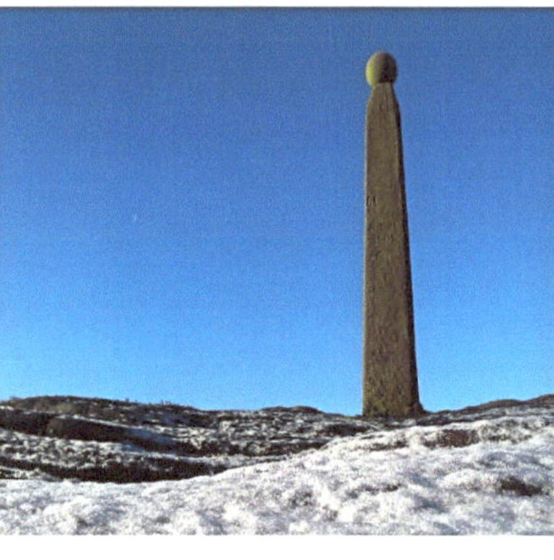

Route Description

1) The easiest place to start is by parking in the Peak Authority car park next to the Robin Hood pub. Take care not to park in the pub car park but in the area just to the right of the pub which is now pay and display. GR SK279 721. Start the walk by going past (the hopefully not open yet) pub heading down the A619 on the pavement on the right handside. After a couple of hundred meters you see a stile over the stone wall on your right that gives you access to some open countryside. A path takes you in a north westerly direction as it slowly climbs through scattered birch trees. You will start to get views east over to Birchen edge and Nelson's monument (see later). However, more interesting are the views over Chatsworth edge that can be glimpsed through the trees over on the western edge of the enclosure.

Photo Location – the Southern Tip of Gardoms Edge

10.30am 16th April – It was great to get up close with the gritstone boulders that litter the area.

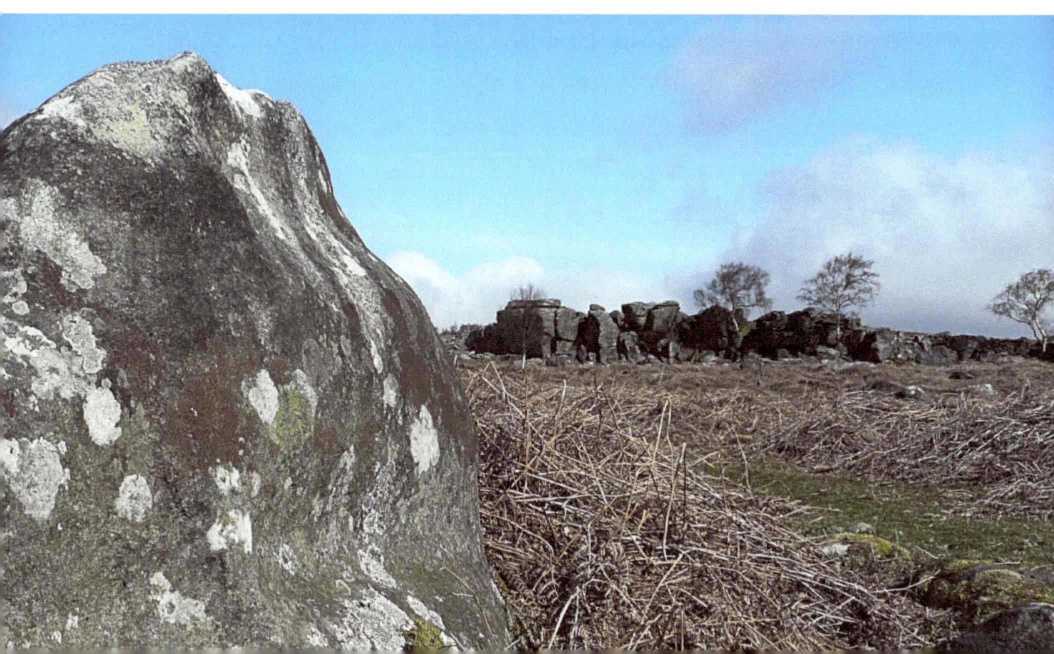

The path comes to a rise at an open gate which is an impressive vista for such minimal effort. The view over to Chatsworth Edge and the Chatsworth estate is particularly fine and can be explored later on. Do spend time looking around the small outcrop of rocks to your right as they not only have good views back over to the often bleak looking Gibbet Moor to the south but also offer interesting close ups of the rocks themselves.

Whilst the main route heads off north along the start of Gardom's edge, just after crossing the open gate a short detour can be made by following the path down through the woods in a north westerly direction. Whilst the trees hide the rocks that form the edge to your right, they offer interesting woodland shoots under a range of seasonal and lighting conditions that you might experience.

2) After you have finished here, head back up to the viewpoint and turn left before you reach the stone wall. This is the start of Gardom's edge. Follow the wall for a hundred meters and then head through a large gap in another stone wall in front of you. Three piles of stone lay ahead. These are known as the Three Men which are 18th century additions to a Neolithic barrow.

To the left along the top of the edge the initial outcrops do not look very promising as they hardly rise above the trees that cloak the lower slopes. However with a bit of effort you can seek out some of the numerous viewpoints that balance themselves precariously along the top of this outcrop.

My first visit to Gardom's edge was on a climbing trip and we were there to do a route called 'Birthday Crack' as it was Liz's 50th Birthday celebration. After the climb we spent the evening enjoying the sunset from the top of the edge and tucking into a great picnic. I remember the magical feel of the place and looking forward to my next visit to check out the photographical potential of this hidden gem.

This section does require some clambering up and over rocks to reach the very edge and there are some steep drops to be aware of. If that's not your thing, keep to the main path.

Photo Location – Mid Section of Gardom's Edge

The path heads through a wooded section and through a gap in a second drystone wall where more accessible views open up to your left. The trees just before this wall give a good indication of the prevailing wind direction here and are a great focus for some images. Head through the gap in the drystone wall and over to the edge on your left. The ground drops away at your feet which gives you a superb panorama.

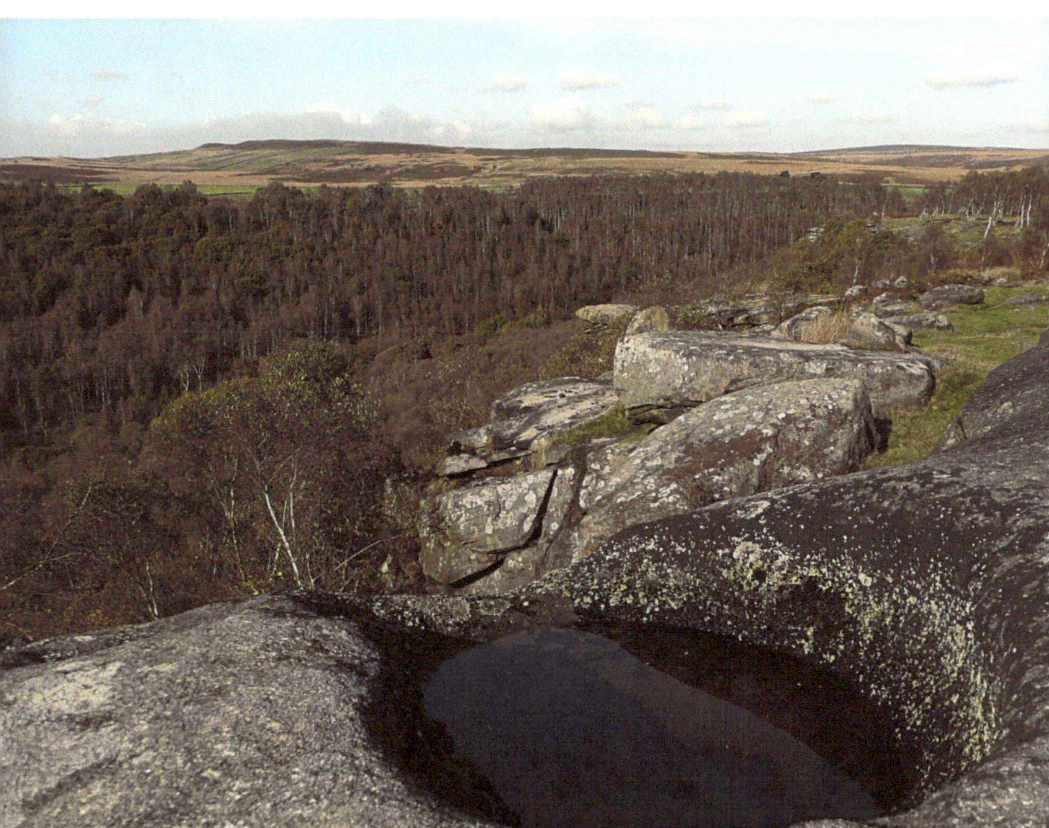

15.10pm 12th October - standing on this promontory of rock looking out at this timeless landscape was a real joy. It was also rather special to be sharing these views with my family, Sally and Sophie, on this occasion.

The lichen covered rocks and surrounding silver birch trees make for plenty of interest also. However, in the right light the views from the top of the edge over the tree lined valley below are wonderful. This is a place to savour and really immerse yourself in these glorious surroundings.

The area around this drystone wall is simply stunning and has a wild remote feel despite being only a few hundred meters from the main road below you. It is a great place to soak up the atmosphere and with some luck, enjoy some solitude in the often rather crowded Peak District.

After crossing this open area the path veers away from the edge and you walk though some more silver birch woods. A rough path goes through a gate and heads across open moor land in a north easterly direction. There are a couple of access stiles to a fenced area to your left. Climb over one of them to check out the last outcrops of the edge as these rocks have interesting shapes and pools on their flat tops. Back on the main path you are aiming for the road junction up ahead (note you can start the walk from this junction if you like).

3a) **Route extension 1:** This route can easily be extended half way round if you're keen to experience some more fine views. After leaving Gardom's Edge and on towards the road junction, instead of heading back straight away to Birchin Edge, go through the gate at GR SK278739 and turn left down the minor road to a crossroads. Head straight over and follow the minor road leading to Curbar. After 200m pick up a bridleway off to your left. This takes you along the top of the opposite side of the tree lined valley that you could see from Gardom's Edge.

Photo Location – Wellington's Monument and the Eagle Stone

Just after 1 km of flat, easy walking you reach a large stone cross on your left which is Wellington's Monument. Whilst this stone obelisk is not in such a commanding position as Nelson's, which you'll visit later, it is still an interesting link to the past.

12.00pm 12th October – the morning's mist was slowly burning away to reveal the valley below us

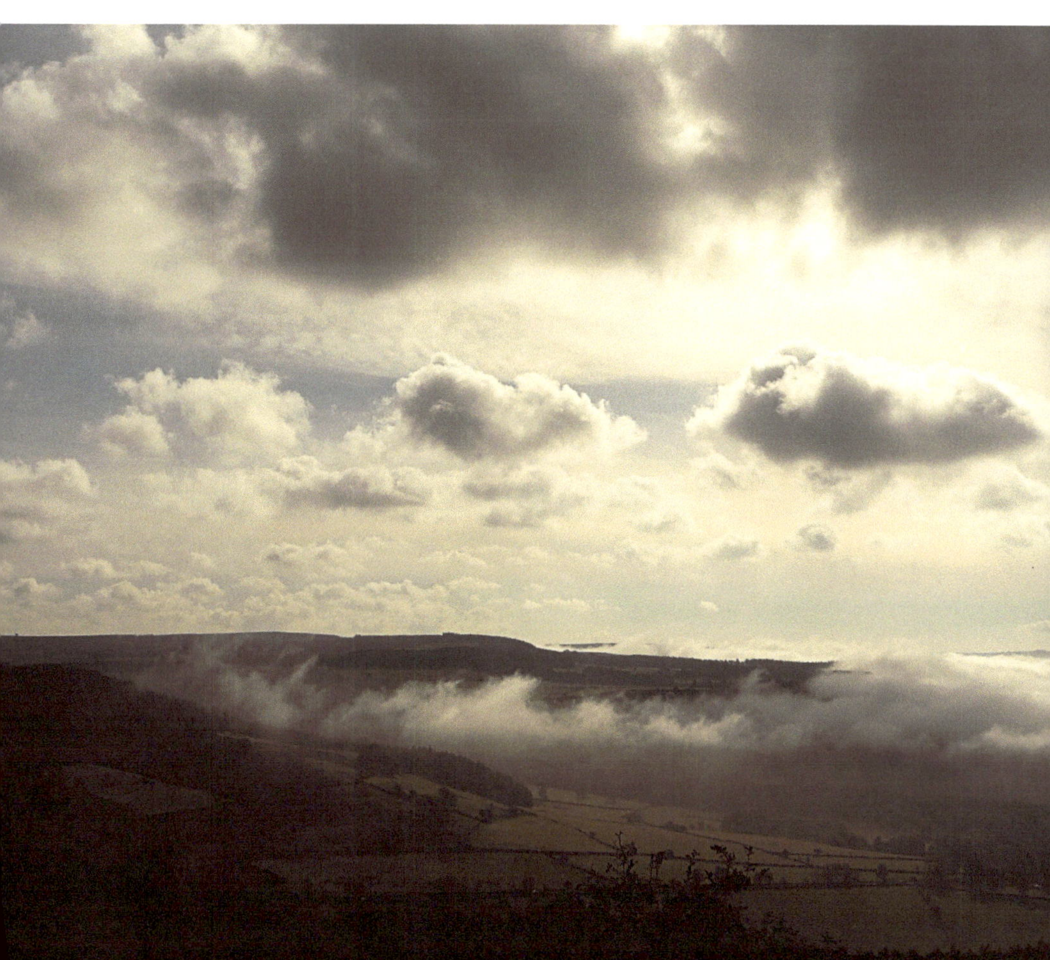

Wellington's Monument was erected in 1866 by E.M. Wrench to commemorate Wellington's victory at the Battle of Waterloo in 1815. Mr Wrench must have felt he wanted to provide some balance to the memory of Lord Nelson's monument that is only a mile away.

If you continue on about a hundred meters west further along the edge you get superb views over the deep tree lined valley below

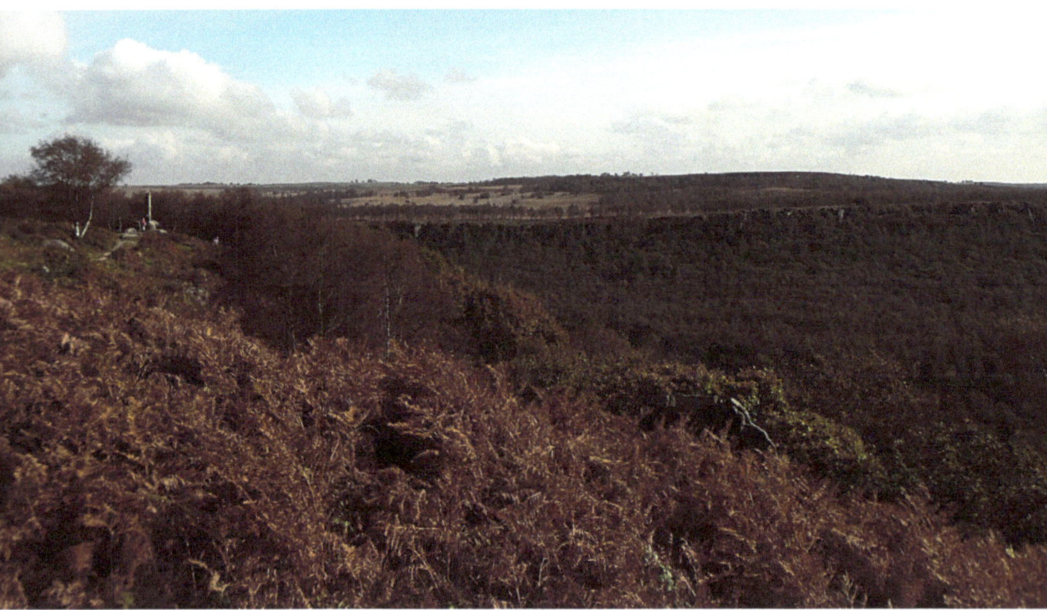

12.25pm 12th October – we decided to stop for lunch at the monument which gave the mist time to completely disappear. This opened up the view back over the valley to Gardoms and in the far distance Birchin Edges.

From the monument there is a path heading off across the moors to your right. On taking this you soon reach a huge, weather sculptured boulder, called the Eagle Stone. This stands out starkly from the surrounding bleak moorland and makes for some interesting close ups or if the sky is good, a great landscape shot.

The Eagle Stone is steeped in local folklore. The name could have possibly been derived from the Norse God Aigle, who was well known for throwing large rocks around. One of the many stories is that local men wanting to get married had to prove their manhood by climbing to the top of the stone. There are also many stories about the stone turning or moving on certain days of the year. It all adds to the mystery of this rather intriguing boulder.

From the Eagle Stone it is well worth heading north-westwards for just over a hundred meters or so to pick up the top of Baslow Edge. This edge is another wonderful spot to enjoy far reaching westward views especially towards the end of the day. However, do remember you will need to backtrack to the road junction and head over Birchin Edge to reach the car again!

So depending on your time and energy you can either return by the same route to the road junction or head northwards to the carpark at Curbar Gap. From here drop down left on either the road or a footpath before picking up the path that heads south below Baslow Edge. Towards the end of Baslow Edge, at a junction of paths, you head south east up to a quarried area. Here you gain good views southwards as you have reached a fine ridge. Follow the bridleway as it climbs up in a north east direction, where you will regain the top of the edge at Wellington's Monument.

You'll now pick up the track that led you out on this route extension. So follow it back to the road junction before heading on up to the delights of Birchin Edge.

3) Just before reaching the road, take a path that heads south across boggy ground. After 200m be sure to take the left fork which starts to gently climb the northern reaches of Birchen edge, again crossing a rather damp and muddy area. On climbing above this area, a small path rises though the heather to bring you out at a trig point. This is the start of Birchen edge, although the best views do not appear until you reach Nelson's Monument a couple of hundred meters further on.

Photo Location - Nelson's Monument and the Three Ships

The monument was erected in 1805, some five years after Nelson's death, by a local businessman. Just meters away, set back from the edge, are three large gritstone boulders known as the Three Ships. These natural rocks have the names carved into them of the three ships that were in Nelson's fleet– 'Royal Soverin', 'Defiant' and of course 'Victory'.

6.20pm 18th April – I'd arrived at Birchins with just enough time to scramble to the top and enjoy the sun as it burst through the clearing cloud. It had been a grey day, in more ways than one, so it made this shoot even more special.

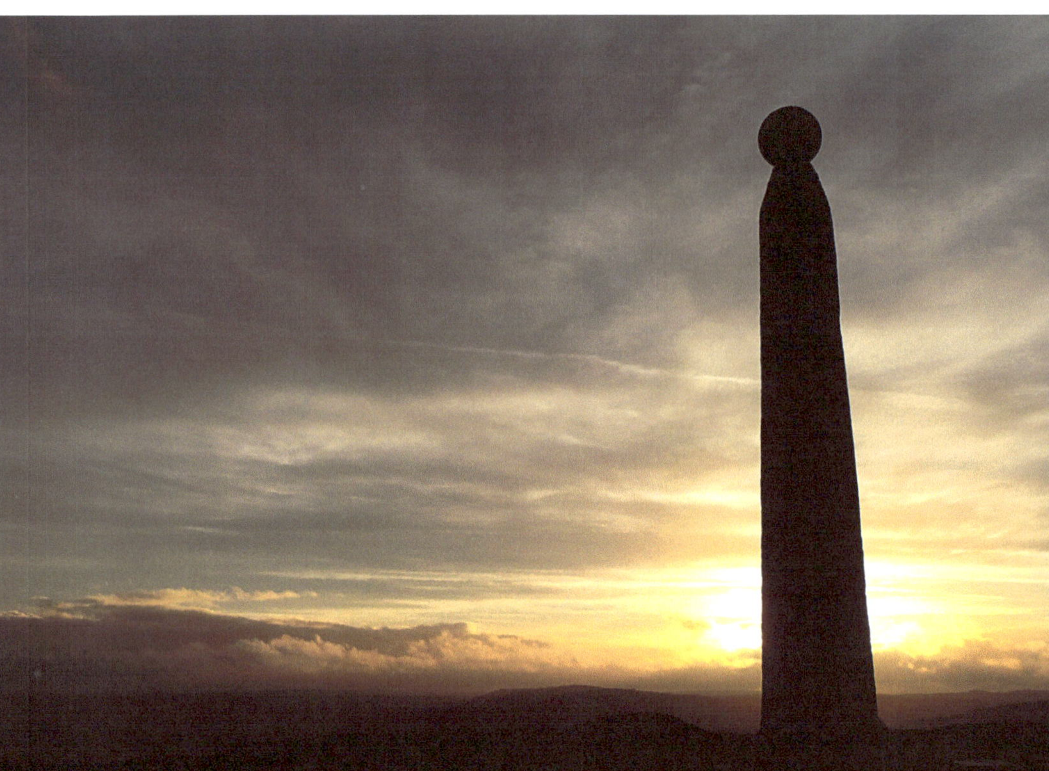

This is a wonderful place to shoot from, as it offers a range of subjects in a compact area and a chance to get creative with your picture taking. As it is westward facing it is also a fine spot to take in any late evening light and sunsets. As this is a popular crag with climbers, it is also a great place to get some action shots. The Monument area is good location for this as there are a number of exposed routes with good access to them.

Whilst there are a number of routes down from the monument, it is often worth following the path along the top as it winds its way south. This gives you an extended opportunity to take in the views over Gibbet Moor. About half a kilometre or so after leaving the monument take the sharp right turn in the path that drops you quite steeply down the last part of the edge. This brings you out on a well trodden path where you turn left. An easy amble takes you down to the road. Go through a gate and carefully follow the road back down to the carpark and a now (hopefully) open pub.

4) **Route extension 2:** If you happen to arrive back at the carpark and still have time, energy and good light, then a short there and back to Chatsworth Edge makes for an interesting route extension.

From the carpark head back down the road again, like you did at the start of the walk, and look for a footpath off to the left signposted 'concessionary path to Chatsworth'. This is just before you reach the path that you took off to the right earlier in the day. Go down some steep stone steps to a bridge over a stream. Cross the bridge then follow the stone flagged path through an often boggy, overgrown area. Climb some more steps which bring you out on a track. Head straight over the track on a grassy footpath signposted ' Beeley via Swiss Lane' to a stile next to a fenced off woodland. Cross the stile and you are quickly on top of the rather fine Chatsworth Edge. After clearing the woods to your left the views start to open up over the top of the edge where there are a couple of airy viewpoints. The path gently drops to a stile which you go over. Follow the wall in front of you for a few yards before going through a gap. Keep to the path as it bears left, to go over another stile that leads you into a large field. Follow the grassy edge on your right which leads you passed some trees before reaching a high stone wall with a ladder stile. Clamber over the stile and head for the high ground in front of you.

Photo Location – Chatsworth Edge

This quarried area offers stunning views over the wilder side of the Chatsworth estate. Beautiful old oak trees line the lower terraces and there are also a couple of millstones to be found at the bottom of the rocks. This is another excellent spot to enjoy a sunset, although do leave yourself enough daylight to walk back as the path has some steep drops

6.50pm 18th April - After a quick calculation I reckoned that I had just enough daylight to make it over to Chatsworth Edge for the sunset.

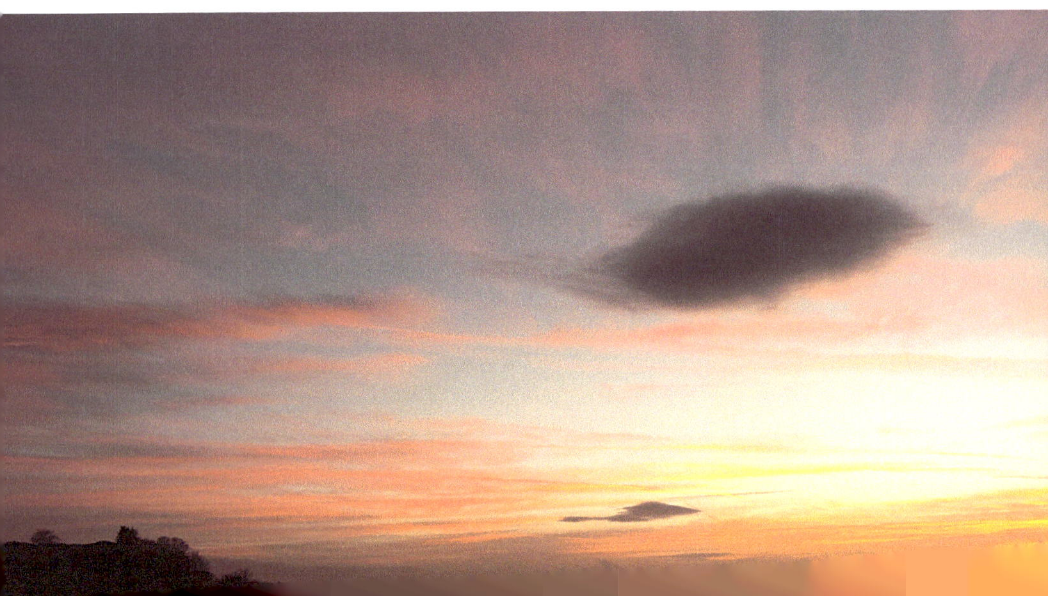

It is also a great place to enjoy some of the local wildlife.

On a visit to Chatsworth edge we were lucky to spot a deer in amongst the high ferns. This sighting was not terribly surprising being in the grounds of a country estate but felt pretty special being in a more 'natural' wilder environment. On another occasion, after enjoying a fine sunset, I heard some rustling from the undergrowth and peered down to see a badger pulling some fresh bedding back into his set. Apart from my nocturnal friend I had the place to myself and felt privileged to enjoy this small moment of nature at its finest.

So enjoy spending some time exploring this special place as it has a lot to offer the photographer. You can extend the walk further by entering the woods that surround the upper reaches of the estate and head over to the folly or even the rather grand house itself. A return route can be taken by clearing the woods to the south and heading over the fine, wild, open moorland of Gibbet Moor. However, returning back the way you came also makes for a good option. Either way you'll be glad you made the extra effort of visiting this hidden little gem.

4.2 Bamford and Stanage Edges

Focal Point – the view from Great Tor has it all. An elevated viewpoint that offers a sweeping panorama over the Derwent valley and excellent foreground interest.

Route Summaries

Full route – a traverse of Bamford Edge before crossing Moscar Moor and returning via Stanage Edge

11 km; 280m ascent

Shorter route – a there and back to Great Tor, the high point on Bamford Edge

3 km; 70m ascent

Why Try this Route

Bamford Edge is a little bit off the beaten track and as it has more famous neighbours it sees few visitors. This gritstone edge just gets better and better, climaxing where you reach its highest point, the stunning viewpoint of Great Tor. The vista opens up below your feet to include the Derwent reservoirs and the shapely Win Hill across the valley. There is also a wide range of foreground interest to include in your shots as the rocks have been eroded into some rather interesting shapes. By taking in the full route you also get to experience some far reaching views along Stanage Edge with some classic millstone foregrounds and Dark Peak scenery.

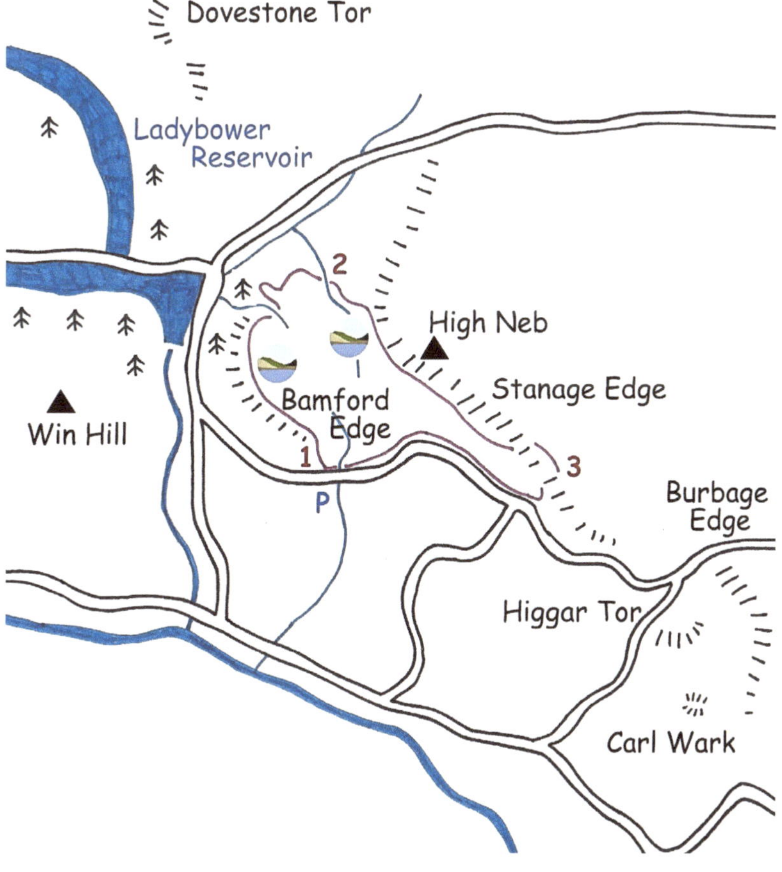

Clockwise from top left:

Ahmed getting creative on the 'Table' Stone, Bamford Edge... The view south from Great Tor... Looking south east along Stanage Edge... Aaron and Paul enjoying a Stanage shoot... The view over a misty Ladybower Reservoir from Great Tor, ... Weathered gritstone on Bamford Edge

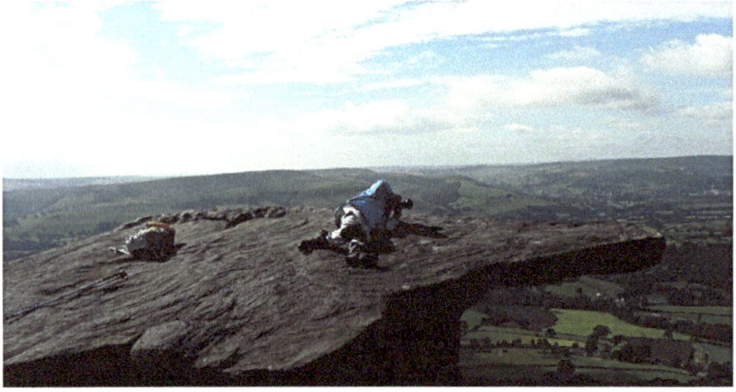

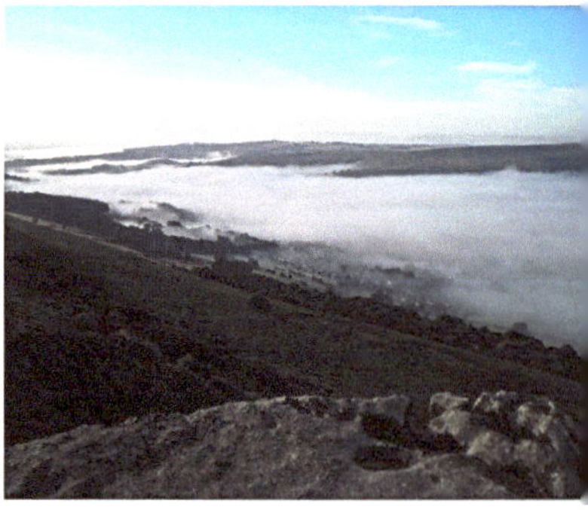

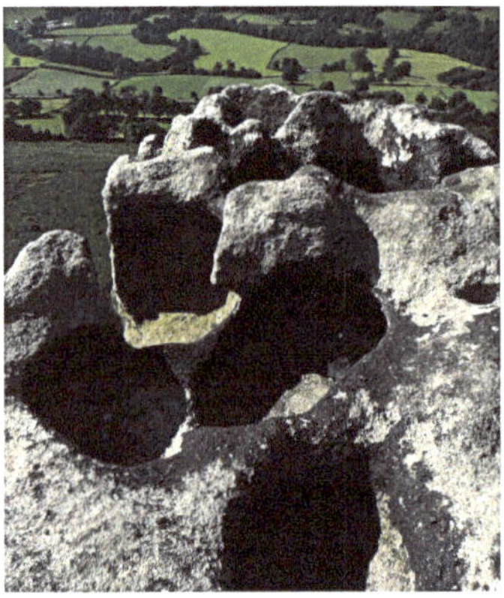

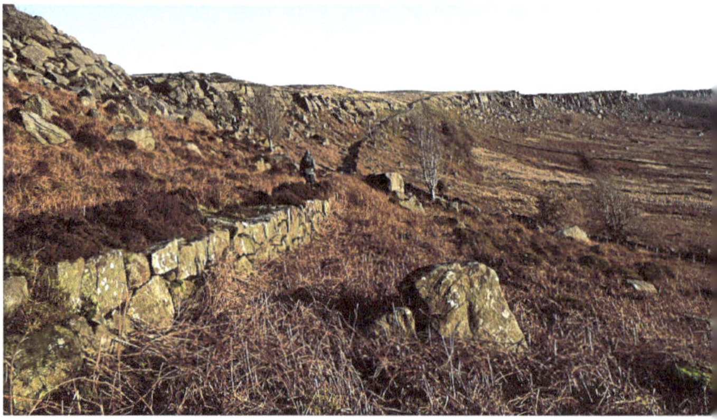

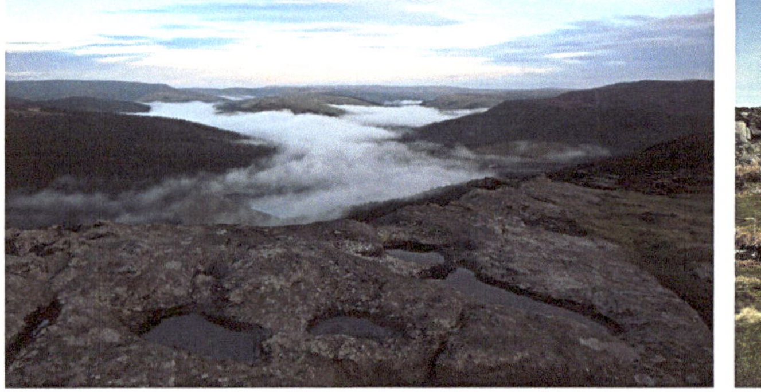

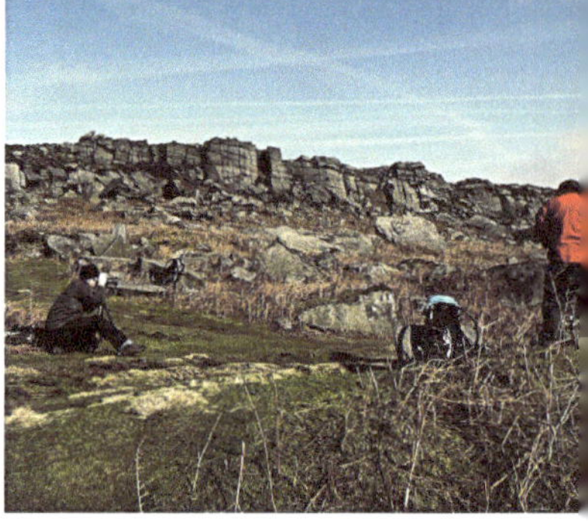

Route Description

1) Starting at the roadside pull in at GR SK215 839, just before the brow of the hill, hop over the stile and take the north westerly (left hand) path for ~20m before taking the right fork that climbs quite steeply. As the gradient starts to ease, bear right over heather to the top of an old disused quarry. The whole of Stanage Edge, and the latter part of your route, stretches out in front of you across the bleak Bamford Moor. Back tracking to the path again, follow the beginnings of Bamford Edge and continue to skirt around a large shallow scooped area. Near the top of the scoop you can cut across on a faint path through the bracken on your left. This brings you out to the start of the edge proper and the fantastic 'table stone'.

Photo Location – The Table Stone and The Great Tor

11.10am 16th September – with a big drop below us it was exciting to be looking over to Shatton Moor from the 'table' stone.

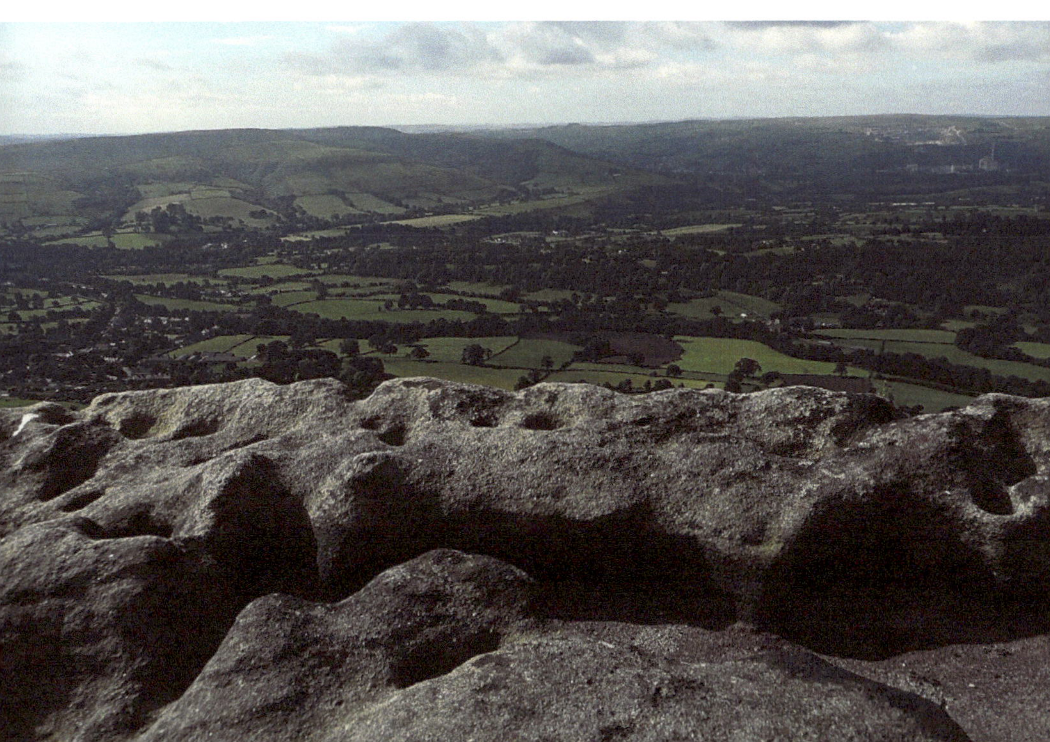

Follow the ever steepening edge until you reach the fabulous 'table' stone that allows you to get creative with your images. It not only acts as a natural vantage point but also has beautiful weather sculptured hollows that make an interesting focal point.

Once finished here, it is just a short amble over to Great Tor which is the highest point on the edge and also where it changes direction slightly.

This opens up the view to the north for the first time and makes a stunning viewpoint. The reservoir contrasts well with the rolling patchwork of the pastures and the heather moors that encircle it. It is worth carefully dropping down to the middle section of the edge so you can also shoot from a lower vantage point and get closer to the treeline. A relatively easy way down can be found just before the high point and this leads you to a wide grassy ledge.

09.10am 13th September - The mist hung like a heavy blanket, hiding the reservoir below. This accentuated the intricate network of valleys that radiated off in all directions. It was a real joy to be able to share the experience with my 7yr. old daughter Sophie, her friend Mitchell and his father Simon. A truly memorable experience.

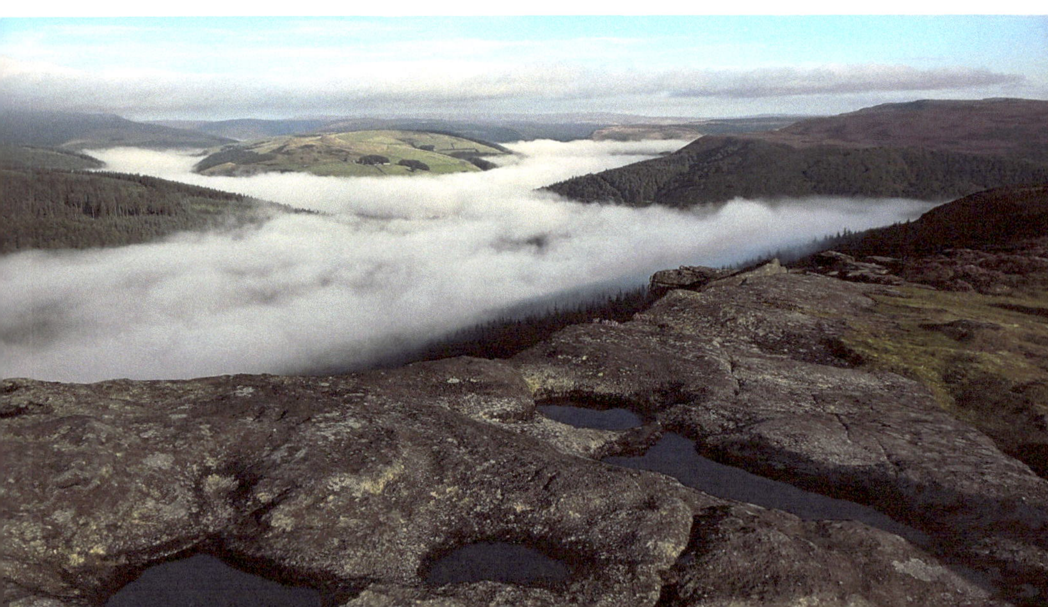

Back up top you can easily reverse the route to your car if you've had enough or have left it late in the day and have enjoyed a sunset shoot. However, for those after more adventure, follow the edge north for just over 1km where you reach a small valley with a stream at the bottom. Contour down to the stream and back up out of the little valley to a meeting of drystone walls. An interesting viewpoint over Ladybower Reservoir can be reached by following the north western wall down to a point just above the treeline at SK 206862. Returning to the stonewall junction, follow the wall that heads north then bends north east crossing one small stream, then to a much larger stream lined valley called Jarvis Clough.

2) Make your way down to this second stream and cross it, heading right up a large stalkers track. This next section is quite featureless so it's best to undertake it in clear conditions. Follow the track where it ends on Moscar Moor and head due east aiming for Stanage Edge less than half a kilometre away. Whilst this is quite a bleak spot it can be a good place to stop and see what conditions prevail.

A hazy cloud cover drifted over Stanage on the horizon but we decided to stop for a rest and wait for a break in the clouds. The desired break never fully materialised, however, it was great to experience the changing colours of the open moors.

As you approach Stanage the gradient steepens slightly but by working your way to the top you gain a great vantage point over the moor you have just crossed.

Photo Location – Crow Chin, Mid Section of Stanage Edge

Whilst you can follow the top of the edge south along its full length, where it kinks south eastwards at Crow Chin, drop down to the area below. You will find a huge number of millstones that litter the heather moors either side of the path around here. The use of millstones as foreground interest can be regarded as a bit of a cliché. However, these beautiful hunks of gritstone, of varying completeness, are fascinating to shoot in their own right and act as an interesting link to this area's historical past.

The next section, following either the high or the low path south eastwards along the edge is a real joy, especially towards the end of the day when the shadows start to lengthen.

15.00pm 2nd January – After exploring the millstones below Crow Chin, Edward and I continued along the path below the edge. The path and Stanage itself seemed to stretch far into the distance. However on a cold crisp winter's day it was a joy to have so much to explore.

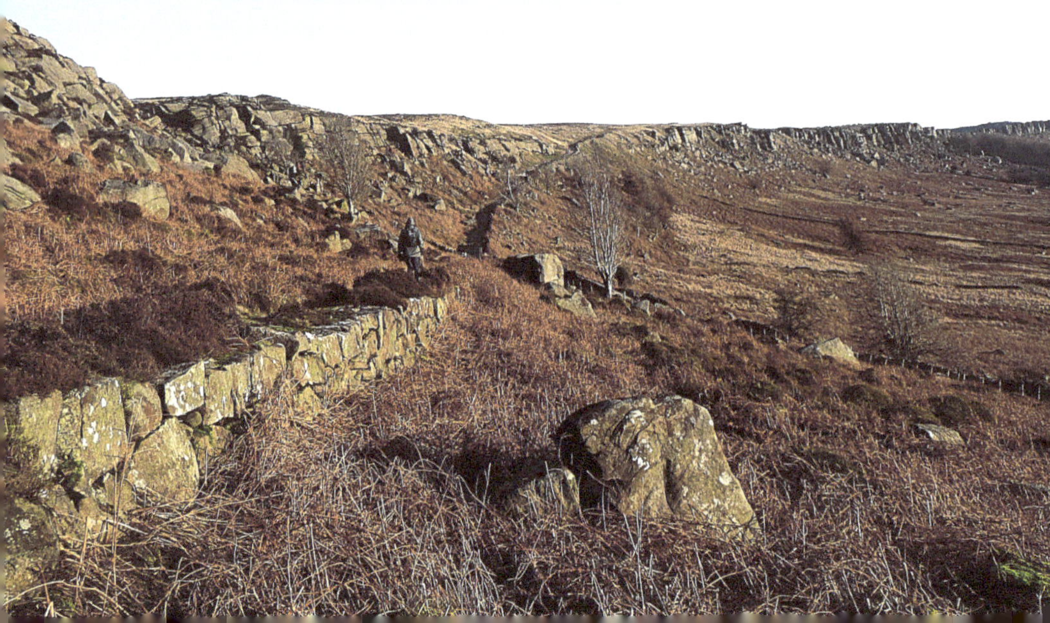

The path makes for an interesting lead in line along the enormous stretch that is Stanage Edge. The steeper, blocky sections of the edge itself act as good focal points for more abstract monotone pictures. Also as this is one of the most iconic places to climb in the UK you can usually find some climbers to add a splash of colour to your images.

If you have taken the lower path follow the heavily eroded and controversial Long Causeway to the top of the edge again. This offers a fine viewpoint down the length of the edge and is a fitting place to leave the high ground.

3) Drop down the bridleway that leads through the Stanage Plantation which is popular with boulderers who climb these amazing rocks.

At the bottom of the Plantation path you reach a large carpark which sometimes has a mobile café that offers excellent hot drinks and cakes. Turn right onto the minor road which has a number of interesting viewpoints along the return route. Be sure to take the right fork after 2km and follow the road up a small incline. This gives you good views down the wooded Hurst Clough to your left. A short downhill and one final, short climb brings you back to the start of the walk and completes the circuit.

Like Gardom's, my first visit to Bamford Edge was on a climbing trip and I remember the feeling of delight on discovering this magical place. Whilst the climbing was superb, the views were even better so I was eager to return to explore it further. Having re-visited the area in both rain and shine it has fast become one of my favourite haunts.

4.3 The Kinder Plateau and Alport Castles

Focal Points – Ringing Roger offers panoramic views over the whole of the glorious Edale valley. The Alport Castles are an outstanding natural wonder and a real photographic gem

Route Summaries

Full route – ascend onto the southern edge of the Kinder plateau by the delightful Ringing Roger ridge. For the adventurous, a crossing of the plateau and its bleak peat bog acts as a great contrast. This section whilst short, is largely pathless and can be navigationally challenging in poor visibility. A pathless descent takes you down to Alport Bridge where you can amble down Alport Dale to the likewise named Castles. The return route takes you along Rowlee Pasture and over the brooding Crookstone Hill.

22 km, 910m ascent

Shorter route – both Ringing Roger and the Alport Castles can be savoured individually if you prefer.

Ringing Roger there and back

6 km, 360m ascent

Alport Castles there and back by Alport Dale

6 km, 240m ascent

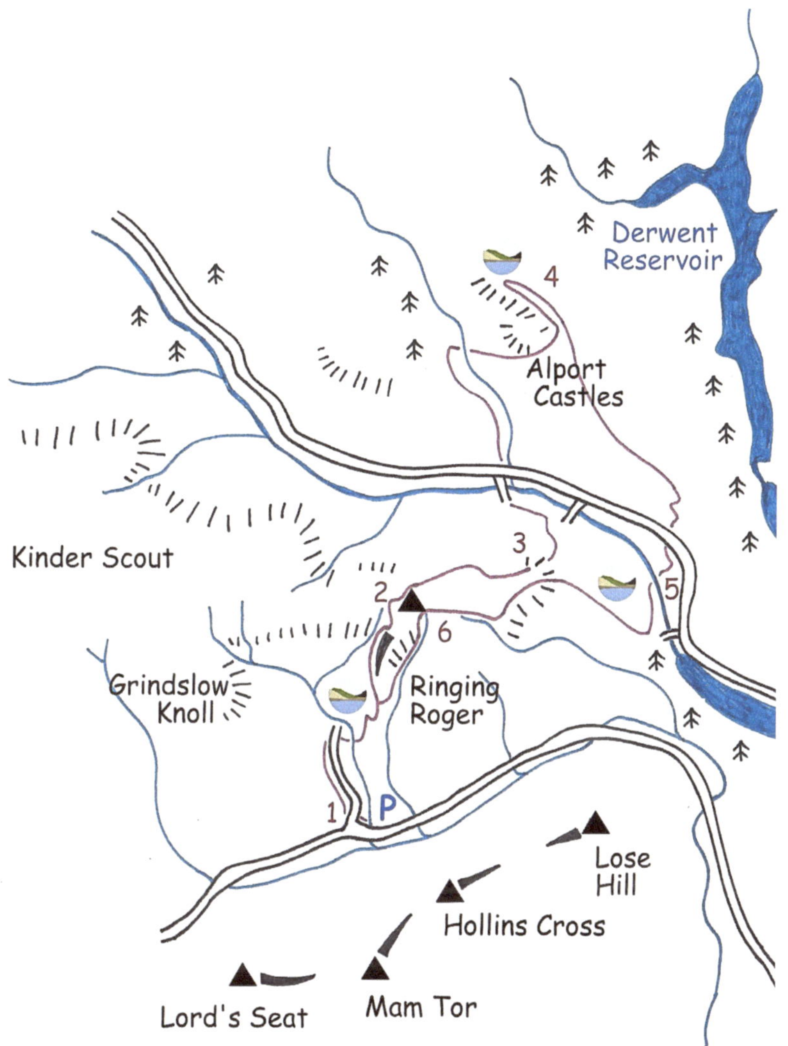

Why Try this Route

The Kinder plateau may appear on the map to be a bleak, featureless bog, however there are numerous fantastic viewpoints along its elevated edges. Ringing Roger is one such viewpoint, although in fact it offers numerous viewpoints on its ascent. Each one offering subtle changes as you gain height. Being a ridge you also get to benefit from the choice of view either side. Off to the west, the deep cleft of Grinds

Brook grabs your attention, as does the contrast between the upland moors and the lush green patchwork of fields that flank Grindslow Knoll. Turning round to the south and the east, the neighbouring ridge of Rowland Cote Moor and the shapely Hollins Cross make for a fine vista. On reaching the edge of Kinder Scout your landscape immediately changes as you look into a wild plateau of bog and heather criss crossed by peaty streams. At first this might not appear to be somewhere you would want to explore but in the right light and with the right navigational skills, it offers something quite unique.

A visit to the Alport Castles later on in the route has to be one of the real highlights of the Peak District and it has a timeless, other worldly feel. As you approach from below it allows you to get a feel of the place and build up the anticipation. On reaching the top of the cliffs and heading over to the viewpoint that looks over The Tower you can't fail to be thrilled by the view at your feet.

Clockwise from top left:

The Tower, Alport Castles... The Vale of Edale... Little Moor from the ascent of Alport Castles ... Mist clearing from the slopes of Grindslow Knoll... The trees on the approach to Crookstone Hill... Andrew on route to Rowlee Pasture

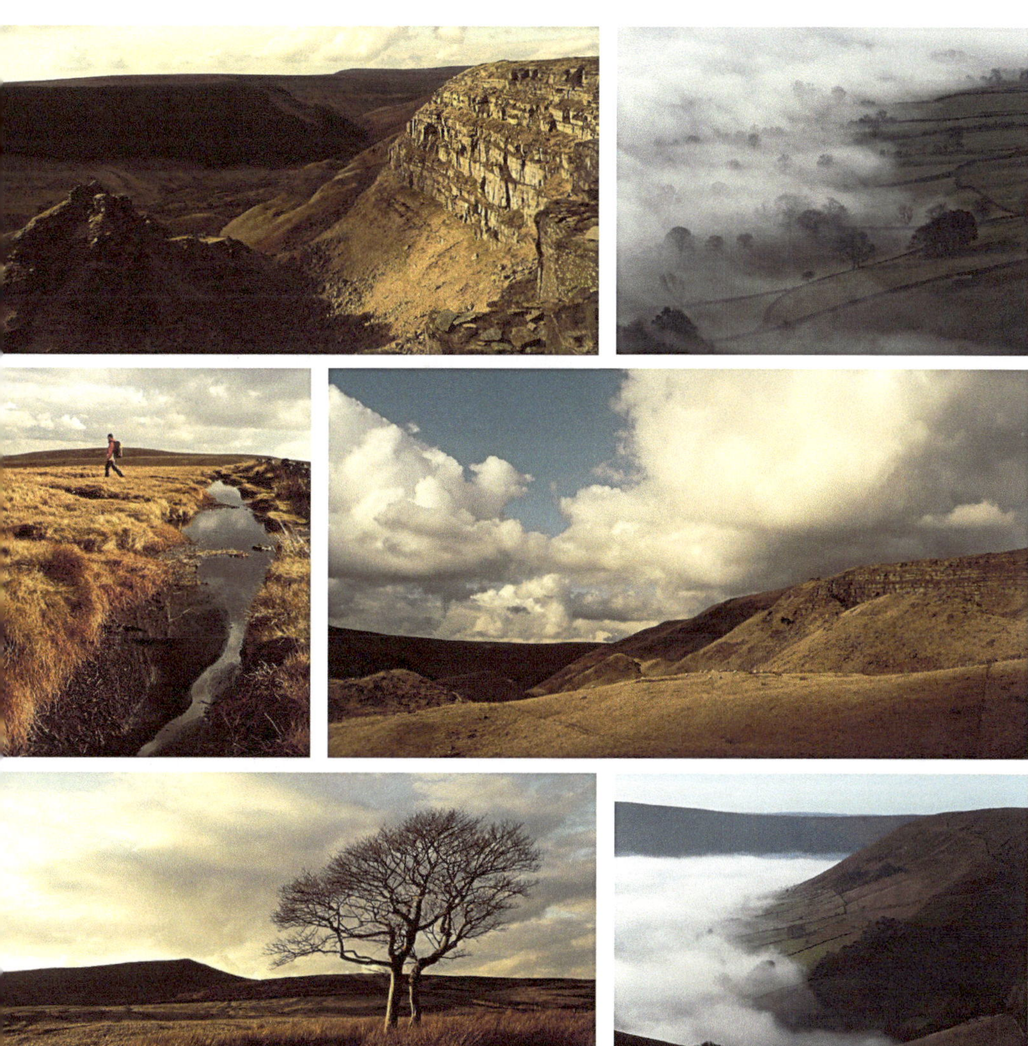

Route Description

1) Start your walk in the beautiful village of Edale which is popular for all sorts of outdoor activities and has a number of good facilities including a railway station, two campsites and two pubs. If arriving by car there is a large car park (GR SK 123853) in the village, which does however fill up fast, especially at the weekend. Leave the car park on a path to the left of the toilet block and turn right up the road that heads into the village proper. Pass the first of the pubs and the campsites where you start to get a view of the Kinder skyline beyond the church spire. Continue to follow the road beyond the Old Nags Head where you soon reach the end of the tarmac. Pick up a footpath to your right, signposted Grindsbrook. Drop down to the aforementioned stream, cross over the bridge and then up the steps on the opposite side. A stone flagged path leads you out into open pasture where after a couple of hundred meters you head off to the right up a good path that starts the ascent of The Nab. Continue through a gate and follow the path up to a sharp turn to your right. At this point you should start to get fine views along the shapely curve of Grindsbrook Clough off to your left.

The climb was steep but with a crisp spring morning in the offing we were keen to reach the first of the stunning viewpoints on the ascent.

Continue up round this corner before reaching The Nab (GR SK 125866). The main path kinks back off to the left, however, be sure to walk over to a grassy spot to your right for a superb view over the Edale valley. It is worth leaving the main path here by taking a small track that leads you up the grassy ridgline in front of you. The view starts to open up to the east taking in the skyline of the neighbouring Rowland Cote Moor. The gradient starts to ease as you reach a large, flat area where the path leads you through the heather towards the rocky outcrops of Ringing Roger. Just before the rocks you re-join the main path coming in on your left which you can follow to the top of Ringing Roger. However, it is more entertaining to leave this path as you cross below the bottom of the ridgeline and pick a line up the easy angled slabs. This brings you out amongst the rocky tors that make up the rather superb Ringing Roger. The rocks not only have great photographic potential but they also make for a sheltered spot from where you can fully enjoy your surroundings.

Photo Location – the Ascent of Ringing Roger

Thankfully there are many viewpoints on the ascent to Ringing Roger which gives you a great excuse to stop and compose some images.

08.30am 23rd December – Roger and I had started the walk in thick mist but were ever hopeful that it was all low level cloud and we could climb above it. The race was on to get into position before the sun could burn it all off. So after a hasty ascent we were rather excited to pop out above the cloud and see the mist gently clearing from the valley floor.

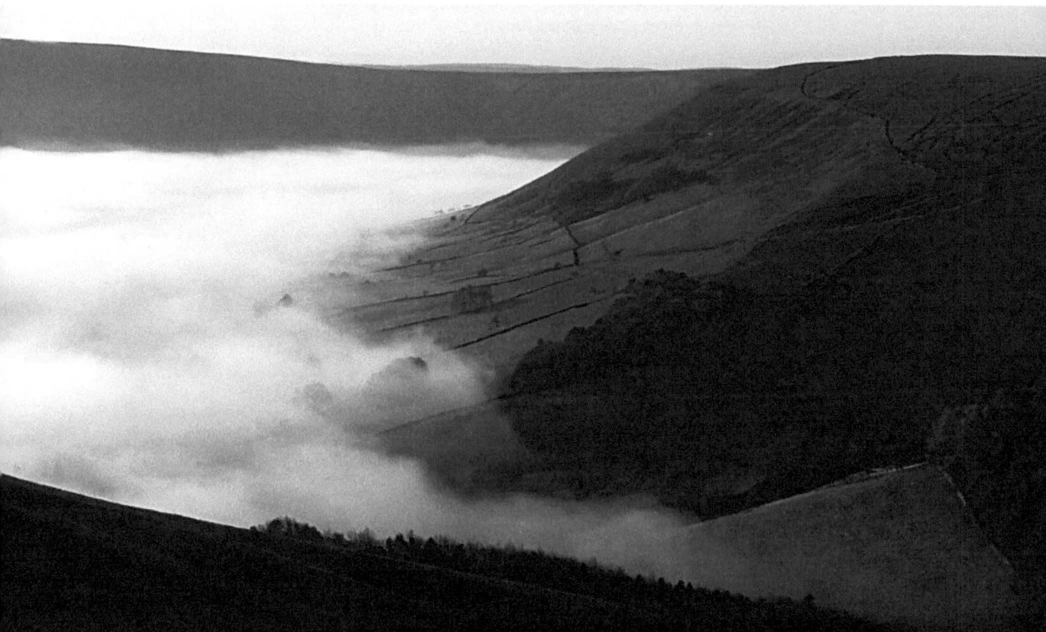

The earlier views down into the deep cleft of Grindsbrook makes a good lead in line around the shapely Grindslow Knoll. Look left and the southern heartherd flanks of the Knoll merge beautifully into the green valley floor. These lush pastures are divided by a patchwork of drystone walls and clumps of trees which are a delight to shoot especially when any mist is starting to clear in the valley. The viewpoint from The Nab comes next. This offers an elevated view down the Edale valley with the Hollins Cross to Mam Tor ridge forming the skyline opposite. On reaching the outcrops of Ringing Roger a full 360 degree view unfolds below you and it is often difficult to know where to start aiming your lens. You get elevated angles on your earlier views which can give you more depth to your shots by being able to take in more of the rock and heathered foreground at your feet.

On reaching the top of Ringing Roger we took a number of shots and then settled down in a sheltered spot to enjoy a well earned break. Sometimes it's good to just sit down and spend some time appreciating a place.

Follow the ridge to its end where it merges with the upland moor; here you are faced with a route decision.

If you do not fancy the pathless tramp across the Kinder plateau or simply do not want to walk too much further then one of the best options is to head over to the top of Grindsbrook Clough. So pick up one of the many paths that contours above Golden Clough to your left and follow the main path that heads west along the edge. Follow this easy going but interesting section for around 2 km before you reach a stream that drops steeply down to Grinds Brook below. You can descend here but it is easier to cross over this stream and head south along the edge to the top of Grindsbrook Clough. The rocky clough drops down to the east before an easier angled path is reached alongside the attractive stream. Follow this all the way back to the village of Edale.

2) To follow the full route from the top of Ringing Roger head for the high ground to the north, aiming for the top of Golden Clough. Pick up the stream and follow it into the rather different world that is Kinder Scout. You enter a more monochrome, two dimensional landscape which has its own, rather unique, photographic potential. Shapely peat groughs, contrasting shades and textures and some rather interesting wildlife all make for quite a rich environment.

Whilst meandering our way round the peat bogs we heard numerous grouse clattering out of their heather hidey holes. Then peering across the moor we caught a glimpse of a mountain hare clad in its fine, grey winter coat. It was only a fleeting encounter but a rather special one none the less.

Here it is a case of choosing your own line, either following the peaty stream, crossing up onto the rough heathered moor or more likely a mixture of the two. This is classic Open Access Land where you are free to roam as long as you respect your surroundings. In fact, Right to Roam really started right here with the Mass Trespass back in 1932. We have a lot to thank these early pioneers for, so enjoy your meanderings.

Head in a north easterly direction working your way around a number of boggy sections before gaining some easier going moorland especially towards the unnamed trig point marked on the map GR SK129878. At this point the horizon starts to open up over the northern edge of the plateau with distant views to the rather bleak Bleaklow. From the trig point, continue in a north easterly direction towards Blackden Edge. Keep an eye out for a faint path along the edge that you should reach after a few hundred meters or so. Turn right onto this path heading to the north eastern corner of Kinder just short of Crookstone Knoll.

3) Here you have a pathless descent heading north east along a line of grouse butts and then north on a faint path on the right hand side of a stream in a gully, aiming for some farm buildings below. Just before reaching the farm turn right for 100m on a good track and bear left down to a gate, an access point at GR SK144891. Cross the ladder stile next to the gate and follow the track down to where a footbridge will take you over the River Ashop. Regain the track to your right then follow it up to the main Snake Road. Cross the road and go through a small gate to pick up a footpath (signposted Alport Hamlet) that runs along and above the River Alport to your right. After 20m cross over a stile in a wall and continue on the path that runs alongside the fence, up a steady rise. Cross a further stile and head on up to a wide track.

Turn right heading north for just over 1km up to Alport Farm. Halfway up this track you start to get some good early views, off to your right, of Little Moor and the Alport Castles. This should whet the appetite and give you an incentive for the short climb to come.

As you approach Alport Farm go through a gate/stile on your right and go immediately through another gate before turning right at the river to cross the bridge. Follow the footpath left and then right up a bank and continue up a rather pleasant climb as the path takes you past a few clumps of trees.

After visiting the area in somewhat poor conditions on previous occasions it was a real delight to arrive at the Castles in a golden, late winter afternoon light. The sun broke out of the clouds striking the escarpment that stretched out from under our feet.

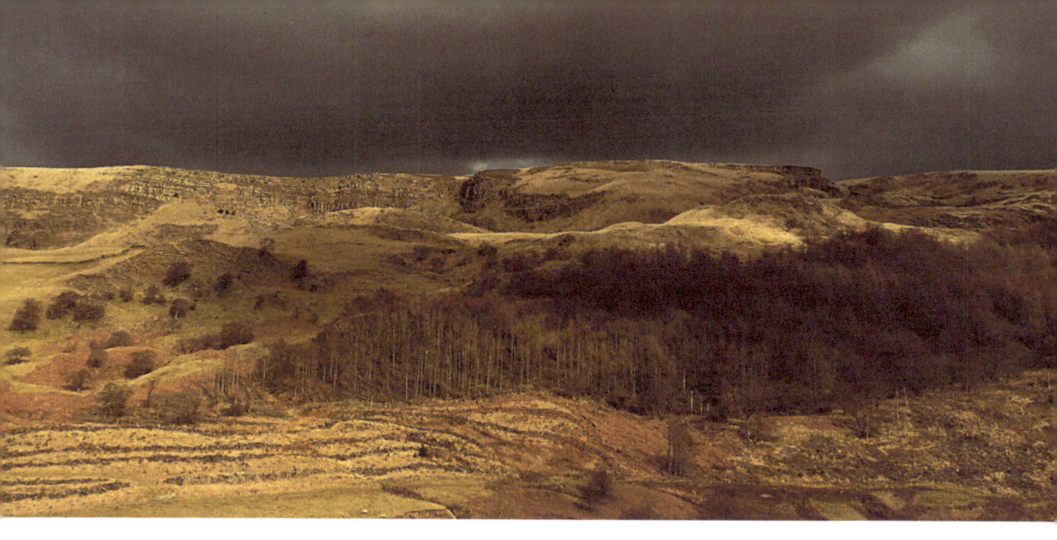

Photo Location – Alport Castles

15.10pm 2nd March – Looking up to Alport Castle from the valley we were concerned that the dark clouds were starting to gather. Would we get a view from the top or would we be stymied by the weather.

After a slightly steeper section the gradient eases off and it opens up to your left, allowing you some good views towards the cliffs above. This area is a good place to stop, have a break and enjoy your surroundings.

16.00pm 2nd March – it seemed somewhat perverse to stop before getting to the top, where we knew the view would be fantastic. However, we couldn't just rush through this amazing landscape without spending some time to take it all in.

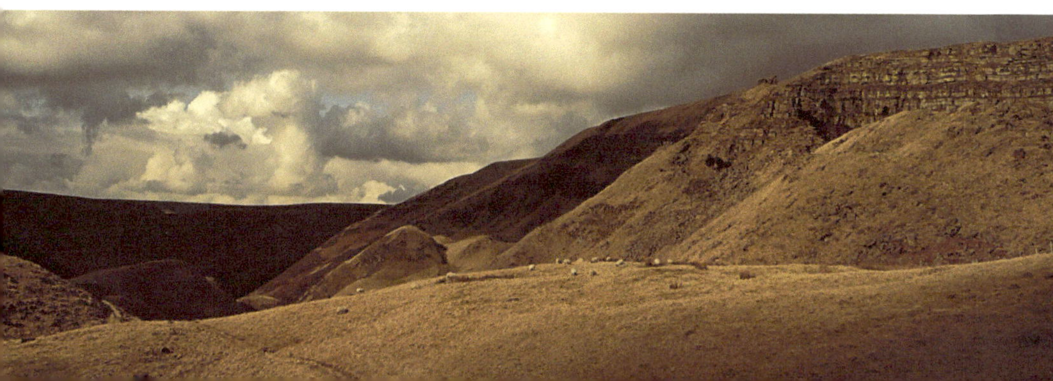

After following the stone wall on your right for a while you'll come to a narrower section and then a ladder stile that takes you over the wall. Follow the path round to the left where it narrows again before opening out just below the cliffs. From a grassy knoll on your left you get an interesting perspective of The Tower as it appears between Little Moor on the left and the cliffs on the right. Head on up the last few steps to the top and turn left along the escarpment edge for 200-300m. By following the escarpment, the view just gets better and better until you reach the stunning viewpoint over the Alport Castles.

Along the escarpment you'll start to get an excellent view over Little Moor. This is a fascinating grassy table top of a hill encircled by a back drop of your return route; Rowlee Pasture and Crookstone Hill. The network of channels that have cut into the table top contrast well with the surrounding smooth moor and make for a good focal point. Moving further north west along the top of the cliffs brings The Tower into view. This pinnacle of rock is surrounded by a mass of boulders that fill the grassy valley whilst the layered cliffs to the right balance the image nicely. For a good contrast there are some excellent panoramic views to be had over the bleak moors to the north and east of here, especially in any late afternoon light.

4) However, there is still a fair bit of walking to do so if you are heading back to Edale it is worth tearing yourself away from the Castle once you've had your fill. The next section, heading along Rowlee Pasture is a real joy as it is easy going and gives you expansive views over the surrounding area. So, back track along the edge of the escarpment, where you'll no doubt stop to take a few more images and head along a good path in a south easterly direction. Keep following this path over Rowlee Pasture for just over 3km where you'll drop down to a field boundary. Go through the gate, crossing a field and then go through a second gate. Keep heading down to a big junction of paths about a 100m away. Pick up the track signposted Hagg Farm which zigzags quite steeply down through a wooded hillside. When you reach the minor road near Hagg Farm (an outdoor activities centre) follow it down a short way to the main, A57 road. Cross straight over and down another steep track that levels out as it crosses over a large bridge over the River Ashop.

5) The next section takes you up through the Woodlands Valley forest. After crossing the bridge turn right onto a track then left up into the trees on a stoney track. After a long straight uphill section turn right on another track that comes in from your left. Go through a gate to leave the woods and keep on the bridleway following along the edge of the forest for another 400m. On reaching a crossroads turn right onto another track signposted Alport Bridge. After a further 200m go through a gate then leave the track, entering Open Access land again. Follow a faint path that heads west up towards Crookstone Hill. After 400m or so of gentle climbing you soon reach a couple of shapely trees.

We had fortunately made good time from Alport Castles and had arrived at Crookstone Hill in a gorgeous evening light. I had remembered visiting this spot some years ago on a grey overcast day and was keen to shoot it towards the end of the day in more flattering conditions.

Photo Location – Crookstone Hill

The view looking west towards Crookstone Knoll is very atmospheric. The two shapely trees complement the distant slopes of the Knoll and the wild moorland adds both colour and texture to this composition.

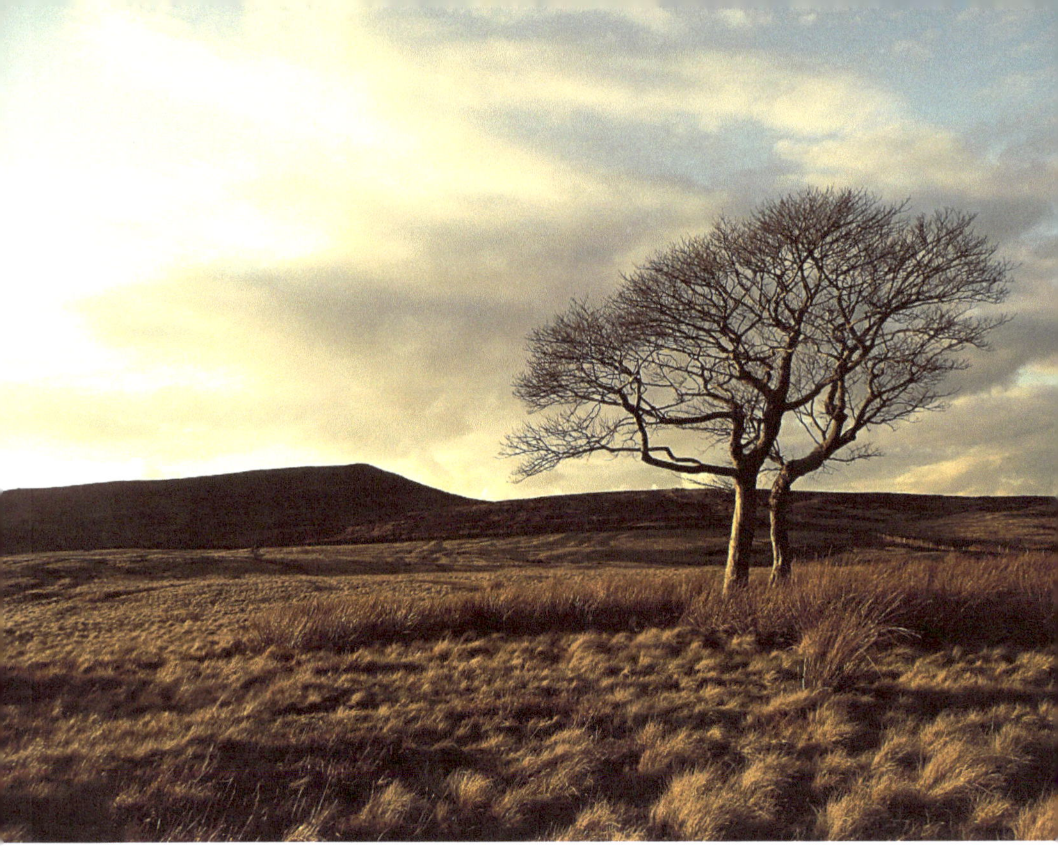

17.00pm 2nd March -Occasionally a planned shoot comes together; the right timing, the right weather, in the right place.

The opposite view, looking east, also has its potential with the bulk of Win Hill making a good backdrop.

From the trees on Crookstone Hill continue heading in a north westerly direction. The path contours left below Crookstone Knoll. A short climb above a crag on your left brings you out onto the Kinder Scout edge again. Keep heading in a south westerly direction along the edge and you'll soon cross the top of Jaggers Clough, a small stream that drops off steeply to your left. After crossing the stream take a path off to your left which heads across a less well defined section of the edge. You'll soon cross another small stream, Lady Booth Brook, and the path gently climbs up to the top of Rowland Cote Moor.

On reaching the rise at Rowland Cote Moor the vista of the Ringing Roger ridgline makes for an excellent mid-ground, backed up by the brooding Kinder Scout. A great spot to take in the last light of the day.

6) Follow the path around the top of Ollerbrook Clough and just before you reach Ringing Roger pick up a path that heads south west down towards the Nab. As you emerge from below the ridge you'll find yourself on the broad saddle of moorland that you crossed on your ascent earlier in the day. Pick up the path that heads south back down to the Nab and then follow the wide path that zigzags you all the way down to the bridge over Grindsbrook again. Cross the bridge and on reaching the road head back down through the village of Edale. You'll now face the tough choice of which pub you want to stop at before heading home, although you could of course visit both just to be sure.

4.4 A Circuit of Burbage, Carl Wark and Higger Tor

Focal Points – Burbage Edge offers excellent views along its entire length and over to the shapely Higger Tor and Carl Wark

Route Summaries

Full route – Starting along Burbage North the walk takes in the whole length of this gritstone edge before heading over to Carl Wark and then climbing up to Higger Tor. An easy descent brings you back to the start again.

7 km, 210 m ascent

Why Try this Route

This is a classic route taking in the picturesque length of Burbage Edge which in its northern half offers far reaching views over the deciduous woods that cloak its lower slopes. On joining South Burbage there are complimentary views back over to its northern counterpart. However, the real gem is the views over to Carl Wark and Higger Tor from a number of less visited viewpoints away from the main tracks. There are also a few millstones dotted around this area which make for useful foregrounds to these views. Crossing over to the ancient site of an Iron Age fort at Carl Wark you get a new perspective on Burbage Edge and Higger Tor. A final clamber up to Higger Tor is a great way to finish the day as there are expansive views over to Stanage and Kinder Scout.

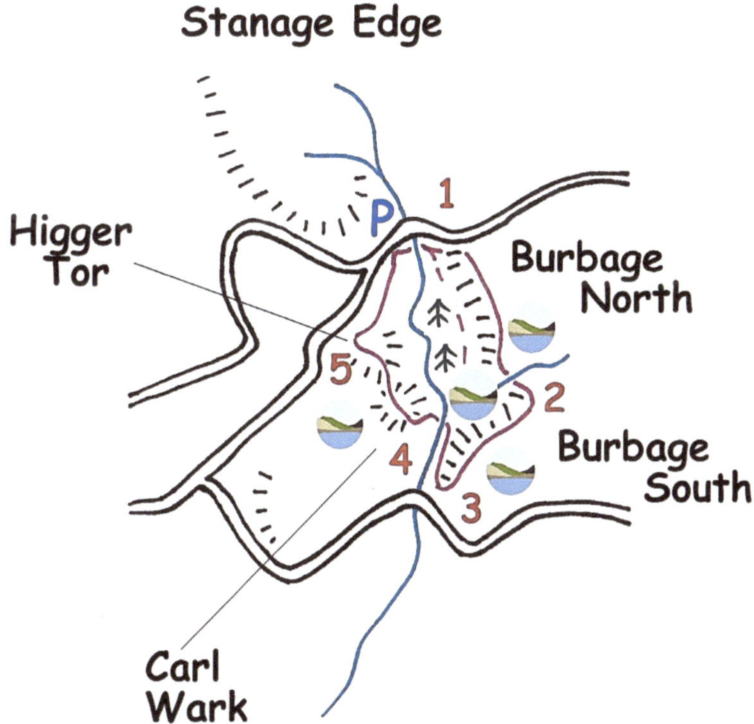

Clockwise from top left:

The view down Burbage Edge... Sunset over Higger Tor... Carl Wark and Higger Tor from the foot of Burbage South... Carl Wark and Higger Tor from the foot of Burbage South, near woods... Higger Tor from Carl Wark... Sculptured rock on Carl Wark with Higger Tor in the background

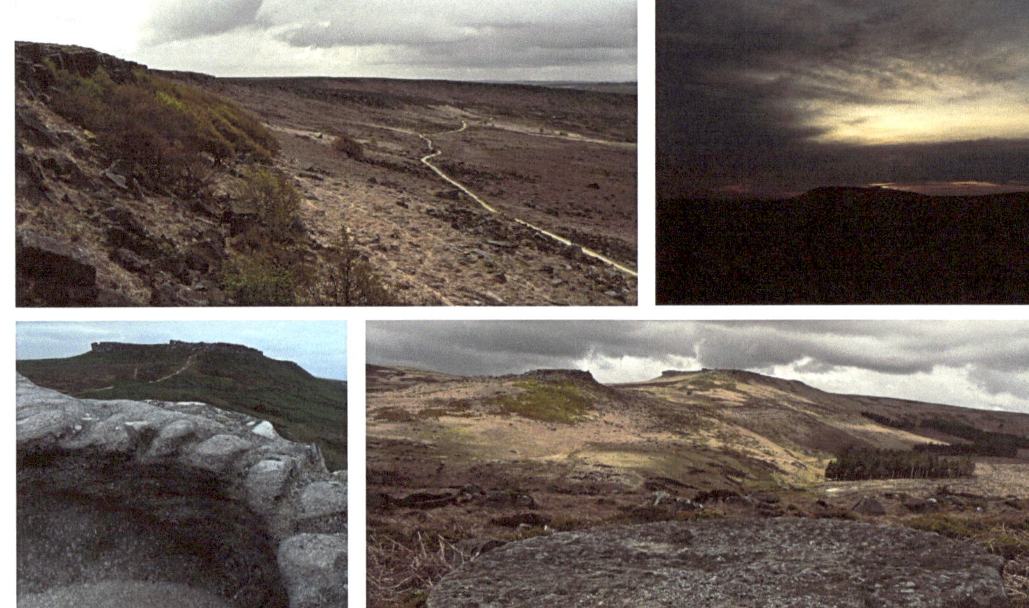

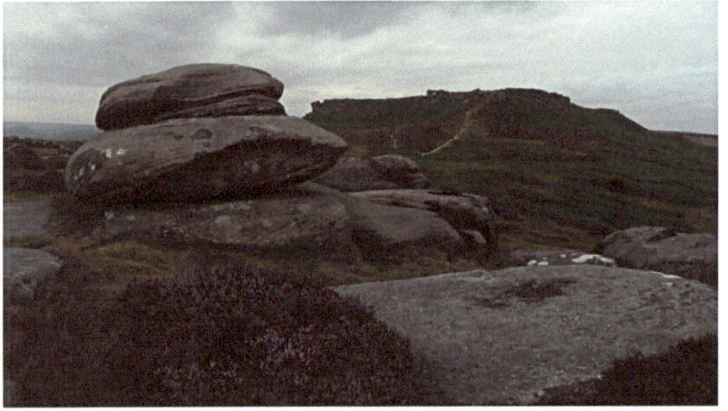

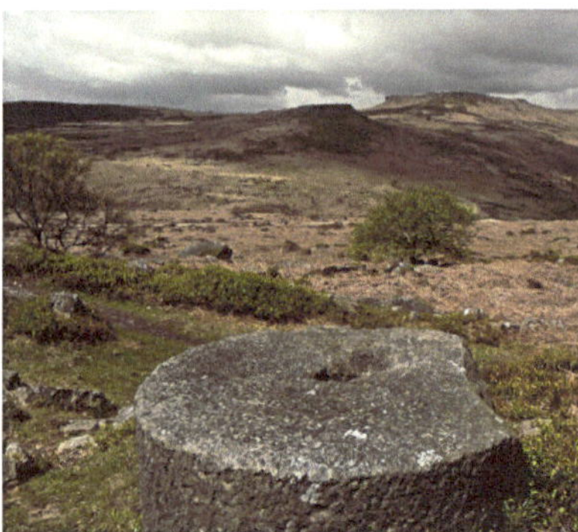

Route Description

1) Start from the main car park at the northern end of Burbage Edge on the Ringinglow Road SK260829. Go through the gate and head east down a path that crosses two streams before it climbs up towards the pull in parking area. You can of course avoid this section by walking along the road, especially if the streams are in spate and the stepping stones are covered. On reaching the start of Burbage North you have the choice of taking either the high or the low route. The low route follows a well made and largely level track which makes life easy. It offers an excellent view down the length of the edge especially as it sweeps round to the southern section. However, the route along the top of the edge does offer more expansive views and is usually quieter. This description will focus on the higher path. There is a faint path through the heather that follows the top of the edge. You get plenty of time to take in the view over to Carl Wark and Higger Tor across the valley which is handy if the conditions are quite variable. Towards the middle section of Burbage North trees have taken hold around the jumble of rocks at the foot of the edge.

Photo Location – the Middle and Lower Sections of Burbage North

There are a number of fantastic viewpoints along this half of Burbage and with some care you can perch yourself on the very edge to give you some rather airy vistas. A good covering of deciduous woods around the middle section makes for a colourful contrast to the gritstone blocks and the moors below.

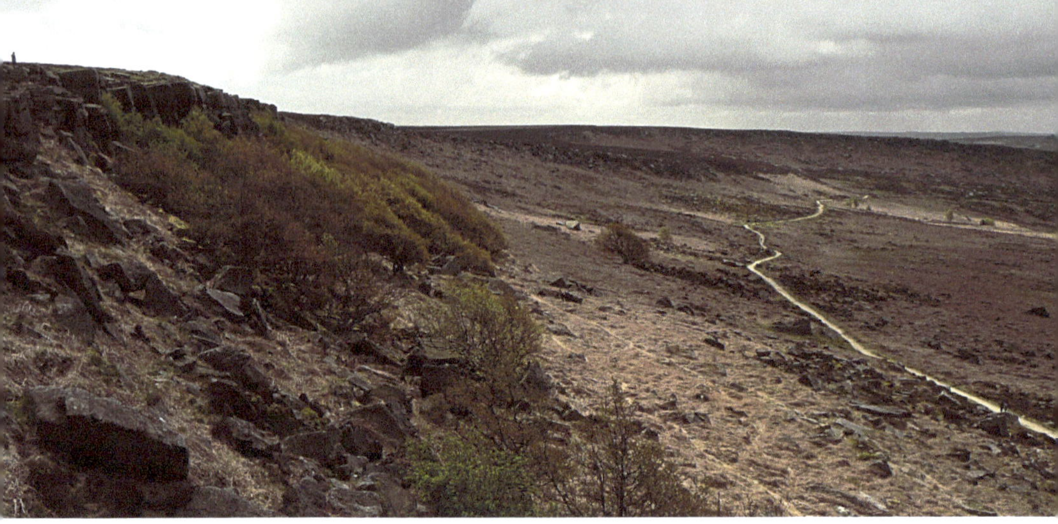

11.30am 20th May - Spring had finally reached this part of the Peaks and the trees were starting to come into leaf. However, the weather was more April showers than late May which had us diving behind the rocks to take shelter on a number of occasions.

As you continue south the edge starts to fizzle out into a mass of smaller boulders dotted amongst the heathered slopes. This is a great spot to take in the views along the edge in either direction. The view south benefits as the last remnants of the edge act as a final elevated viewpoint.

This is a great place to try and spot Ring Ouzels as they often nest around these parts. In fact whilst I was snapping away Sally spotted a couple where the rocks blend into the high moor.

2) As the gritstone edge along the northern half of Burbage starts to fade away the path drops you down to cross a small stream. You can head down the stream to pick up the main track from here if you'd like to shorten the walk. If happy to continue after crossing the stream follow the path as it climbs up to the left towards the top of Burbage South. This section starts to give excellent views over to Higger Tor. Towards the lower part you pass around the top of two precipitous quarries.

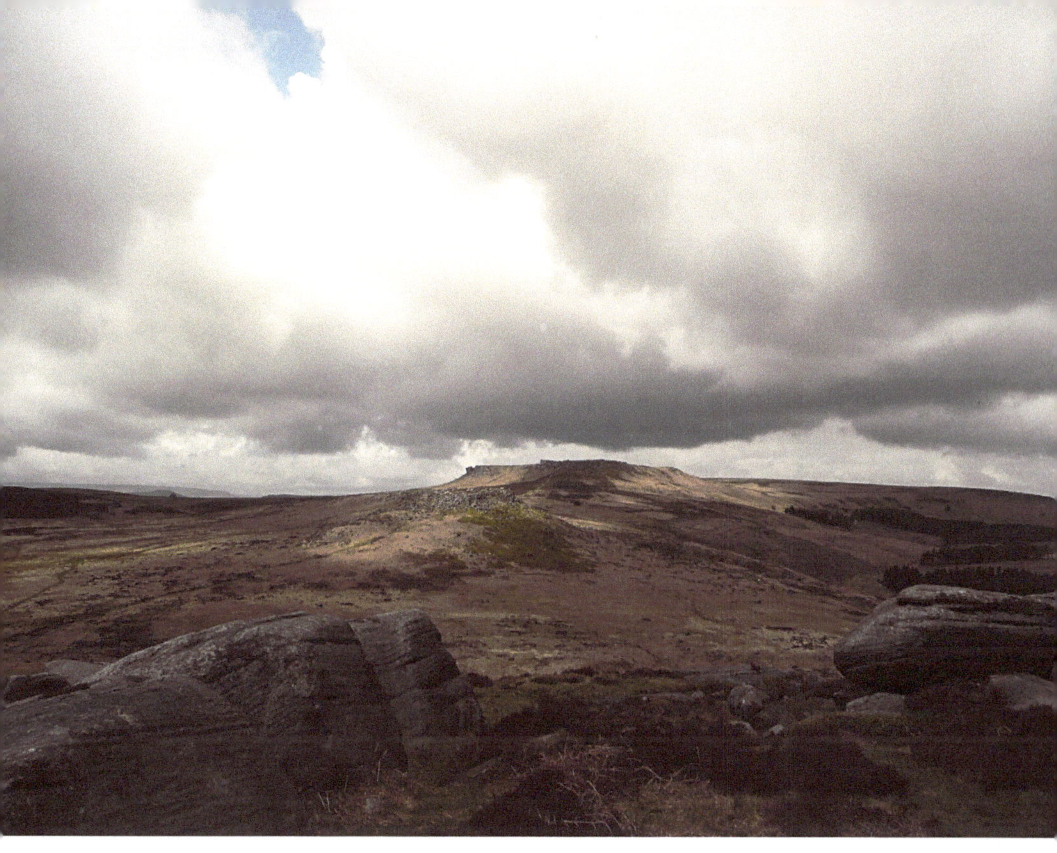

12.40pm 20th May – After a particularly heavy shower had finally cleared, the sun started to break through, lighting up the slopes of Higger Tor.

Photo Location – the Lower Section of Burbage South

The quarries and the slabby rocks along the top of the edge are useful foregrounds as you look out across the valley. The profile of Higger Tor is particularly fine from here as it dominates the skyline.

However, to get the best of both Higger Tor and Carl Wark you need to drop down to the foot of the edge. A lower vantage point brings the profile of the ancient Iron Age fort above the horizon.

3) As the steep edge to your right starts to peter out, look to join a good track that skirts round the bottom of the cliffs. This track was presumably used to access the quarries as it gently climbs north eastwards back towards them. As the track reaches a rise, just before the trees, pick up a path that leads down towards a large scattering of boulders.

Photo Location – Below Burbage South

Just before you pass the woods there are a couple of millstones lying amongst the heather. The view over to Higger Tor and Carl Wark is particularly fine from here and the millstones can be used to add to the foreground. By continuing on the path towards the larger boulders there is another millstone that is also useful.

13.30pm 20th May – You could really make out the stone carver's chisel marks on the millstone and could start to appreciate the amount of work it took to shape this link to the past.

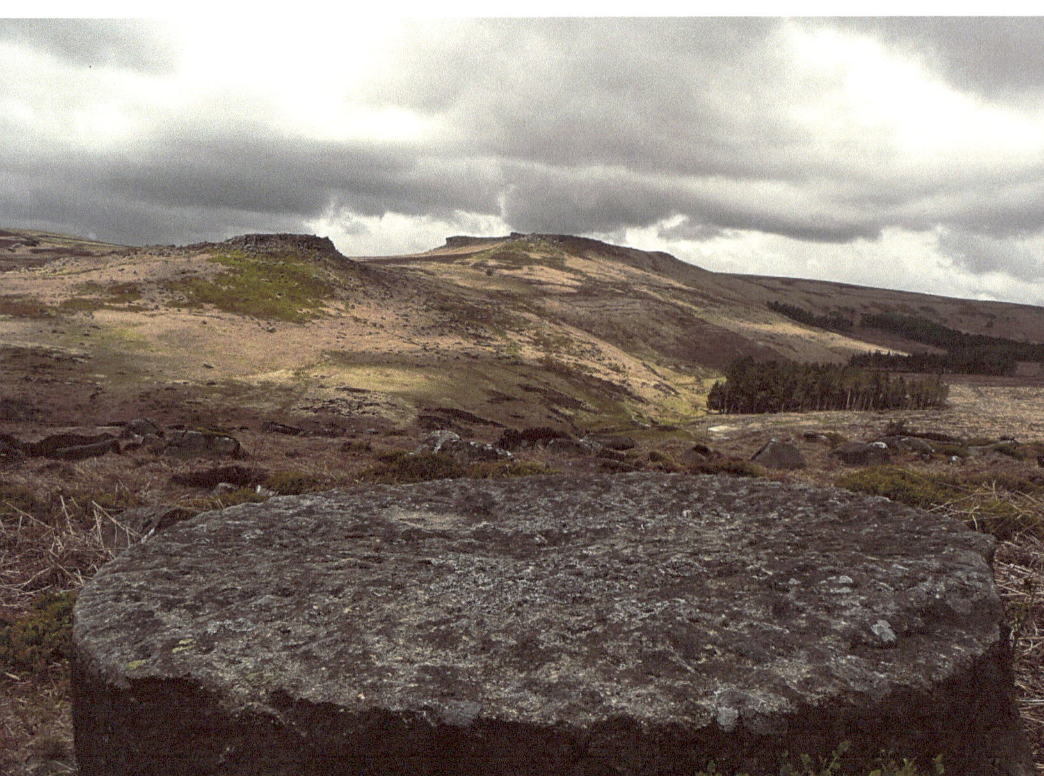

As you reach the main boulder field there are a number of beautifully sculptured rocks that make good subjects to shoot.

4) On reaching a large boulder, covered in pock marks and sitting next to a large flat table topped slab, you can drop down to the left to pick up the main track. This track can be followed all the way back to the car park and allows you to examine the lower slopes of Burbage Edge. However, the pull of exploring Carl Wark and Higger Tor will probably be too great, so pick up a path that drops down to the stream to your left then climb up onto the former.

Photo Locations – Carl Wark and Higger Tor

Carl Wark is a wonderful place to explore with numerous excellent vantage points around its perimeter. It looks like a natural fortress and in fact was used as a hill fort in the Iron Age. The exact use and by whom is a mystery but this only adds to the drama of the location. The view back over to the quarries around the southern end of Burbage Edge is interesting but the most dramatic view is probably from the northern edge looking across to Higger Tor. Be sure to seek out some beautifully weathered rocks along this section that make dramatic foregrounds for the Tor.

To head over to Carl Wark's imposing neighbour Higger Tor drop down on a good path that leaves the north west corner, near the end of the Iron Age wall fortification. A short amble across the connecting moor and a little clamber over some rocks brings you out onto the large plateau that is Higger Tor.

Spend some time here enjoying the views from all its sides, especially off to the north-western corner where you can take in a distant

Stanage Edge and Kinder Scout. For this, follow the left hand, southern edge all the way to the end where there is a grassy promontory. The road may only be just below you but it is a wonderful spot from which to watch the sun go down.

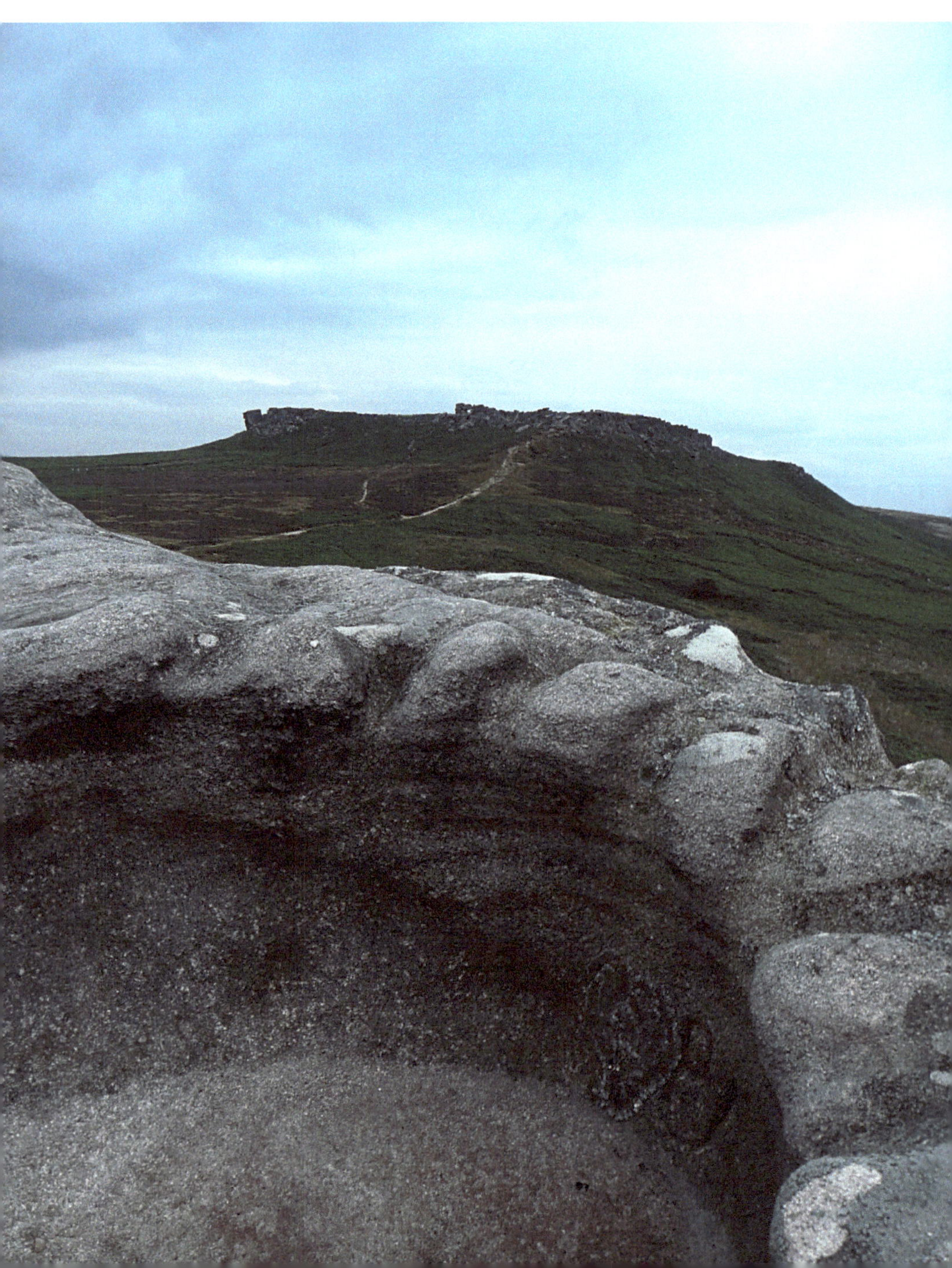

17.15pm 5th August – It was a bit of a precarious stance balancing on the sloping rock but sometimes you have to stick your neck out to get the shot.

5) To return back to the car park, pick up a path that heads off north east from the Tor as it drops down some rough steps. The path runs parallel to the road to your left. As you climb your last few meters for the day look over your shoulder for one final outline of Higger Tor. A bit of rock hopping, or weaving around the boulders that litter the path, brings you back to the car park and the end of this interesting take on a classic route.

As the sun was dropping down behind the shapely profile of Higger Tor we realised we had timed our return rather well. It reminded me of some of my climbs at Burbage which usually ended in a hasty retreat from the edge as the gathering of dusk descended. Time for a chip supper in Chesterfield.

The Northern Pennines and The Howgills

Geographically the Northern Pennines and the Howgills fall between the Lake District and the Yorkshire Dales, the latter two being some of the most visited areas in the UK. On first glance these 'in betweener' hills might not appear as dramatic as their more popular neighbours, but, if you know where to look there are some stunning gems to be discovered.

5.1 A Photocircumnavigation of High Cup Nick

Focal Point – High Cup Nick is a geological wonder and a large one at that but this means there are numerous fantastic view points to take in all of its angles.

Route Summaries

Full route – taking in a traverse of the northern side of High Cup Nick and across the wild moors to the outstanding waterfall at Cauldron Snout. Then double back to the head of the Nick, with optional wild camping. The return route takes in the less visited southern edge.

30.5 km; 670m ascent

Shorter routes - a there and back along the Pennine Way to the head of the valley

14 km; 400m ascent

with an alternative return by the southern edge

15.5 km; 450m ascent

Why Try this Route

If you thought that the Pennines were just a group of dull, boggy, rounded hills that didn't warrant a visit then read on. There's gold, photographic gold to be found in those hills. You just need to get off the well beaten path. A full circuit or photocircumnavigation around High Cup Nick is a real feast for the eyes and should be on every landscape photographers must visit list. You also get to experience a fine section of the Pennine Way which includes bleak moors and an outstanding waterfall. So grab your gear and go and explore this real gem. You'll soon discover a different side to the Pennines.

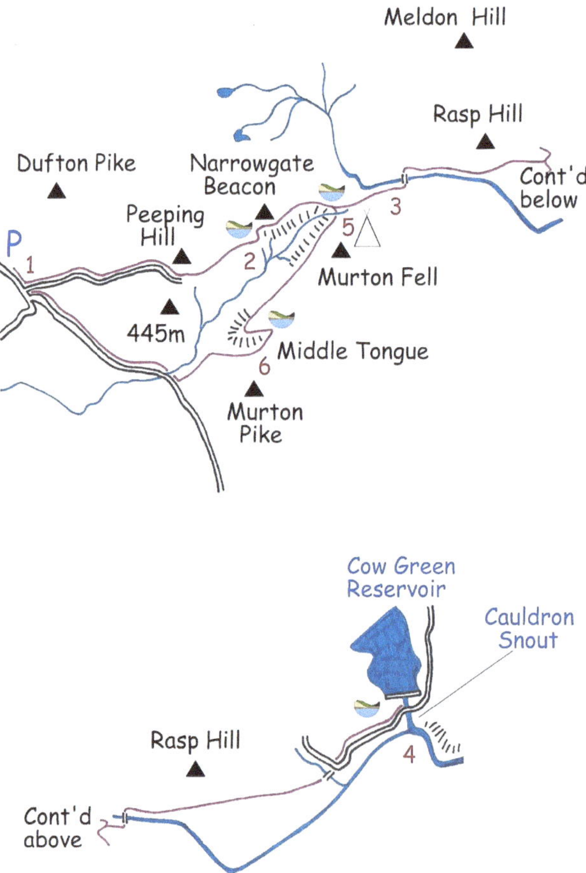

Clockwise from top left :

This way to something special – the signpost in Dufton... Wild camp at High Cup Nick... Chris and Liz on their way towards Middle Tongue... The northern arm of High Cup from the head of the valley... Approaching Cauldron Spout, the Upper Teesdale valley... Exploring the cliffs of High Cup

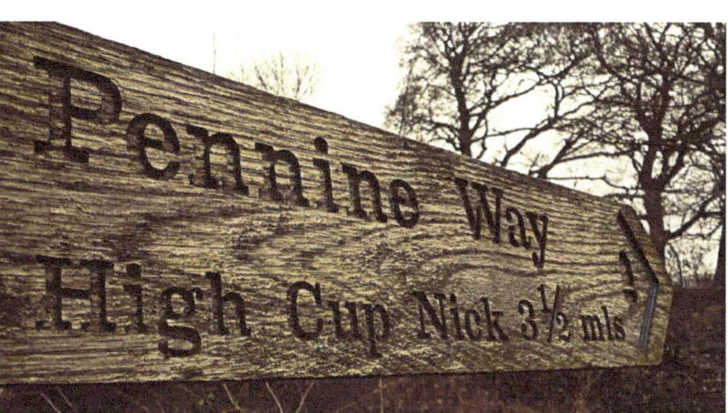

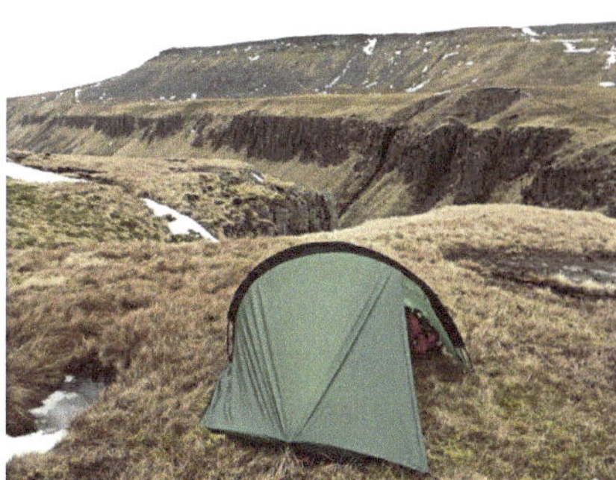

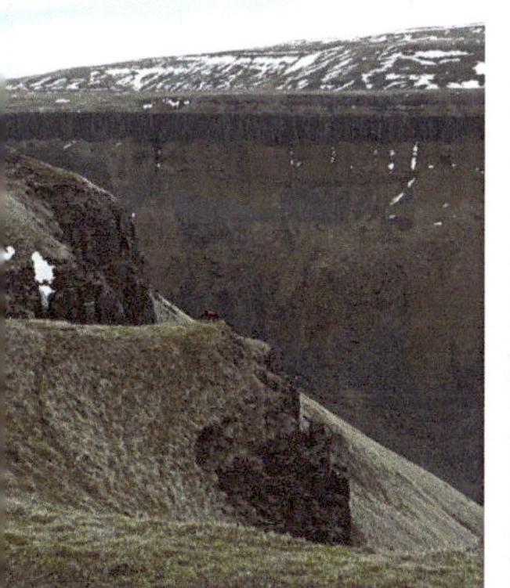

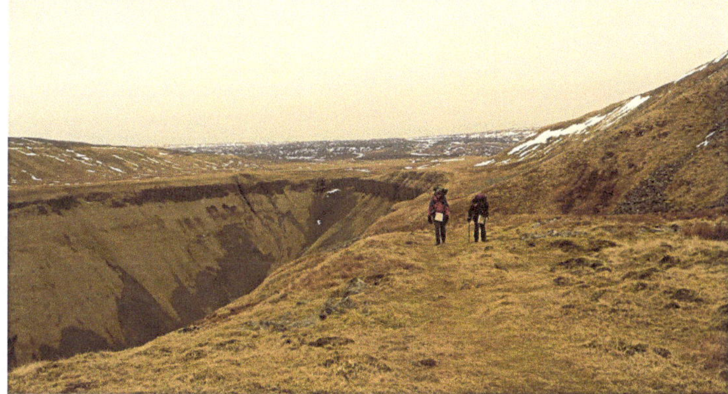

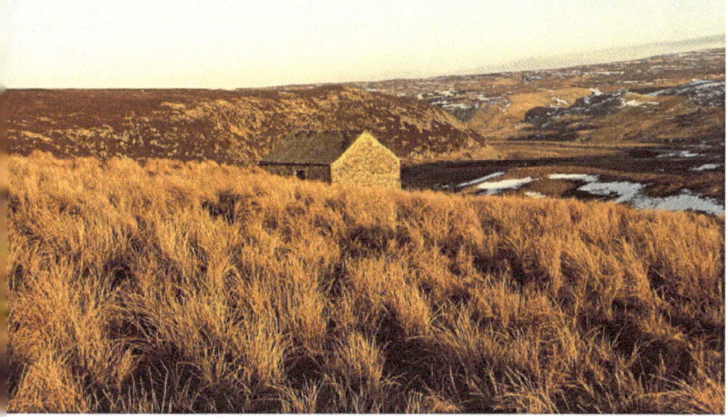

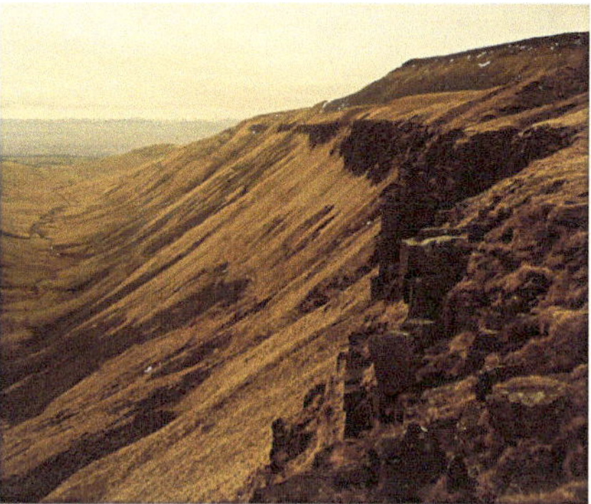

Route Description

1) Start from the attractive village of Dufton where there is a small car park (GR NY 689250) and also a cracking pub called the Stag Inn. Turn right out of the car park heading south east down the road to Murton. On the outskirts of Dufton look out for a large track on the left with a finger post signposted Pennine Way, High Cup Nick 3.5 miles.

Follow this wide track for about 3km as it climbs the southern flanks of the delightfully named Peeping Hill. At the end of the track go through a gate and continue along the Pennine Way.

Photo Location – Early Views of High Cup Nick

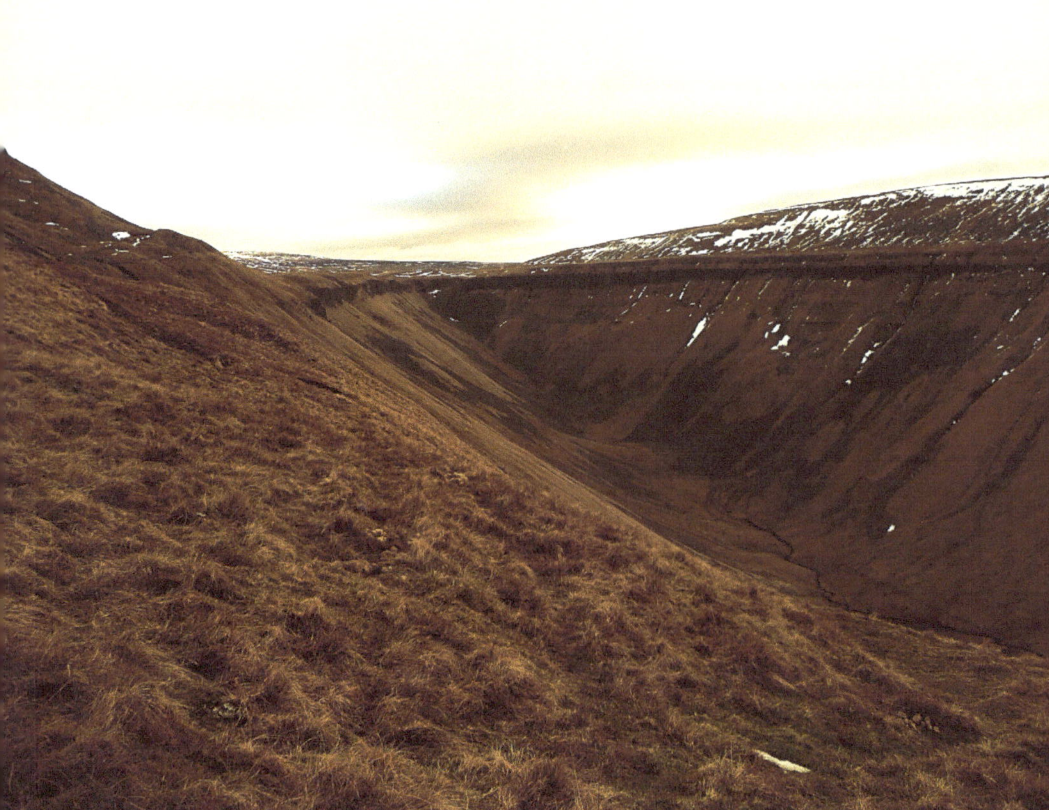

08.00 am, 2nd March - We'd spent an extremely cold night camped out on the hills and were keen to get a first glimpse of High Cup. From this vantage point we were able to get a sense of its sheer scale and beauty and we knew we were in for a special trip.

To get an early and exciting view of High Cup Nick leave the path approximately 300m after passing through the gate. Contour east and slightly downhill to a small flat grassy area (GR NY728249) that has a rock cairn at its far end. Being below the level of the cliffs gives you an interesting perspective and your first impressions of the Nick.

08.20 am, 2nd March – Penny the dog checking out one of the dramatic views. There were still a few last patches of snow left and considering the air temperature they weren't going to disappear anytime soon.

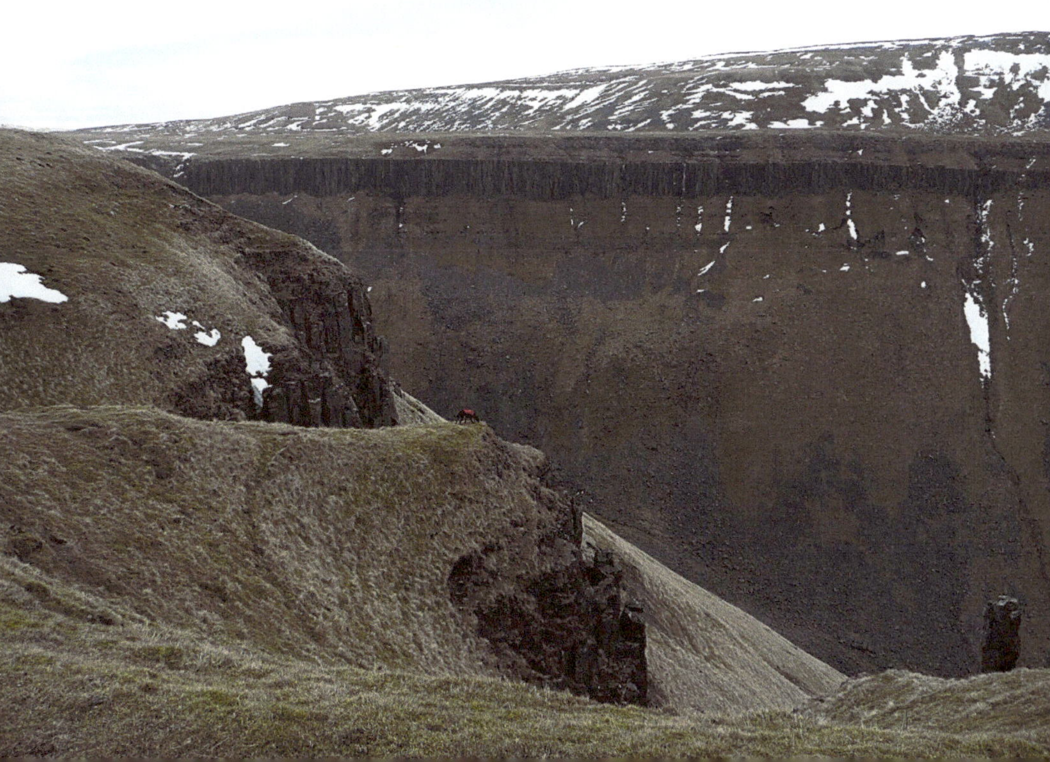

2) Regain the Pennine Way by heading up a short sharp grassy slope that can be made somewhat easier by tacking up leftwards first to clear the steepest ground. When you reach the path again continue gently climbing in a north easterly direction. As the path squeezes between the steep slopes of Narrowgate Beacon and the Nick you reach the cliffs proper. This next section is a real joy. Flat, easy walking allows you to focus on your photography.

Photo Location – High Cup Nick

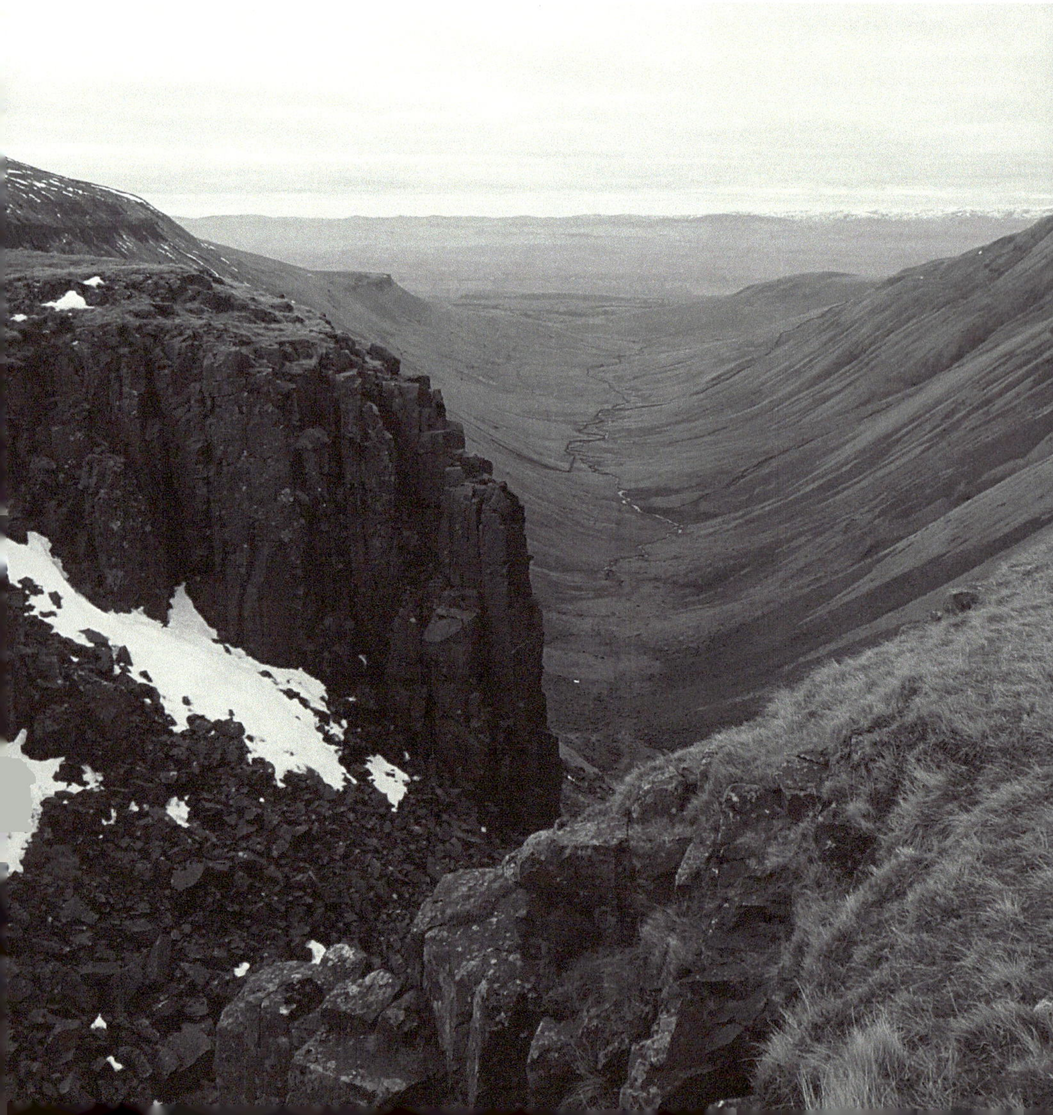

08.30 am, 2nd March – Standing at the head of High Cup Nick the photographic opportunities were so numerous we decided we would head back here later in the day to camp out.

When you reach the head of the valley, the tip of the 'V', where a small stream trickles down the cliff, you get a real sense of the scale and beauty of this place. You'll need your wide angle lens to capture the full panorama, although taking each 'arm' as a focus works as well. The sweeping lines of the cliffs and contrasting textures make for an exciting shoot.

The view from here is multi-layered. High Cup Gill weaves its way along the base of the valley as it leaves the high ground of the Pennines. As the escarpment cliffs peter out, the fine bastions of Middle Tongue and the unnamed peak (445m spot height on the map) appear to guard the entrance of the valley. Finally, in the distance the superb High Street range of fells can be seen if the skies are clear.

08.30 am, 2nd March – This view felt like it had a timeless quality to it, especially as there was no one around and little sign of any human presence.

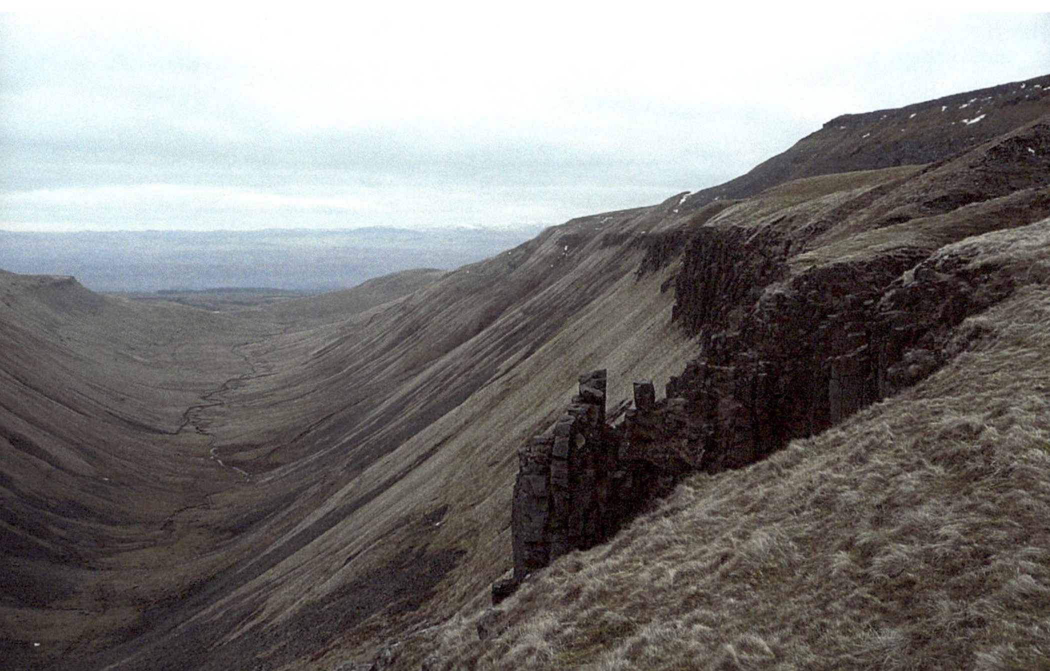

You now have a couple of options.

The quickest route back is of course to return the way you came. If you want to take in a bit more of a walk but not the full 'out and back' to Cauldron Snout, the south section of High Cup is a real joy and is described later in section **5)**. However, if you're up for the full route and a bit of an adventure read on.

3) To reach the Cauldron Snout waterfall you'll have to undertake a 16km out and back romp across the moors. This might sound a bit excessive but if the weather is fine and you have plenty of time, then it makes a real contrast to what you have just experienced. The route follows the Pennine Way which for the most part is easy to follow, if a bit boggy at times.

You only have to walk a few paces from the edge of High Cup and you realise you have entered the type of terrain for which the Pennines are more famous; Wild rolling moors, that in the right light are stunning in their own way. After a kilometre you reach the attractive Maize Beck which acts as a constant partner for the next section of the walk. After just under another 2 km be sure to cross the bridge to the northern side of the stream or you'll be encroaching onto M.O.D land with restricted access. The path continues alongside the stream for another kilometre before it takes a short cut over the flanks of Rasp Hill. As you drop down to another bridge, pick up a track heading north east and pass a farm house (Birkdale) on your left.

Whilst this last section isn't too exciting you soon reach an old farm building on your right offering great views over to the ever expanding river valley below.

Photo Location – Cauldron Snout Area

On rounding the next bend you start to hear the roar of the waterfall some time before you can see it. It is worth leaving the track here and heading over to the edge to get an airy view of the Snout and the meandering valley below. The upper Tees river has cut through the bleak moors to form the stunning Falcon Clints cliffs. You can gain access to the far side of the river by crossing the bridge above the waterfall and carefully following the path down to the confluence of Maize Beck and the River Tees.

14.40 pm, 2nd March – Upper Teesdale; We reached Cauldron Snout just in time for dusk. The waterfall itself was already in shadow but it was a glorious spot offering extended views down the river bluffs of Upper Teesdale. As we didn't have much daylight left and as we wanted to camp up back at the Nick it was time to get moving. We got back to Maize Beck before the headtorches were donned. This added a new dimension to our Pennine experience.

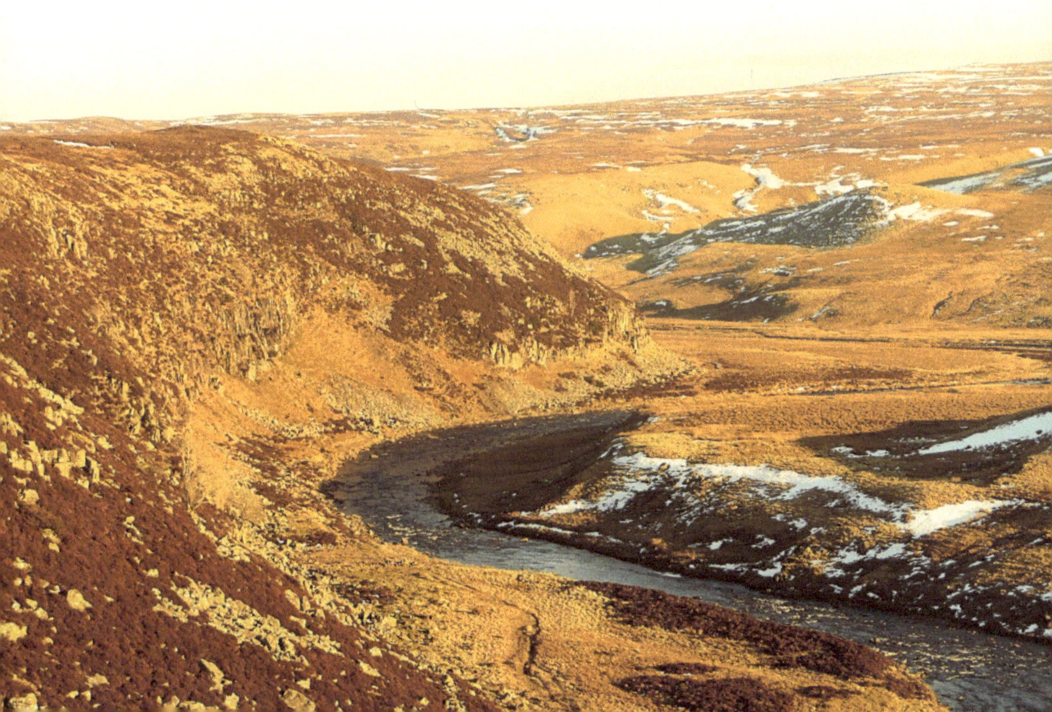

4) The only realistic way back from the Snout is to return the way you came. Psychologically this can be quite tough but to spur you on you'll have the attractive prospect of reaching High Cup Nick again, no doubt under somewhat different lighting conditions.

On reaching High Cup, if you are planning on camping out there are numerous flat spots on which to pitch up. One such spot is a few meters south from the place where the stream drops over the cliffs.

We spent a remarkably quiet, if rather chilly night on the edge of the Nick with high hopes of a sunrise from this spectacular spot. However more grey skies were on offer with little promise of any golden hour. Still, it had warmed up a touch making it easier to hang around camp. We were packed up and ready to go pretty early so we planned to take in the less visited southern edge of High Cup Nick. This gave us a great opportunity to complete a full 360 degree tour of High Cup Nick before leaving the high ground and heading back to the lovely village of Dufton.

5) There is a faint path along the southern arm of High Cup and by taking this route you get to view the cliffs above which you walked the day before. By following the escarpment to its obvious conclusion you reach a flat, raised plateau called Middle Tongue.

Photo Location – Middle Tongue

This gives you one final, elevated viewpoint up the length of the valley and an impression of the scale and grandeur of the place.

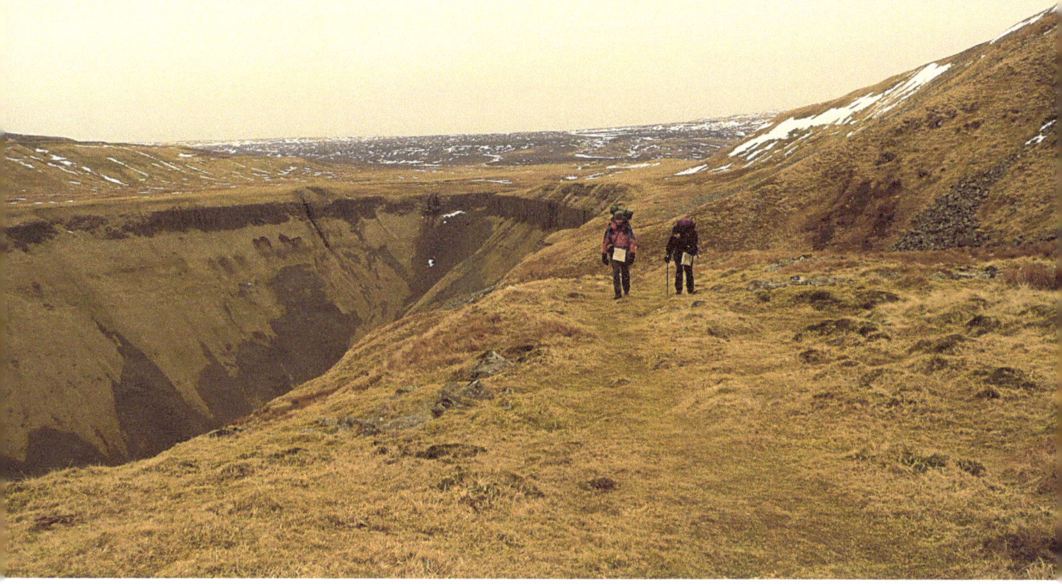

07.40 am, 3rd March – On route to Middle Tongue. Chris and Liz enjoying a fantastic start to day 3.

There are numerous viewpoints along the top of the cliffs of the 'Tongue'.

08.05 am, 3rd March – We spent a leisurely half hour or so enjoying the views from this remarkable spot before it was time to finally leave the high ground.

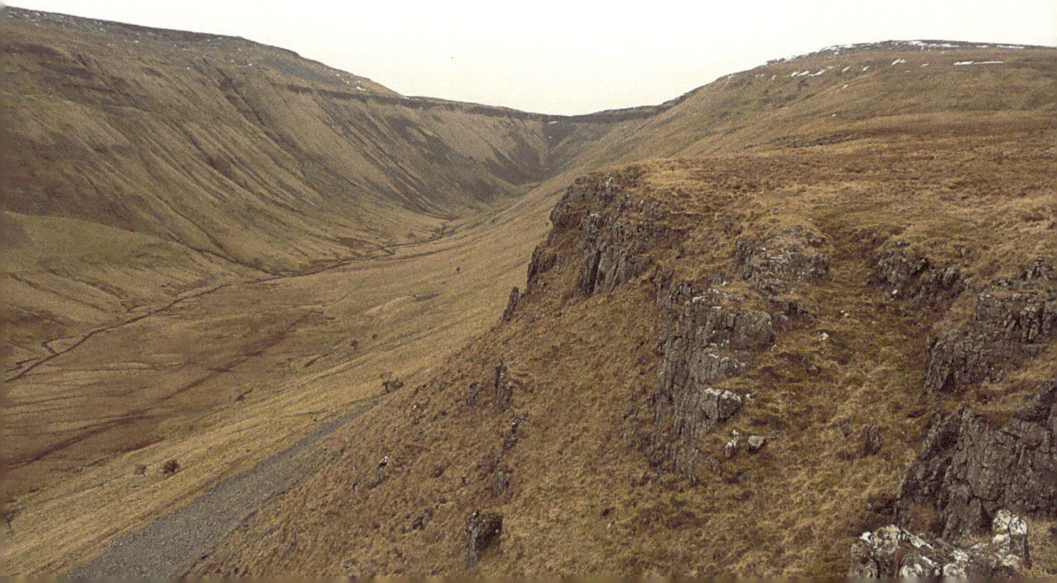

The sinuous form of High Cup Gill leads nicely up to the head of the valley. Also, if conditions prevail there are some fine views in the opposite direction over the Eden Valley and on to the distant Lake District fells.

6) Head east along the southern side of the plateau to clear the cliffs and then pick up a faint path which drops you down to the valley below. A good track then takes you across a stream and down to a large farm, Harbour Flatt. Head through the farm on the signed path and take the track down to the road. There are ways to avoid the section of tarmac back to Dufton but it is a quiet road and is also a gentle way to bring you back to civilisation.

Despite it being a pretty fine weather window in early March we only saw two other walkers over the whole weekend. If the Nick was in the Lakes it would be a different matter. It just goes to show that there are still some cracking locations waiting to be explored.

5.2 Exploring the Howgills

Could the Howgill Fells possibly be the most overlooked range of hills in England? As you drive north up the M6 on a trip to the Lake District or Scotland you might notice their shapely contours and fleetingly consider exploring them at some point. However, if you never get round to spending some time in this area you are really missing out. They form a compact range of hills centred on the highest hill, The Calf. A number of broad ridges radiate out from this central summit and are separated by deep, stream laden valleys. One of the few areas of really steep ground is home to some very fine cliffs and a picturesque waterfall, all of which you explore on this walk.

Focal Point – Cautley Spout waterfall and the surrounding Cautley Crag form the focus of this walk. The latter provides a dramatic vista that takes in the waterfall and its watershed.

Route Summaries

Full route – an easy start along Cautley Beck takes you up to the base of Cautley Spout. A steep ascent on a good path takes you alongside the waterfall to the top of Cautley Crags. Traversing south along the top of the crags brings you out onto the rolling high ground of Great Dummacks, Calders and onto the highest hill in the area, The Calf. Follow the north west ridge off The Calf over Bush Howe and then on to Fell Head. Reverse the route for the return.

17km; 990m ascent

An extension can be made to take in the viewpoint of Simon's Seat before or after a visit to Fell Head

adds 4 km; 150m ascent

Shorter route – A there and back along Cautley Beck to the base of Cautley Spout.

5km; 60m ascent

Why Try this Route

The area around Cautley Spout is rich in photographic potential. By climbing its steep flanks you gain access to the sweeping cliffs that encircle the valley below. And by following the crags to their southern end you access one of the finest viewpoints in the area, and one which does not see many visitors. This devious route to the high ground takes in the wild rolling moor which contrasts dramatically with the steep valley you have just climbed. The well worn path over The Calf is another contrast to the faint tracks that lead you over to the outlying peaks of Fell Head and Simon's Seat. Being outliers these two hills offer excellent views back into the range. Additionally they offer excellent vantage points over the lush green fields of the lowland valleys and on to the distant Lake District, which from here is seen in all its wide angle glory. Also, as they have flat grassy summits surrounded by steep sides they make remote locations for a high level wild camp. All these attributes mean they are ideal spots to enjoy a sunset and sunrise in rather special and tranquil surroundings.

Clockwise from top left:

Yarlside from Great Dummacks,... The Lune valley from Fell Head... The infant Cautley Beck above the waterfall... The route to Simon's Seat... Sunset over the Lake District from Fell Head... Cautley Crags from their southern end

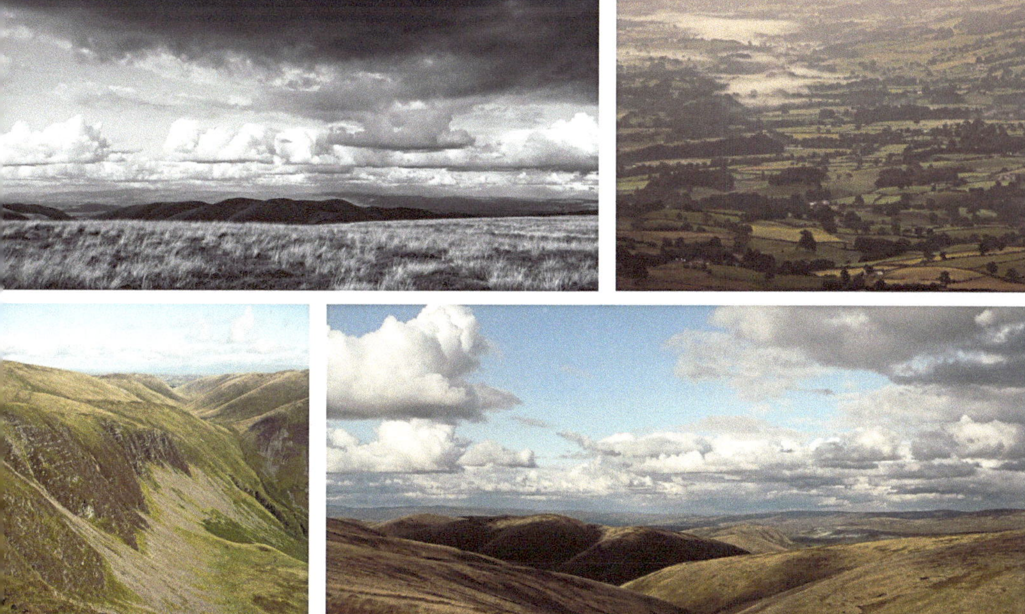

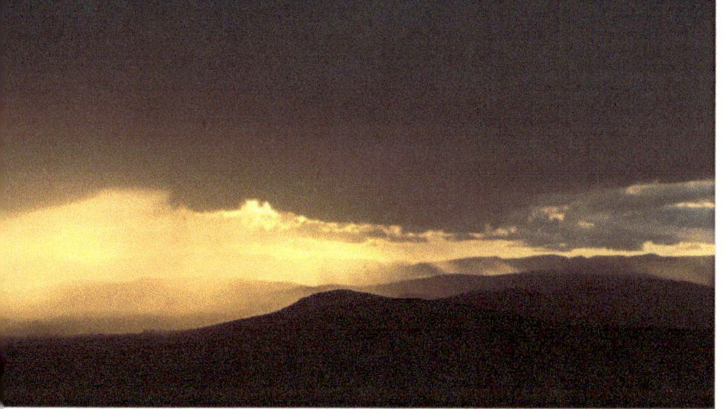

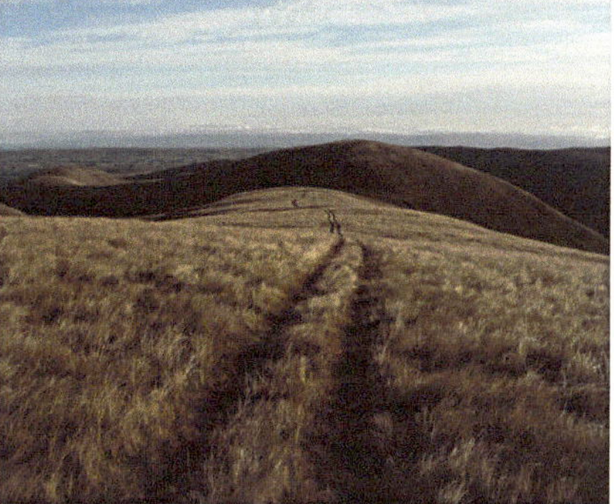

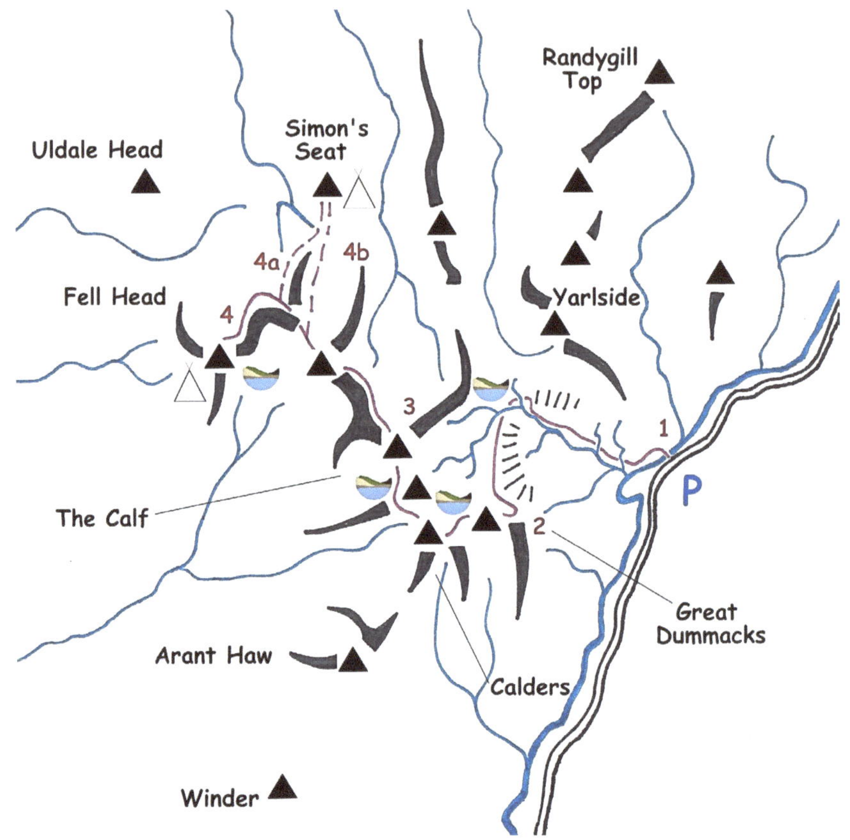

Route Description

1) Start from the lay-by, a few meters north of the Cross Keys Temperance Inn, GR SD 697969. Leave the pull in at its northern end where a signpost to Cautley Spout points you down some steps to a bridge over the river Rawthey. Cross the bridge, taking in this fine valley and turn left on a good path that follows the river for 500m or so. Just before another bridge the main path bears right, leaving the larger river, to pick up the gentle ascent of Cautley Beck. This is good, easy walking; however the view of the waterfall tumbling down the steep cliffs of Cautley Crags, is sure to quicken your pulse.

As I entered Cautley valley, despite knowing what to expect, the view in front of me stopped me in my tracks and had me reaching for my camera.

Just before the ground starts to really steepen drop down to the stream on your left and follow it for a 100m or so to a small waterfall. This is the first of many idyllic waterfalls, the main two being half way up the climb. So pick up a sheep track that heads up a grassy bluff slightly off to your right and you soon rejoin the path. Follow this as it steepens, always keeping the beck to your left. Although the climb is hard work the flagged steps make ascent more manageable.

About half way up the climb you reach a point that is just above the first of the main waterfalls. From here you can gain some pretty amazing positions just yards from the path. The drops here are steep so obviously some care is needed in where you position yourself.

Photo Locations – the Top of the Main Waterfall of Cautley Beck and Cautley Crags

From the top of the waterfall the view over the drop is superb with the beck meandering its way far down below to the enclosed pastures in the valley. The steep sides of Cautley Crags and Ben End frame the picture with Baugh Fell as a backdrop.

Continue the climb on the path above the waterfall and as the gorge starts to open up, bear left on a path to cross a feeder stream. Follow the path upwards, then cross Cautley Beck at the end of its upper valley. Here the walk gets really interesting as you reach the top of Cautley Crags. So, after crossing the beck, head on up a faint path that climbs the grassy ridge in front of you. Whilst the climb isn't over the gradient soon eases and the views over the crags are simply stunning. Possibly the finest viewpoint is at the southern, higher end of the crags near the top of a steep scree lined gully. Being east facing this area is best shot in the morning before it falls into shadow.

After the hard climb was over, the view really opened up. However, I was about to be treated to a wintry hail storm which kept the camera packed away this time around.

10.20am 24th August - This was my second visit to the southern end of Cautley Crags on this trip and it was one to savour. The heather was just starting to come into flower and the weather was more typical for the time of year compared to the wintery showers of yesterday.

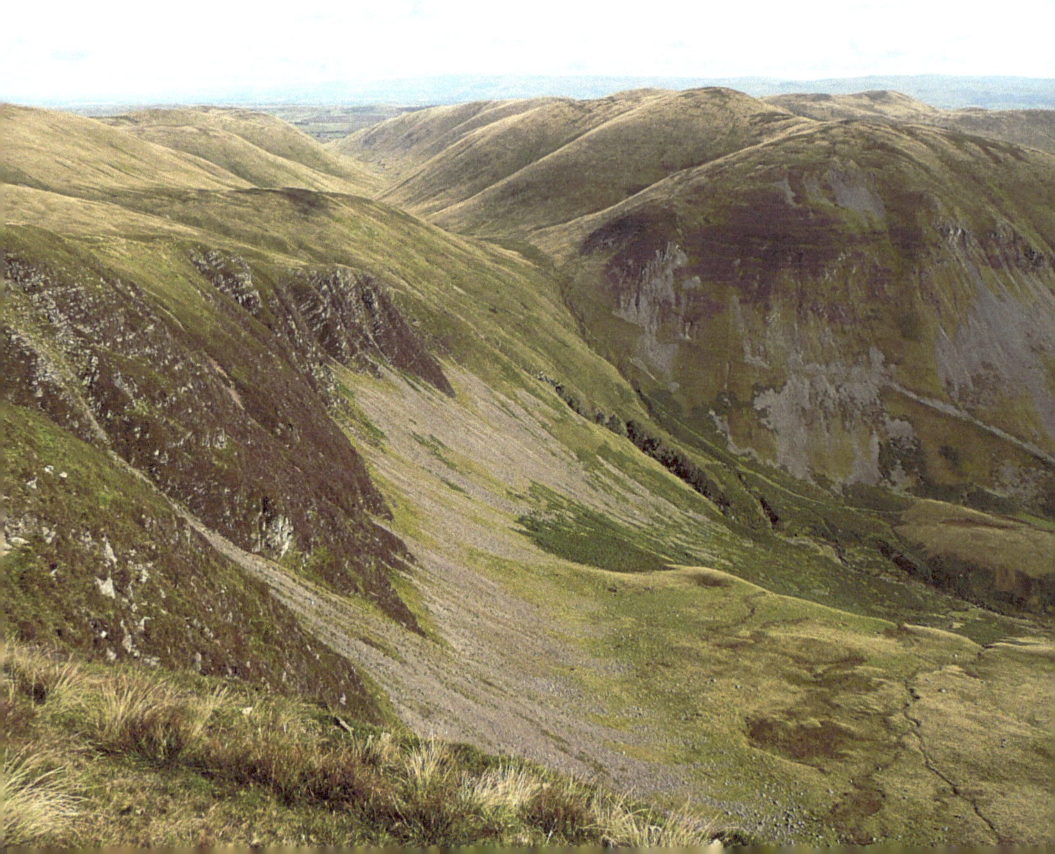

The sweep of the heather clad crags leads your eye towards the gorge, and the layered slopes of Yarlside act as a fantastic backdrop to balance the composition.

2) When you've had your fill of the view over Cautley Crag it's now time for a real contrast. The next section of the walk is quite featureless so would not be so easy to tackle in poor visibility. However, despite the walk across Great Dummacks being rather featureless, the interplay of bleak moor and distant shapely hills can be very rewarding.

So, turn your back on the cliffs near the steep scree gully and pick up a faint grassy track that heads off in a south westerly direction. As you reach the high ground around Great Dummacks it is worth turning round to take in the view back north towards Yarlside. From this position the bottom of the peak is obscured by the foreground. However, this makes for an interesting composition. Follow the path down the western slopes and you should be able to see a fence line in the distance that leads you to the well positioned summit of Calders.

Photo Location – Before Reaching the Summit of Calders

As you reach the fence turn right on a double grassy track. Before you start the gentle climb to the summit of Calders enjoy the view looking back over the way you've just walked.

17.30pm 23rd August – After enduring a heavy shower my reward was a rather impressive sky. This added to the drama of the wild moors I'd just crossed.

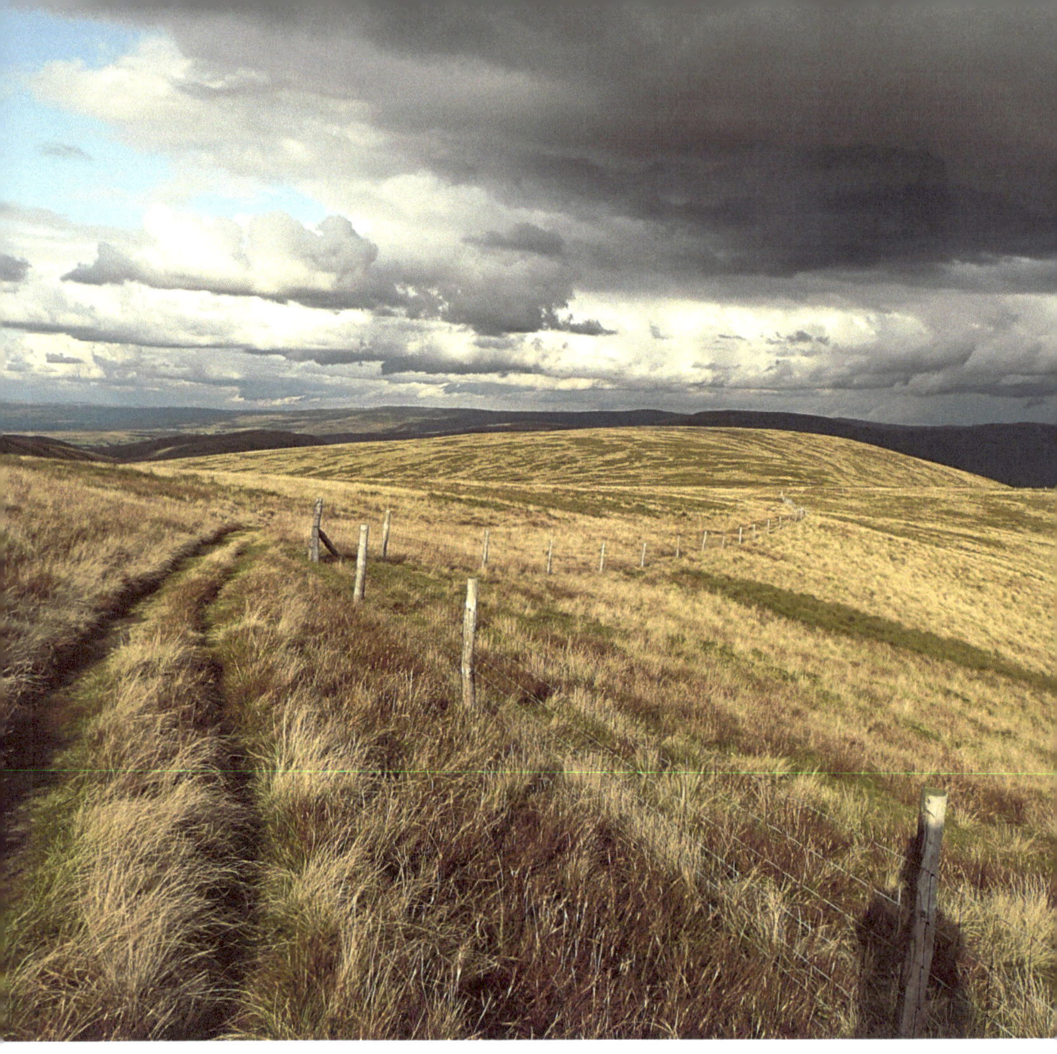

The track and the fence not only make useful navigational aids but also act as a useful lead in line, taking your eye across what might appear a rather bleak open vista. This is a place to appreciate, or sometimes endure, whatever the weather throws at you.

As you start the short pull to the top of Calders the ground drops away steeply to your left opening up a dramatic view. This is a fine spot to enjoy the shapely curves of Arant Haw and the ridgeline leading up to your next destination, the summit of Calders.

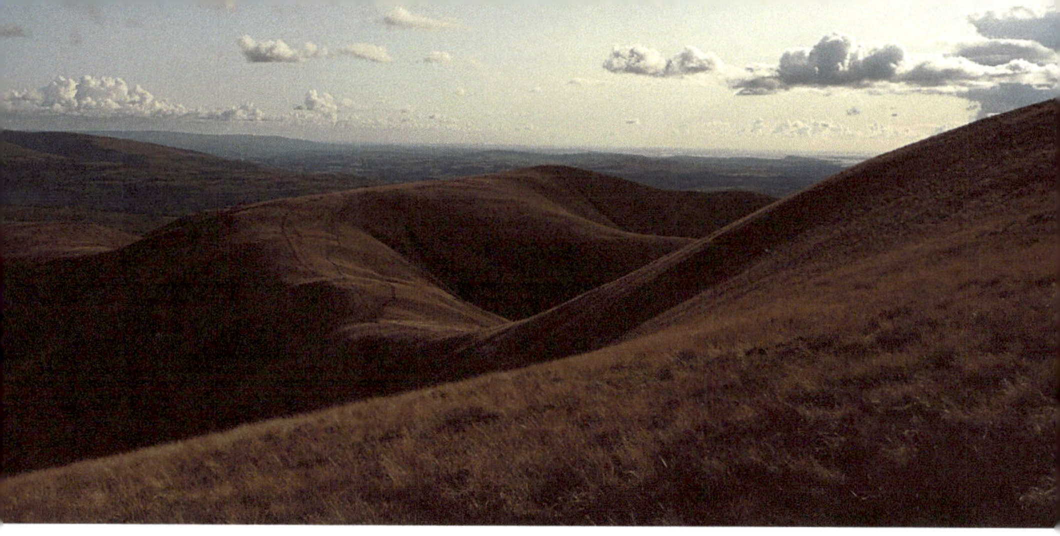

17.40pm 23rd August – Arant Haw and its connecting ridges is one of the fine peaks that make the Howgills rather special. I reached this point as the sun and everyone else were starting to go down and felt privileged to have the hills to myself.

Sometimes it's worth stopping before you get to a summit as the slopes you are on can be a real aid to the composition of an image.

The final pull to the summit of Calders is short and here you get your first views of a distant Lake District. There is a small pile of stones to mark the top and a wide, well made path that is a contrast to what you've been following so far. This signals the main route up to the high ground and you can enjoy some rather easy walking to the highest peak in the Howgills, The Calf. Turn right to enjoy the expansive views reaching down into the Lune valley and beyond.

Photo Location – Between Calders and The Calf

Shortly after leaving the summit of Calders there's an excellent view down the upper Cautley valley. The sweep of the beck forms a striking lead in line to the slanting ridgelines of Yarlside.

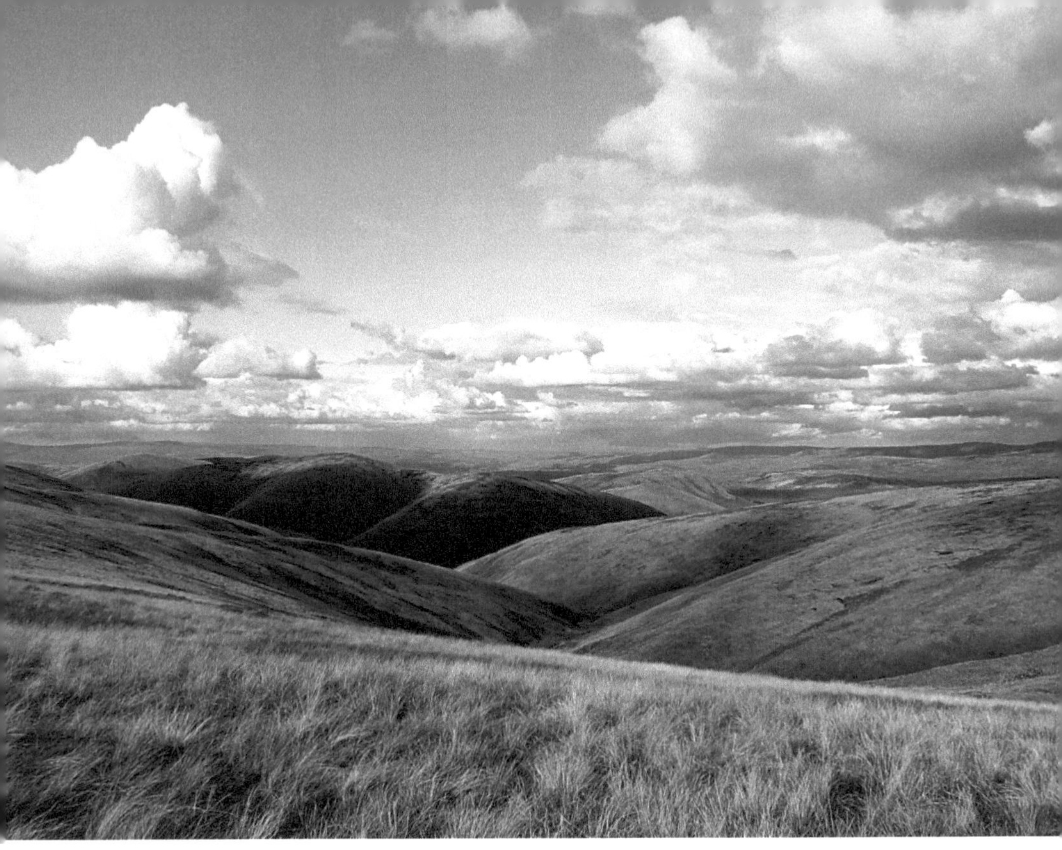

18.20pm 23rd August – This valley lacks interest from the lower end but is a delight when shot from this location above the watershed.

Just to the right of these slopes seek out an interesting limestone outcrop for which it is worth digging out your zoom lens.

If it is busy on this stretch, or you just want to get off the beaten track, you can pick up a faint path to the left, 300m after leaving the summit of Calders. This little detour takes you to the rounded, and in itself, rather uninteresting Bram Rigg Top. What it lacks in interest under foot it makes up for in excellent views that you wouldn't get from the main path. The rolling ridges of Arant Haw to the south and your next objective Fell Head to the north add to the interest.

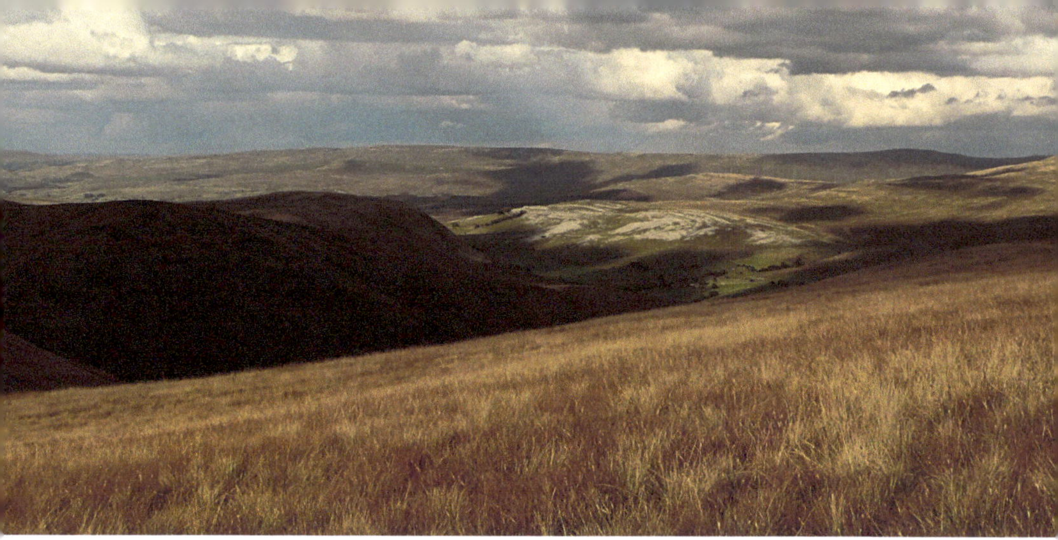

18.25pm 23rd August – The sun broke through the patchy cloud and picked out this contrasting patch of limestone way down in the valley below.

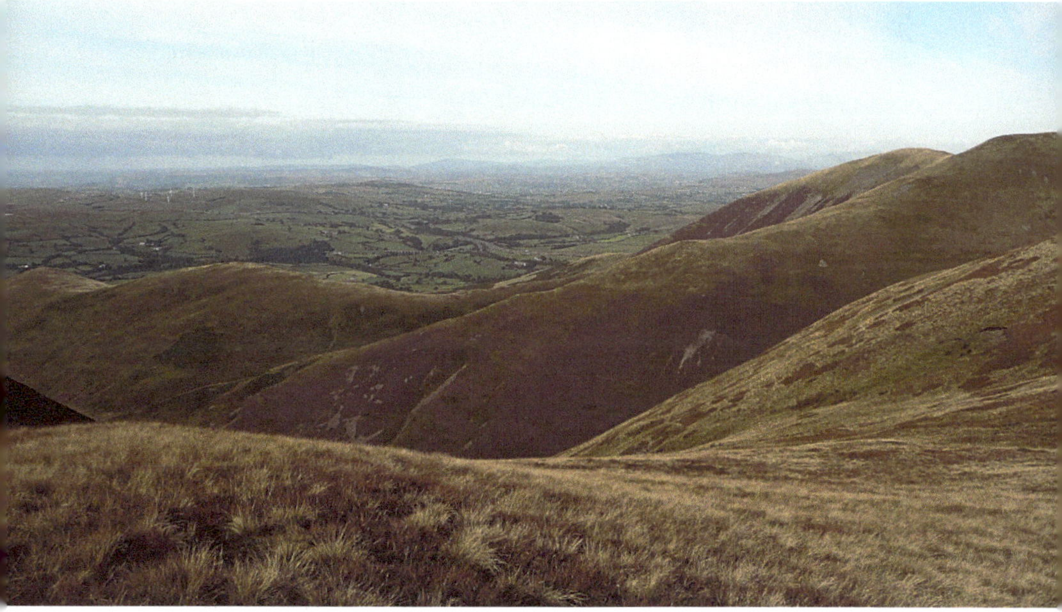

10.05am 24th August – After spending a glorious night camped out on the summit of Fell Head (seen on the far right above) it was great to look back to this peak and put its location into context.

From Bram Rigg Top take a faint path back to the main route. This leads you easily to the trig point that marks the summit of The Calf. Again, this summit lacks much immediate interest but as it sits at the high point of three main ridges it makes an important junction. Our route from The Calf, and probably the most interesting view, follows a grassy path that heads north west. In the distance the Lake District's High Street range fills the horizon.

From this elevated viewpoint I could see that the Lakeland hills were taking a battering from the squalls that were sweeping through. It was fascinating to watch the rain as it appeared to be bouncing off the ground. Then I realised that this weather was heading my way so I set off in some haste.

3) Leave the trig point by bearing left off the main path, heading down the north westerly spur on a good track. Ignore the first left and continue north and then north west again, over the slight rise of Bush Howe. From here you drop down steeply into a grassy pass where you can detour round the flanks of Wind Scarth on your way to Simon's Seat. A direct ascent of Fell Head from the pass is aesthetically preferable, although physically, the climb out is a bit of a pull.

4) Follow the path as it climbs leftwards out of the pass to reach the flat snaking plateau of Fell Head.

Photo Location – Fell Head

Follow the path as it winds its way along the top to the far western end, where there is a small pile of stones. This spot is a perfect place to camp out on, unless of course it is blowing a gale, as it is rather exposed. The steep drop on three out of the four sides makes this an excellent location for a shoot, whatever the position the sun is in, as the vistas are extensive.

As I pitched the tent the next heavy shower swept in so my dog got the lucky job of weighing the tent down whilst I finished pegging it out. The dramatic weather made for a challenging although really enjoyable shoot.

So, spend some time taking in the full 360 degree views from the summit. To the north east the Fell Head ridge stretches out towards the distant brooding bulk of the Pennines. To the east and south east the hills that you walked earlier stand out above the steep valley of Long Rigg and the deep pass you crossed. Looking south and south west, the hills recede down to the lush fields of the Lune valley far below. And of course to the west and the setting sun lies pretty much the whole of The Lake District and its layered skyline. The only fly in the ointment is the M6 motorway, which being only a couple of miles away does distract very slightly from this superb location.

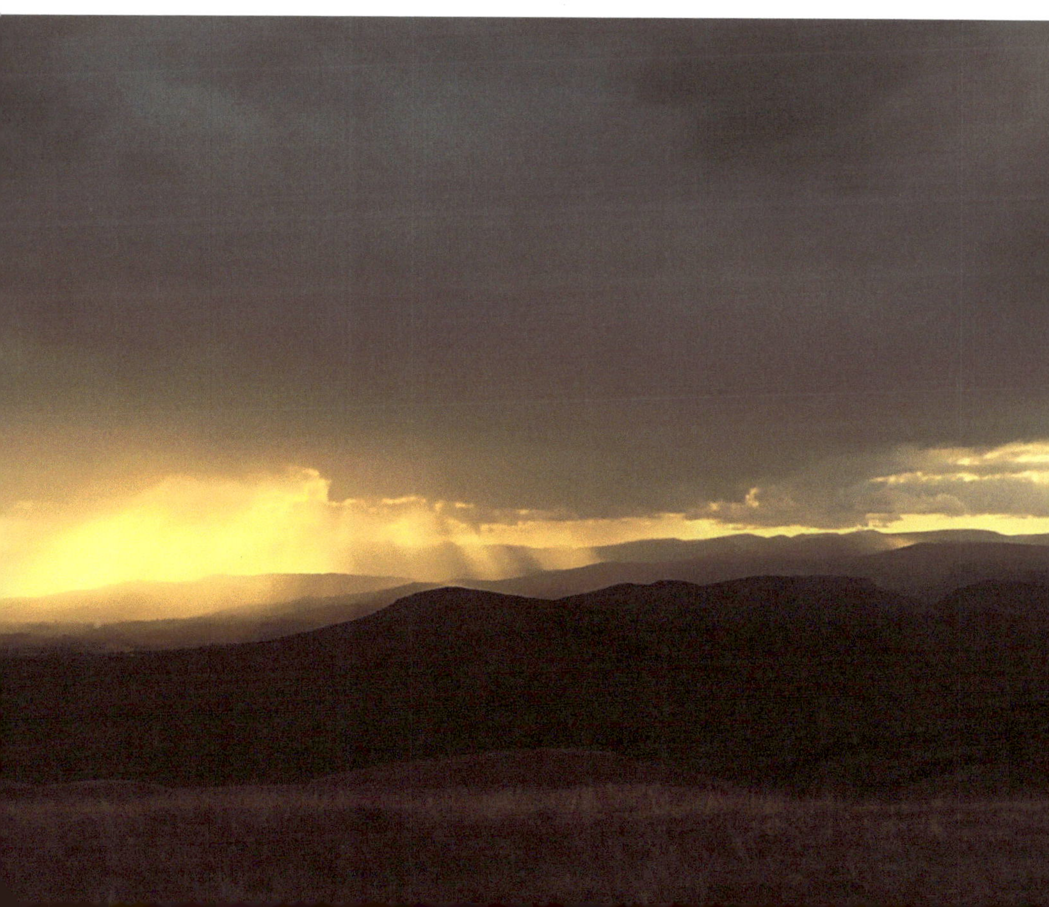

20.10pm 23rd August – It was a great place to watch the sun burst through the rain clouds that engulfed the Lakeland peaks. Finally the clouds cleared as dusk arrived so there was time for one last shoot in the failing light. Just as I was about to clamber into the tent I was treated to a firework display in the valley far below me, which was a pleasant surprise.

Whilst the summit area around the pile of stones is one of the best from which to shoot, be sure to check out all the options. For example, there is a fine subsidiary peak a few hundred meters down the south western spur and by dropping down the surrounding slopes a few meters you gain different perspectives.

6.00am 24th August – I awoke before my alarm went off and with much anticipation I unzipped the tent door. The cold air hit me as I poked out my nose but I was soon scrabbling to put on my boots as the first rays of the sunrise were lighting up the sky. This truly was a very memorable, if a bit chilly, start to a day in the hills.

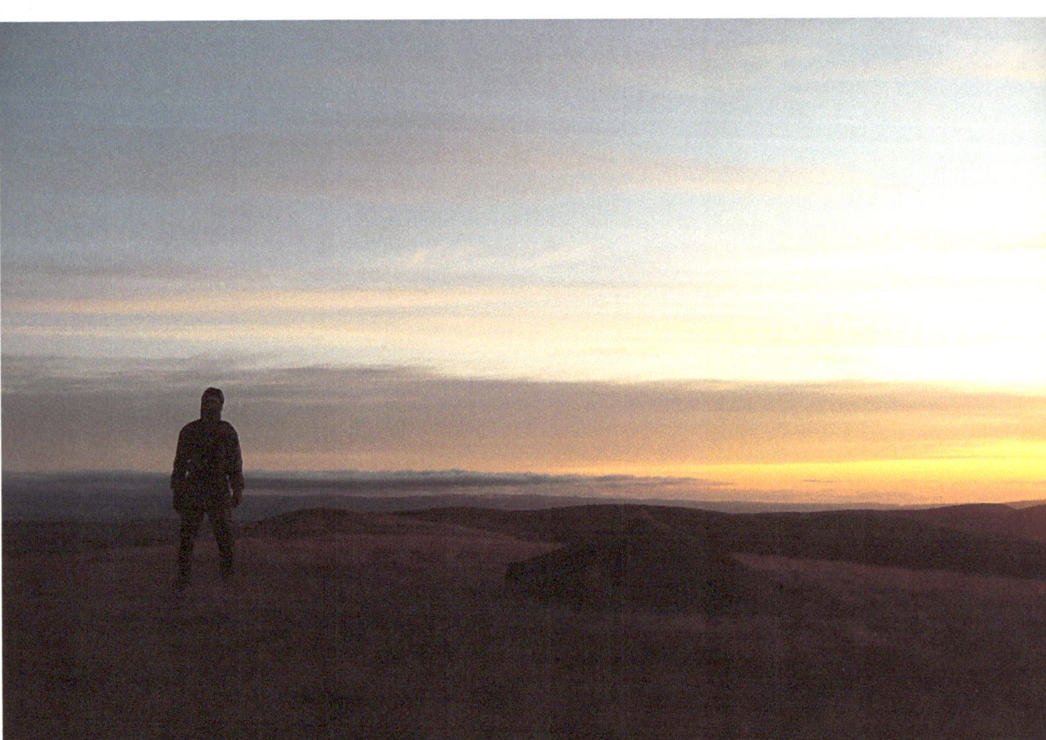

When it is time to leave Fell Head, reverse your steps back to the north eastern corner of the summit ridge.

4a) From here you can make a detour to the small rounded summit of Simon's Seat which offers more 360 degree views. So rather than dropping back down into the pass to your right, follow a broad ridge that heads off in a north easterly direction over Wind Scarth. After 400m drop gently down onto a broad grassy area where there are a number of very small tarns. From here take a right fork in the path which leads you towards Simon's Seat. Before reaching the peak drop down into a small boggy pass and climb out the other side. The direct ascent is rather steep so you can bear slightly left of centre to avoid the worst of it. As the climb eases you soon find yourself on top with expansive views to the north and the Pennines. In the opposite direction you also get a chance to view the heavily eroded stream beds that cover the northern flanks of Bush Howe and The Calf. This is another fine spot for a summit wild camp with ample areas for a tent and jaw dropping views from your doorstep.

Whilst you can head off in any direction from here, the valleys are quite deep and hard going so the best option is to head south down to the boggy pass again.

4b) From here you can avoid the re-ascent of Wind Scarth and the descent to the next pass by contouring around to the left. You end up at the pass between Wind Scarth and Bush Howe and also get a good look at the eroded stream beds that fan down from the slopes above.

Climb out of the pass, on over Bush Howe and easily back up to The Calf. Whilst reversing your outward route might not seem as pleasing as a circular route it does give you the chance to return to the viewpoints in somewhat different lighting conditions. However, if you really don't want to head back over to Great Dummacks, pick up the clear path that heads off to the north east from the trig point to Hare Shaw. From here you can drop down to Cautley Spout and back to the start.

Otherwise, follow the path south from The Calf to Calders before turning left down the fence line. Just after the fence turns right for the second time take the second track on the left that heads to the high ground of Great Dummacks. Then head back over to the southern end of Cautley Crags.

Returning to Cautley Crags a second time was a real treat. As you leave the wide open moors the vista suddenly opens up right at your feet.

You can descend off to the east and the south but they are hard work so the best option is to reverse your route north around the top of the crags and on to the waterfall. You can avoid the steep descent next to the waterfall by heading a bit further north then right down the easier path on the flanks of Yarlside. Either way you drop down Cautley Beck and down to the River Rawthey where you turn left to get back to the bridge and the carpark next to the pub.

I had spent less than 24 hours in the hills and had slept for a good portion of this time. However, I had only seen 2 other people on the high ground, had been battered by hail, rewarded with dramatic skies and then gone on to experience a glorious sunset and sunrise from my summit wild camp. It was a real feast for the senses and I left feeling rather glad I'd returned to this special little range of hills.

The Scottish Borders

6.1 A Walk on the Wild Side – the Galloway Hills

Just the names of the hills in this wild corner of the Scottish borders make a visit worth while. Where else can you find places called Murder Hole, The Devil's Bowling Green and the Rig of Jarkness? This area is often overlooked partly as the highest ground falls just short of the 3000 foot Munro mark. However the hills are stunningly wild and offer the adventurous photographer something rather special.

A Walk on the Wild Side – the Galloway Hills

Focal Point – the remote and shapely Loch Enoch offers both lakeside shoots and far reaching views.

Route Summaries

Full route – a traverse of the wild Dungeon Hills and down to the stunning shores of Loch Enoch, returning over the highest peak in the area, The Merrick.

18 km, 1170m ascent

Shorter route - a 'there and back' taking in one, two or three of the lochs ending up at Loch Enoch and avoiding the high ground.

13 km, 490m ascent

Why Try this Route

The paths are few, the ground is boggy and rough going but the views are simply spell binding. From hidden lakeside shores to rough granite hills this area has huge photographic potential and is also perfect for wild camping expeditions.

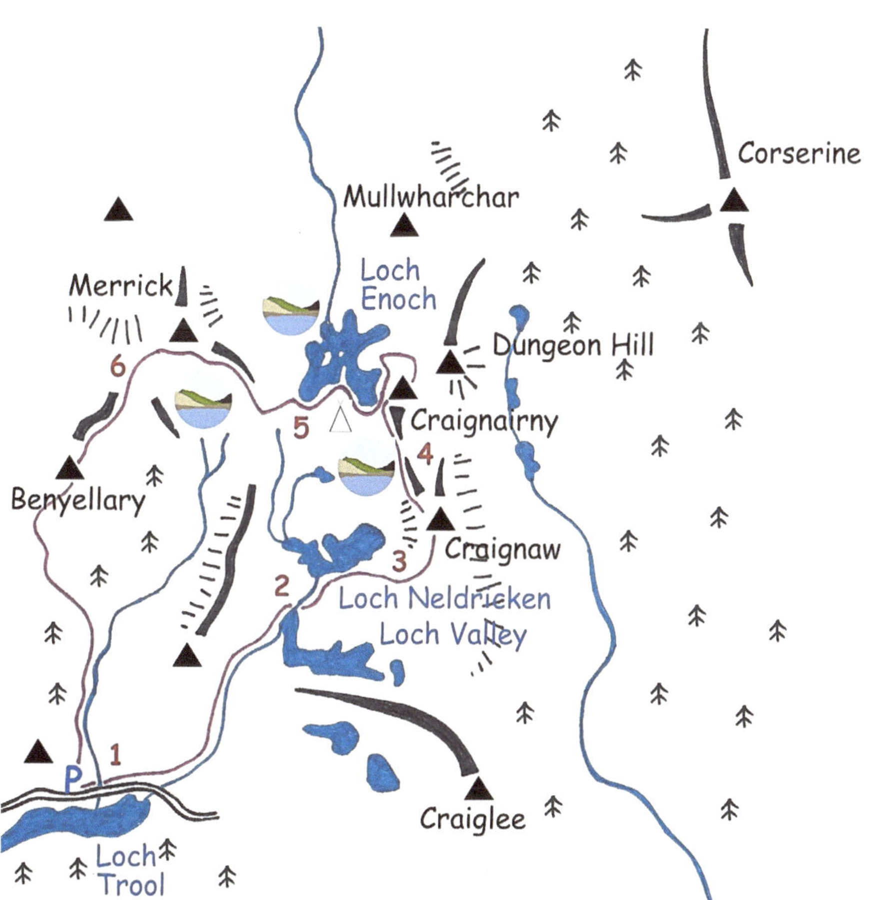

Clockwise from top left :

Sunrise from the Loch Enoch camp... Loch Enoch from the ascent of Redstone Rig... The Devil's Bowling Green... Our beachside camp on Loch Enoch... A distant view of Loch Enoch on the descent from Craignaw... The crystal clear waters of Loch Enoch

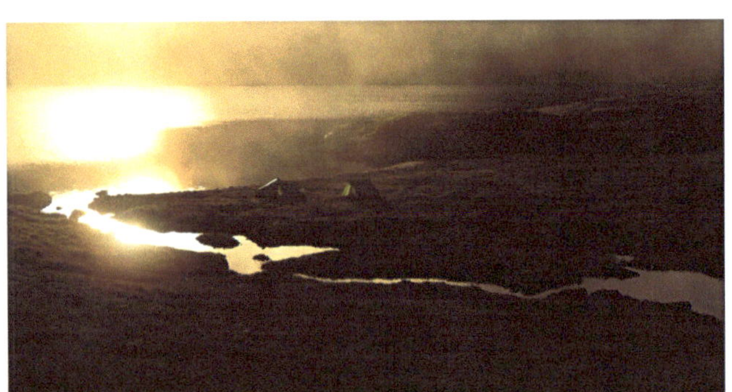

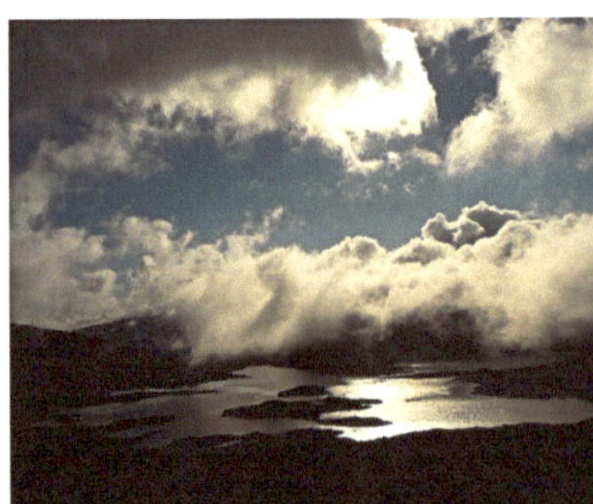

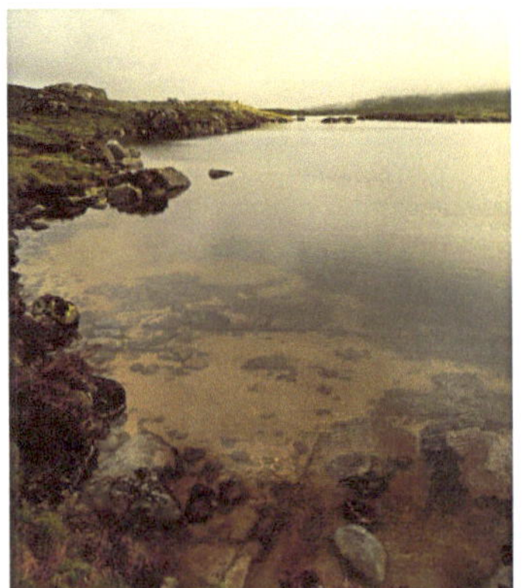

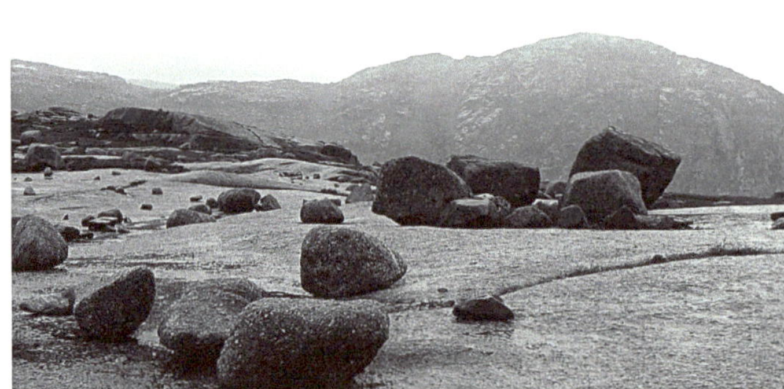

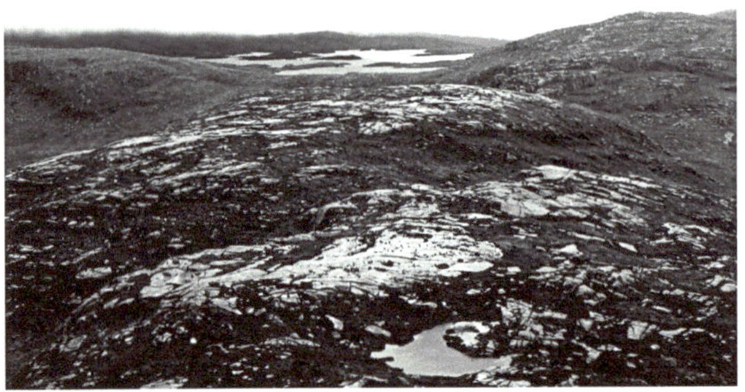

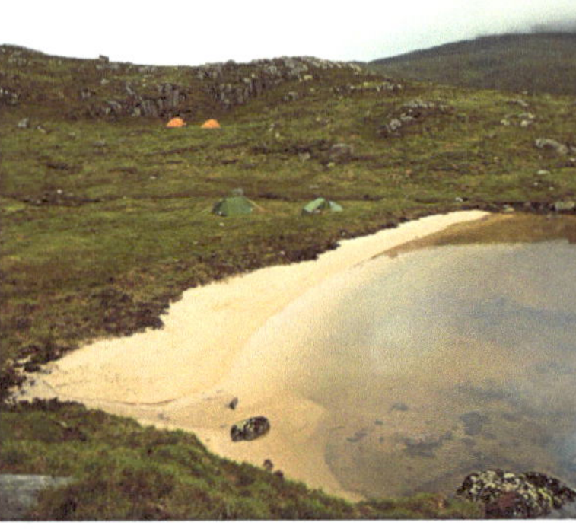

Route Description

1) Start from the trail head carpark on the northern shores of Glen Trool (NX414803) near the Bruce's Stone. Follow the wide track that leaves the eastern end of the carpark, ignoring the path on the left (signed Merrick Trail) which will be your return route. The track descends to a bridge over the Buchan Burn and shortly after that look for a stile on the left. Climb over the stile and take the rough and often boggy path that traverses uphill in a north easterly direction. Continue along this path and you'll eventually reach the upper stretches of the Gairland Burn.

Like all good trips, this one started in a fantastic little pub called the House O'Hill Hotel at Bargrennan. A cunning plan was hatched over a pint before we headed down to the end of the Glen Trool road. Sadly it was now chucking it down with rain and pitch black outside so we quickly headed up the steep valley before pitching our tents in some heathery moraine above a rampaging stream.

2) Follow the stream to the first of three fine lochs, Loch Valley. Continue along its western shore, picking up the inflowing Mid Burn that leads to the second loch, Loch Neldricken.

Just before reaching Loch Neldricken you'll pick up a stone wall and stone enclosure that, along with the cascading burn, make for an interesting foreground and lead in line down to Loch Valley.

It was a blustery, wet night but fortunately the rain had stopped by the time we woke to low scudding clouds. Being optimistic that the weather would improve and keen to see what delights were on our doorstep we hastily packed our tents and headed further up the valley. We picked our way along some sheep tracks and checked out the stunning series of lochs.

You now have a route decision to make, which if you can't cross the stream around here, could be made for you.

The most direct and easiest route to Loch Enoch is by following the path that heads around the western flank of Loch Neldricken to the wonderfully named (but in fact fictional place) Murder Hole. Then continue along the stream that comes down from the small Loch Arron above. This path takes you to a low pass which then drops you down to Loch Enoch's fine southern shore.

3) An alternative high level route, taking in the fine granite peaks of the Dungeon range, can be taken by crossing the Mid Burn stream around where it joins Loch Neldricken. Continue along the loch's southern shores before picking your line of ascent up a broad, pathless, grassy ridge, aiming for the southern end of Craignaw above. As you gain height it becomes rockier with some granite slabs to negotiate.

It was now time to gain some altitude with our first major climb of the day on more pathless terrain. The summit took some time to reach so it was midday before the gradient levelled off and the cairn came into view. Fortunately the rocky top provided us with a sheltered lunch stop.

After a fair bit of work you'll reach Craignaw's fine little summit. It offers superb views down into the wild bog that is Silver Flowe. However, you also get your first real glimpse of the shapely Loch Enoch over some wild, rocky terrain. This is where the route heads next but it's worth spending some time on the summit to enjoy this stunning location.

4) The descent from Craignaw can be a bit tricky to negotiate. However, drop down the steep, grassy north westerly spur, working your way around the rocky outcrops and you'll soon arrive at a beautiful relic from the last Ice Age; the Devil's Bowling Green (NX456837), where the rocks were deposited onto the granite plateau by a melting glacier.

Photo Location-Devil's Bowling Green

The numerous granite boulders scattered around this area make for a fantastic foreground with the surrounding Dungeon Hills as a moody backdrop. This spot has a feeling of timeless, rugged beauty which allows you to get creative with your images.

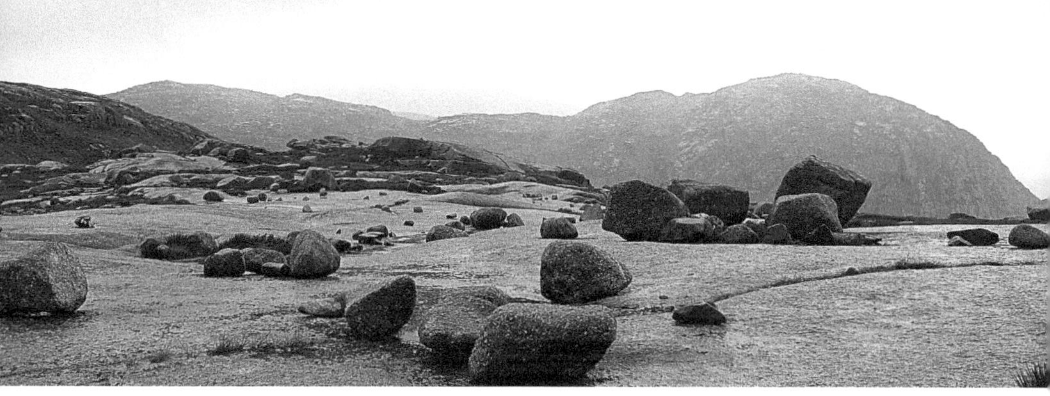

13.30pm 15th June. The next feature to explore was the imaginatively named Devil's Bowling Green. As we arrived the rain returned with a vengeance which prevented us from fully enjoying this remote and beautiful natural feature. Perversely, this just added to the drama and our ongoing battle with the elements.

Heading northwards from the Bowling Green cross a small pass before climbing up to the craggy summit of Craignairny. Continue north from the summit down to a broad flat area where you can pick your way south west down to Loch Enoch

On reaching the shores of Loch Enoch you start to appreciate how wild and remote it feels out here. Follow the southern shoreline westwards on some faint, boggy paths. If you're planning on camping out there are a number of fine lakeside spots around the area of NX445848.

Photo Location - Loch Enoch

There's a perfect granite sand beach here set in a stunningly wild spot which makes for an excellent photographic location. A water level shoot is always exciting and the water is so clear here that it gives your images an extra dimension.

After some further exploration we decided to head down to Loch Enoch and check out a loch side wild camp spot for the night. After choosing a rather exposed beach side location we pitched our tents for a second time. The weather proved somewhat grim but as least this encouraged an early bedtime which at the time of year gave us a decent chance of getting up for any possible sunrise.

6.10am 16th June. As I awoke the next morning I was aware that all was quiet. There was no sound of rain or even wind on the tent and I excitedly unzipped the doors to take a peek out at what we had on offer. Not surprisingly there was a fair bit of mist about but I was hopeful that the sun would make a great shoot when it came up above the eastern hills. So I settled back in my tent to get a brew on with one eye on the changing light outside.

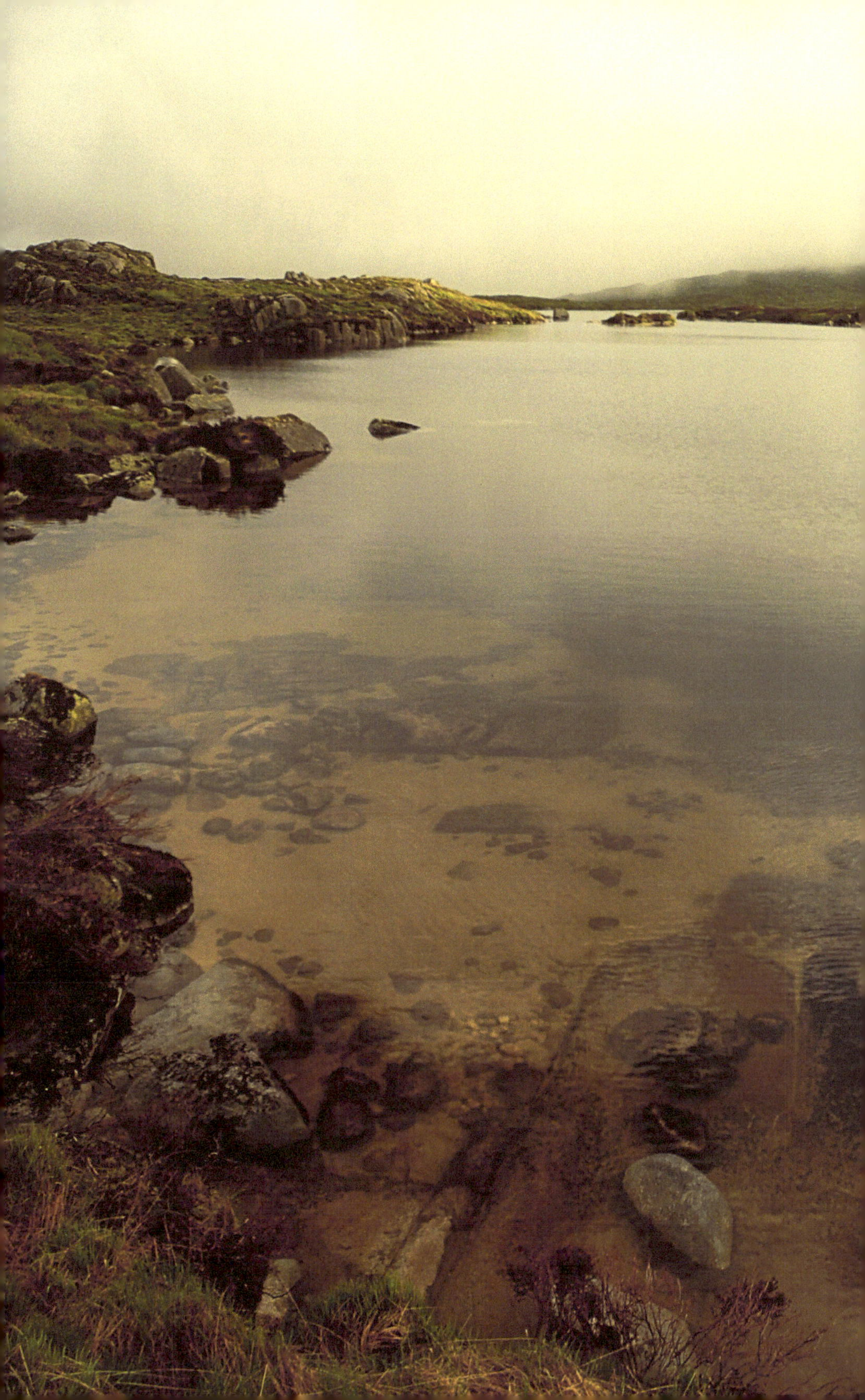

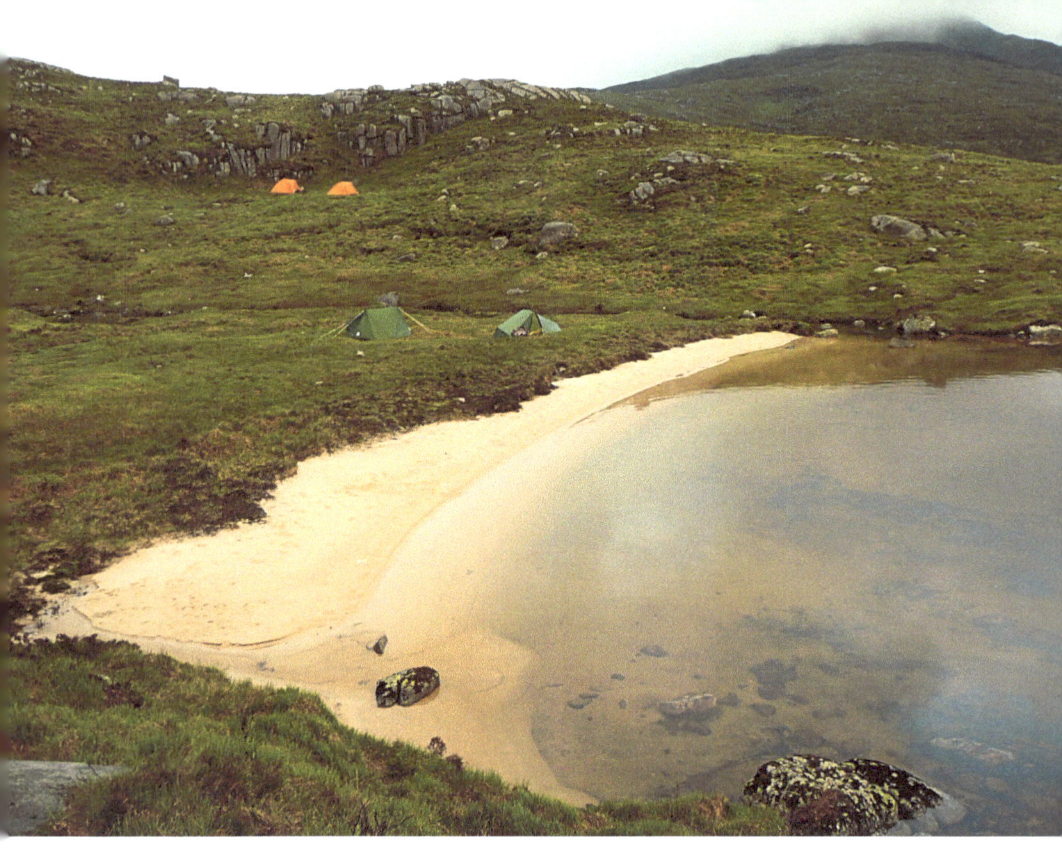

7.40am 16th June. It wasn't long before I was clambering out of the tent clutching my camera and spending a very enjoyable hour shooting the scene as the light steadily improved. All the battling with the elements the day before suddenly became worthwhile.

So spend your time exploring this fantastic loch side location with its bays, peninsula and pristine beaches.

5) Follow the shoreline to the south western corner of the loch where there is the smallest beach you are ever likely to find. From here head up the valley, with your back to the lake, to the start of the broad ridgeline, Redstone Rig. There are a few tracks along the way but the general direction is upwards picking up the easiest line.

Photo Location - Redstone Rig

Make sure to stop and take in the excellent views back over Loch Enoch with its complex coastline and number of small islands. This attractive lake makes an interesting silhouette from this elevated position.

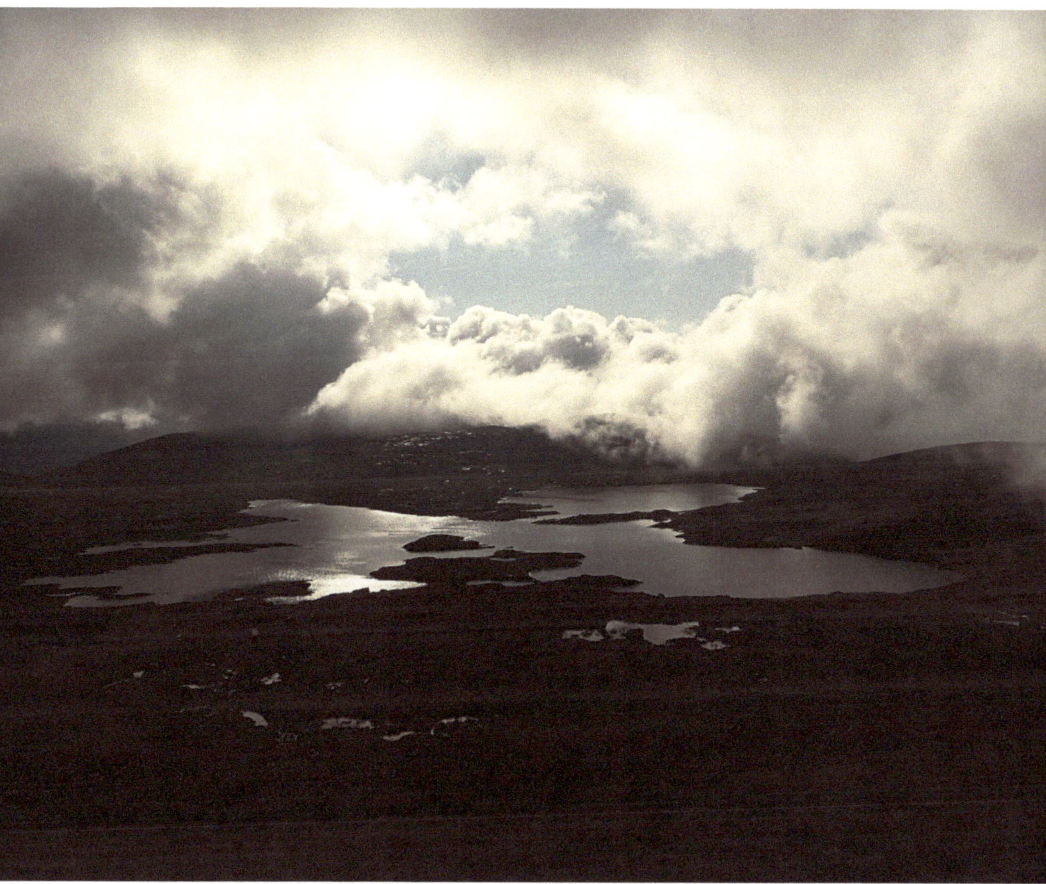

10.10am 16th June. As the mist cleared and blue skies appeared we packed up to take on the last big challenge of the weekend. A climb up Merrick via the less well trod Redstone Rig. The ascent might have been hard going but the extra height gave us an elevated view over the intricately shaped Loch Enoch where we had camped.

The climb up Redstone Rig is a fair pull, especially after all the walking so far on the route. However, the ground soon starts to level out when you reach the large open summit of Merrick. This is quite a popular hill, partly because it is the highest in the area but also as it now has a very good path from Loch Trool. With a bit of luck you'll reach the top long before the crowds start to appear up this path. The views from the summit are pretty stunning but make sure you work your way around the top of the cliffs on its northern side to get some far reaching vistas.

There was still some hill mist hanging on to the summit but we decided to be patient and wait around in the hope that it would clear. The patience paid off as the mist started to burn off, giving us views over the area we had travelled and a number of valleys and hills that looked even wilder.

6) The route off Merrick is very straightforward unless you're sadly there in very poor visibility. Leave the summit in a south westerly direction and you'll quickly pick up a large stoney path that drops you down to a stone wall. This leads you over a narrow strip of land that links Merrick to its neighbour Benyellary. It also has another fantastic name, the Neive of the Spit, and the walking is so straightforward that it allows you to take in the huge number of lochs that are scattered around the area.

With some reluctance to leave the summit we headed down the 'tourist track' which was not only our first real path of the weekend but also later on gave us our first encounter with anyone else on the hills.

On reaching the broad grassy summit of Benyellary you drop down on a decent path before reaching the last of the open ground. Heading through a gated fence you'll quickly start descending south into a steep wooded valley that brings you out at an old bothy, the Culsharg. The gradient starts to ease and you soon reach the Buchan Burn again which is picturesque, if not full of photographic potential. After a kilometre or so of following the stream you reach the trail head at the Loch Trool carpark and your return to civilisation begins.

As a reward for our efforts we decided to revisit the pub again where we got a hearty welcome and some equally hearty hill walking fodder. The pie and mash hit the spot perfectly. Whilst we were sad to leave this beautiful place we knew we would be back. A combination of bizarrely named craggy hills and stunning remote lochs make this an area that begs to be explored again and again.

On a Visit to the Area Why Not Also Check Out These Coastal Options

If poor weather makes a walk in the hills seem unattractive or you've spent a glorious couple of days in the Galloway Hills and want something easier but still interesting why not take a trip to the coast. There are a number of amazing little beaches dotted around this coast and many of them see only a few locals. Here are a couple of options:

Carrick Point NX 576505 on the southern edge of Fleet Bay with its small enclosed tidal beach is an interesting place to explore. There are a couple of small islands, The Islands of Fleet, just off the coast which make great focal points, especially as the sun dips down over the horizon.

Rascarrel Bay NX801480 is wild, rocky and off the beaten track. There's a small carpark at the end of the road. Follow the track heading along the left hand side of the stream down to the sea. Head east along the track and head onto the beach pretty much where you like. There's a good mixture of sand and rocky outcrops to explore with an option to continue on to the beautiful cliffs around Balcary Point

Wild Camping and Landscape Photography

Imagine you've toiled up a hillside in the dark and pitched your tent near the summit. You've gone to bed not knowing quite what to expect when you wake but you sense that it's something pretty special. It's now 5am and your senses are starting to wake up. Your brain is frantically trying to work out where you are and then you remember. You are in your tent, perched on a wild summit with an expansive panorama waiting for you outside. Suddenly it's like being a kid on Christmas morning and you can't wait to take a peek out of the tent. You roll over, unzip the door and peer out to take in your surroundings...

Wild camping in the hills is an experience that is so simple and yet so fulfilling. It takes you out of your everyday routines and makes you focus on simple enjoyable experiences like watching the light change as the sun goes down or just enjoying a cup of tea you've prepared on your stove.

Even if you've pitched your tent in daylight the night before and had a great time shooting a sunset, the feeling of waking up in a remote spot with just you, some friends and a whole lot of views bathed in early morning light never fails to inspire. The freedom of having all you need for a couple of days out in the hills is wonderfully liberating and allows you to experience the hills in what is arguably their best light and without a whole lot of time restrictions. As a bonus, if you choose your location well, you'll get the place to yourselves and get to capture something that no-one else will even see, be that a subtle changing of light on a distant peak or features emerging from valley mist.

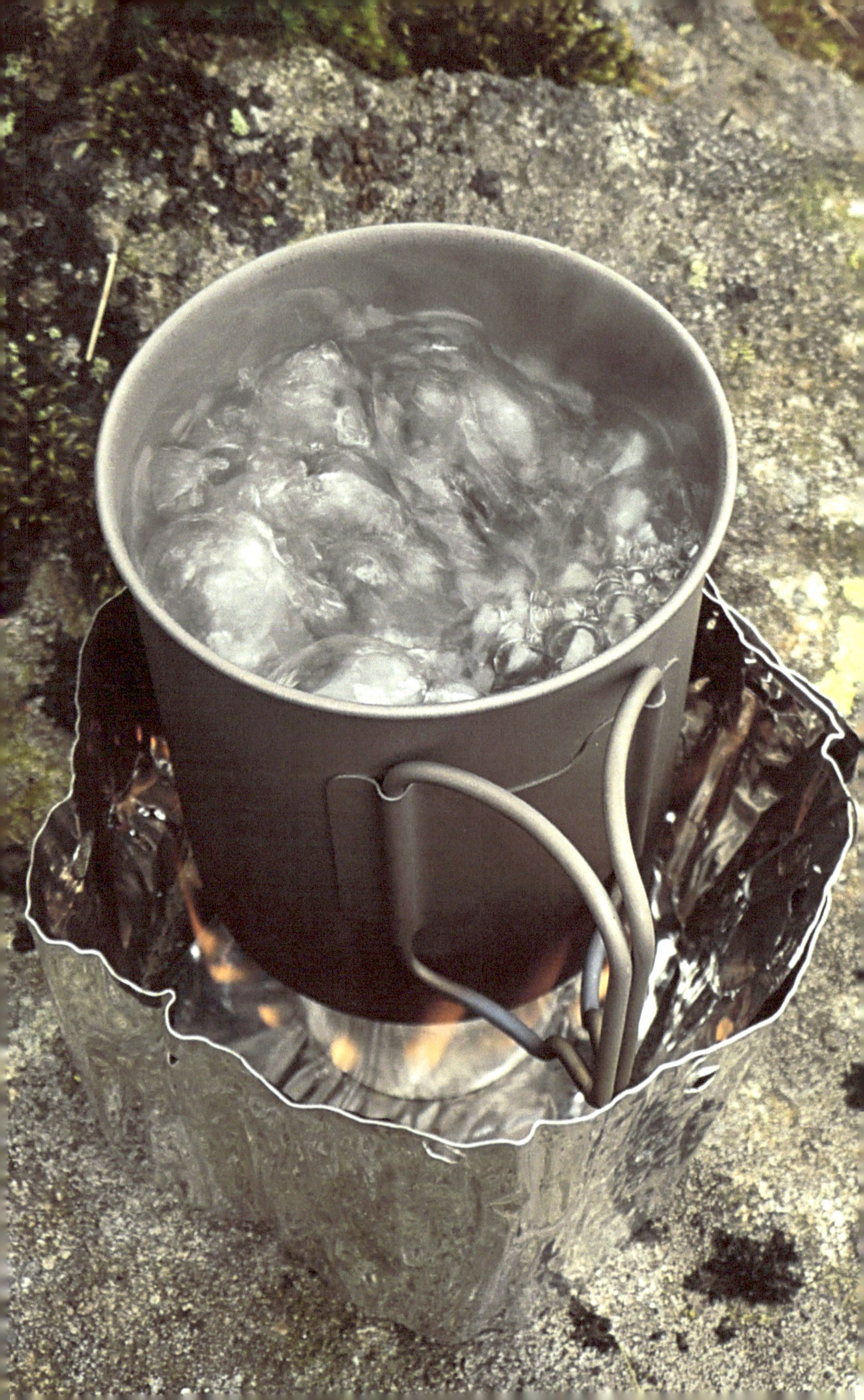

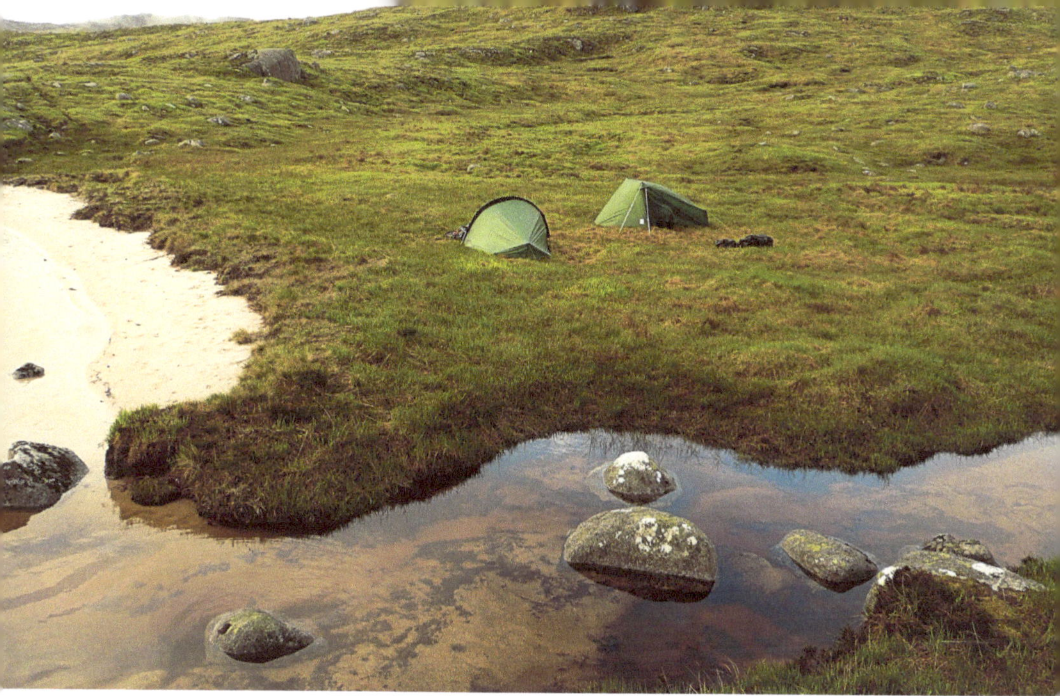

Wild camping in a truly wild setting and with our own beach.

Ok, there are some drawbacks. Waking up with the wind and rain lashing your tent knowing you are miles from anywhere and that your camera will be spending all day in your sack is not great. But with a bit of planning and taking a good look at the weather forecasts you can usually avoid this situation.

Then there's the slight problem of having a load of camping gear to carry along with all your usual camera kit. When packing for your trip you have to get a bit ruthless and work out what you'll really need to have some comfort, get the shots you want but not be weighed down so much you can't even walk. With a bit of practice you will work out what you can live without and what level of comfort works for you.

I started out with a pack weight of 18kg which even when I was a young, fit thirty something was ridiculously heavy. Since then I have shaved several kilos by investing in some light weight gear.

However, it's not all about buying the latest titanium gizmo and paper thin tent. It's really all about going light weight but at your right weight. Small items of gear do all add up to your overall load and just chucking it in your sack thinking you might need it is no good. Think about your key, heavy items like tent, sleeping bag, rucksack and boots (heavy boots take a lot of energy to move over a long day) and consider how you might cut down on the weight of each item. Buying a lighter version is one way of doing this and it's certainly a good idea to consider the weight of an item if you're going to buy a new piece of kit. Lighter versions are however usually more expensive and may not be as robust as their heavier alternatives.

Certain items are a must like your basic camping gear: tent, sleeping bag and mat, warm jacket, stove, mug & spoon

While you can share communal items like the tent, stove and fuel between the group, you will also still need your basic walking gear of waterproofs, warm layer, food and drink.

Water can be a bit of an issue as it's quite heavy and bulky and you don't want to be carrying all you need for the whole trip. In most upland areas, if you are careful where you collect your water (fast flowing streams, away from civilisation, mountain tarns and dead sheep) you will probably be ok drinking it but it is often wise to purify it first. Boiling works well but does require a fair bit of fuel. Water purifiers like a hand held UV unit or a filter pump are really useful if you are going to be camping quite a bit. I usually take a small luxury with me like my iPod for the tent but like a lot of the above it's all down to your personal preferences, discomfort threshold and tastes. Above all, you don't need to invest vast amounts of money to get some great equipment or spend your time being cold, wet and uncomfortable.

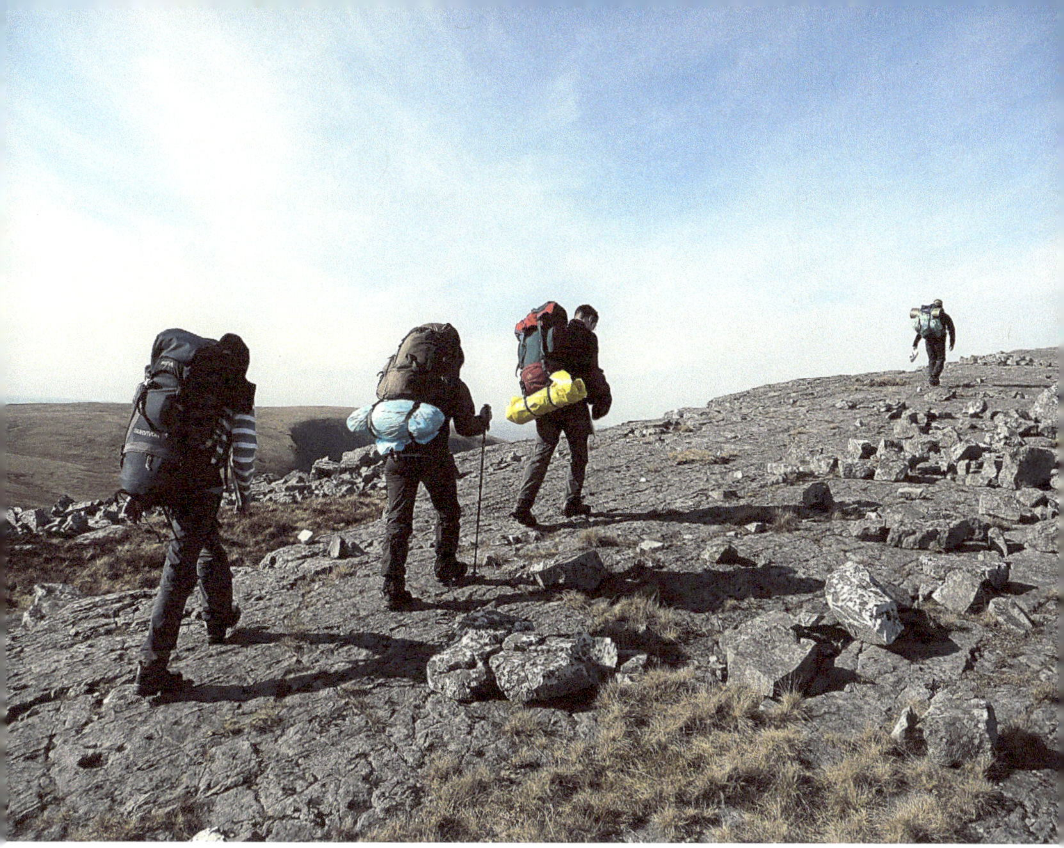

Adrian, Catherine, Chris and Austen sharing the load of wild camping

It maybe cold outside but with the right gear you can be comfortable

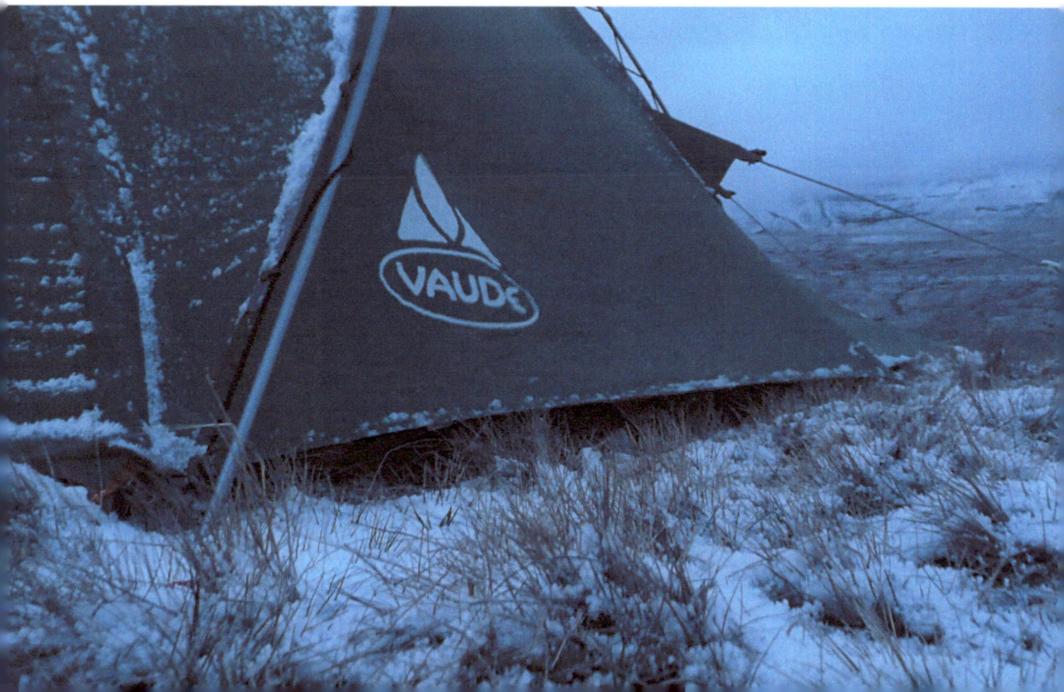

Finally you do have to consider the legalities of wild camping. In Scotland it is generally legal to camp in the hills as long as you are away from civilisation and respect the environment. Whilst in England and Wales, Dartmoor is the only area you can legally wild camp on. Strictly speaking you should ask the landowner wherever possible, although this can prove difficult in most upland areas. You need to be responsible for your actions. Only camp in small groups for one, maybe two nights maximum, take out all your rubbish, toilet responsibly and leave the spot as you find it.

Wild camping can be a wonderful experience to share with friends, whilst conversely a solo trip can be a very fulfilling way to really immerse yourself in your surroundings and forget about the stresses of everyday life. You really get to study a subject over a period of time whilst the light changes without the worry of having to get down before it gets dark.

Whilst we all strive to take the perfect image of a landscape during perfect light conditions we all know too well that being in the right spot at the right time is hard to achieve. However, capturing an image from your chosen wild camp and working with the conditions that you experience can be very rewarding and produce evocative and highly personal results. We all still aim to take that perfect shot but sometimes the process of being there at a stunning location, watching the light and clouds change can give you much more than just some images on your memory cards. Wild camping can be seen as a tool to help you take better landscape shots but it's also about much, much more than just that.

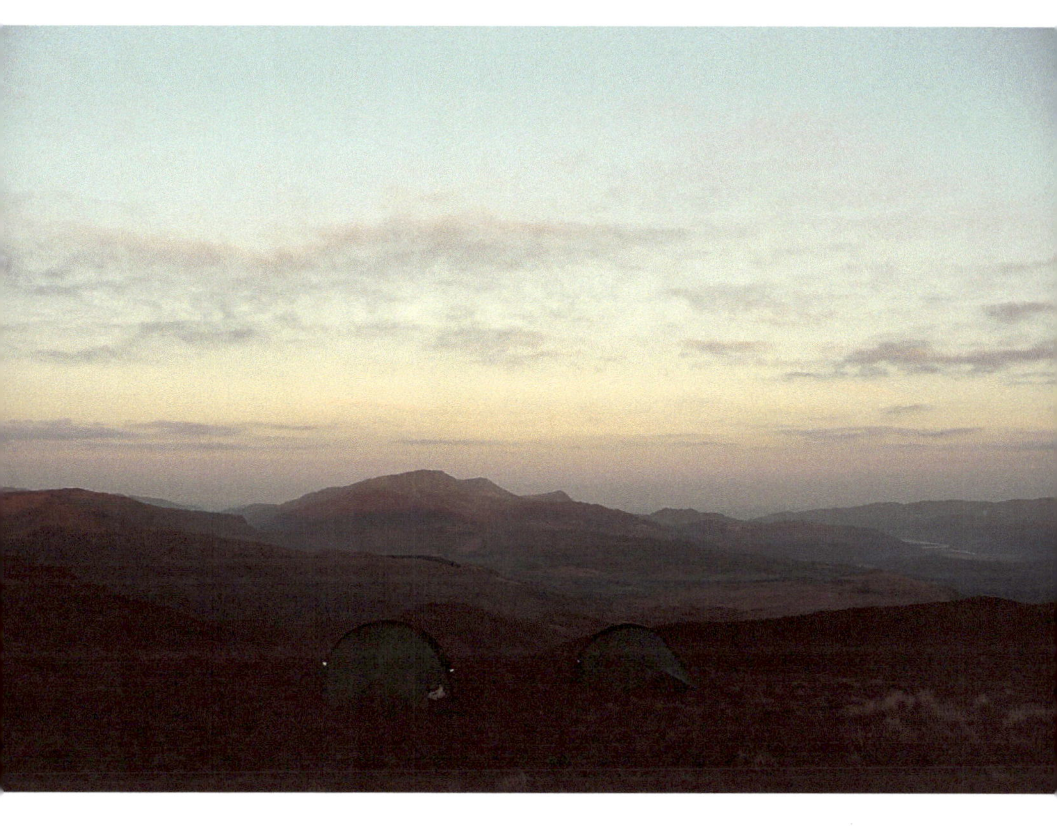

Enjoying a glorious sunrise from our wild camp

www.ingramcontent.com/pod-product-compliance
Lightning Source LLC
LaVergne TN
LVHW072029110826
845147LV00001BA/3

* 9 7 8 1 9 0 9 6 4 4 9 2 2 *